Death Over a Diamond Stud

Death Over a Diamond Stud

The Assassination of the Orleans Parish District Attorney

Christopher G. Peña

PELICAN PUBLISHING COMPANY
Gretna 2018

Library of Congress Cataloging-in-Publication Data

Names: Peña, Christopher G., author.
Title: Death over a diamond stud : the assassination of the Orleans Parish District Attorney / by Christopher G. Peña.
Description: Gretna : Pelican Publishing Company, [2018] | Includes bibliographical references and index.
Identifiers: LCCN 2018000425| ISBN 9781455624164 (hardcover : alk. paper) | ISBN 9781455624171 (ebook)
Subjects: LCSH: Murder—Louisiana—New Orleans—Case studies. | Lyons, Lewis Williams, 1858-1905. | Gurley, John Ward, Jr.
Classification: LCC HV6534.N45 P46 2018 | DDC 364.152/4092 [B] —dc23 LC record available at https://lccn.loc.gov/2018000425

Printed in the United States of America

Published by Pelican Publishing Company, Inc.
1000 Burmaster Street, Gretna, Louisiana 70053
www.pelicanpub.com

For Linda

Contents

Acknowledgments

After writing *The Strange Case of Dr. Etienne Deschamps: Murder in the New Orleans French Quarter,* I never intended for it to be my final book about a famous New Orleans murder. Even before the book was published, I began to collate materials for my next project. To my surprise, some prominent family names showcased in my last book resurfaced in my latest chronicling set fourteen years after the Juliette Dietsh murder.

I would be remiss if I did not mention the following people whose assistance is greatly appreciated. Thank you so much to DeeDee Denise DiBenedetto of St. Amant, Louisiana and Gregory Cho of New Orleans. Many thanks to Beth Davis, Vital Records Section, Louisiana State Archives, Baton Rouge; Georgia Chadwick, former Director and Francis X. Norton, Jr., Research Lawyer/Librarian, Law Library of Louisiana, Supreme Court of Louisiana, New Orleans; Florence M. Jumonville, former Chair, Louisiana and Special Collections Department, University of New Orleans Library; Christina Bryant, Head, Louisiana Division/City Archives, New Orleans Public Library; and Kevin Williams, Archivist, Southeastern Architectural Archives, Tulane University Libraries, New Orleans.

I am especially grateful to Colin O'Key, Knoxville, Tennessee, for reproducing certain newspaper archival images that appear in the book and to my daughter, Pamela P. Smith, Knoxville, Tennessee, for her computer graphic-design assistance. And finally, I would like to extend a heartfelt thanks to my wife, Linda D. Peña, for putting up with me during this and so many other writing projects I pursued over the years. For that and so much more, I dedicate this book to you.

Death Over a Diamond Stud

Lyons's World
New Orleans 1903

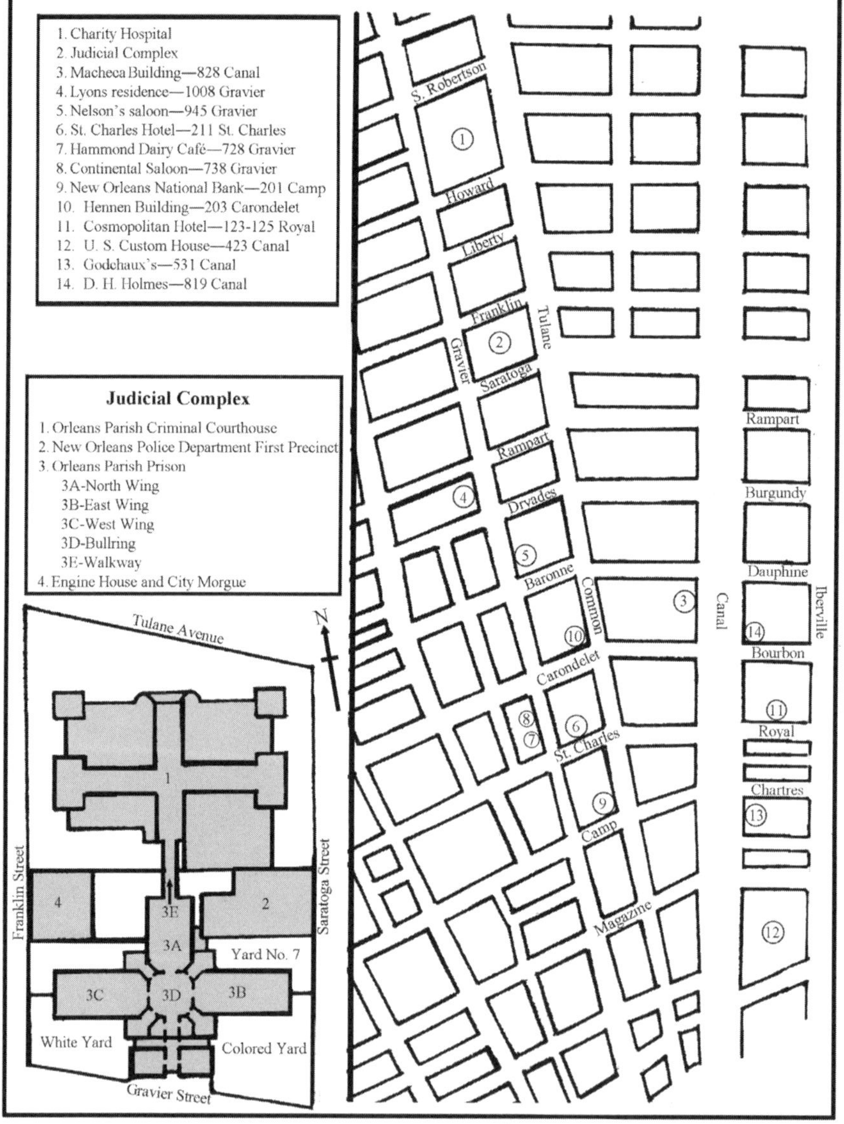

Chapter One

EXECUTION DAY

Try to make a clean job out of it.

Lewis W. Lyons, Jr.

Friday, March 24, 1905, was execution day at Orleans Parish Prison and the sixth judicial hanging since its opening. The prison was part of an elaborate complex of buildings located on a city block bordered by Tulane Avenue, Saratoga (formerly Basin, now Loyola Avenue), Gravier, and Franklin streets. With the nearly sixty-year-old parish prison on Orleans Street in deplorable shape by the early 1890s and a need to consolidate judicial services and other city and parish amenities at one location, city leaders began to plan for a centralized judicial complex. It would contain a new parish courthouse and prison, a new building for the police department's First Precinct Station, an engine house, and a city morgue, the latter the first of its kind in the city. At a cost of $360,000, when the complex opened in February 1894—the prison did not accept its first inmates until January 21, 1895—it was viewed as an architectural marvel. Adding to its magnificence, the complex was bordered by an impressive Schillinger-patent concrete sidewalk.

The three-story courthouse, described in the *New Orleans Daily Picayune* as "entirely void of monotony," was constructed of red pressed brick and exteriorly trimmed with Pecos sandstone, from the Pecos River district of Texas, and terracotta, the latter molded into various architectural shapes and sizes. The exterior resembled an earlier French Renaissance château with its rounded towers, pointed spires, and clock tower. The interior was likewise beautiful, finished in Georgia marble, with doorways and trim made primarily from Louisiana cypress wood with some mahogany features. The first floor was entirely tiled.

The front of the building faced Tulane Avenue and was marked by a wide, stone stairway that led to a triple-arched, columned entrance. The building was divided into quadrants by two intersecting corridors. One corridor ran

Orleans Parish Courthouse and New Orleans Police Department First Precinct Station (1895). (Courtesy Louisiana Division/City Archives, New Orleans Public Library)

north to south toward the prison facility on Gravier Street, and, the other, east to west from Saratoga to Franklin streets. Inside the main entrance, immediately on the right in the northwest quadrant, was the office for the jury commissioners. Farther down the hallway on the left, at the intersection of the corridors, was the office of the chief of police, along with separate offices for his private secretary, clerks, and operators. In addition, there were three rooms dedicated to his city detectives.

In the southeast quadrant, across the east-to-west corridor from the chief of police, were the First Recorder's Court, his clerk's office, and the affidavit office. The recorder's courtroom was conveniently placed to the rear of the police station on Saratoga Street. Down the east-to-west corridor toward Franklin Street in the upper portion of the northwest quadrant was the office of the Registrar of Voters, along with the registrar's private office and a vault to ensure the safety of various official records. Opposite that room in the southwest quadrant was the coroner's office, which consisted of three rooms. In addition, the first floor had assorted offices and storerooms, an elevator, centrally located, and an adequate number of "toilet rooms."

On the second floor, "reached by means of a wide, roomy and handsome stairway," according to the *Daily Picayune,* were two courtrooms utilized by the Orleans Parish Criminal District Court, Sections A and B. (Beginning in 1898, Section A shared its space with the First City Criminal Court when it, along with the Second City Criminal Court, was created to adjudicate lesser criminal offenses. In December 1900, officials moved the lower court to the second floor in the new First Precinct Station.)

Each district courtroom was massive in size, nearly three thousand square feet, not counting the adjoining judge's private office, and had a small, interior third-story balcony initially reserved for lady visitors. In addition, both courtrooms had a private stairway that led to the third-floor deliberation rooms, dining rooms, and private suites when jurors were sequestered. The convenience of these stairways allowed jurymen to enter and leave the courtroom without having to intermingle with the public in the main, second-floor corridor. Across the corridor from the courtrooms on opposite ends were the offices of the clerk of court and sheriff's office, though the criminal sheriff's primary office was initially located in the new parish prison. In addition, the second floor housed the office of the district attorney, the grand and petty jury, and a meeting room for witnesses.

A special feature on the second floor was a fifty-foot-long enclosed bridge that connected the sheriff's office in the courthouse (by way of an iron-barred gate) with the second floor of the prison. The overpass allowed inmates to be securely transported to and from the courthouse, saving time, energy, and expense. The bridge also gave the courthouse access to the prison's kitchen, which provided food for jurors and for inmates jailed at the police station.

Besides the jury quarters, the third floor contained miscellaneous offices, which were accessible by way of the grand stairway. In addition, the floor contained a separate stairway that led to a 150-foot-tall clock tower, the highest point in the building. The double-faced clock, one dial facing Tulane Avenue and the other facing Saratoga Street, became the most recognizable feature of the courthouse.

Though the courthouse was deemed beautiful, it appeared that the 800 pilings driven into the ground to support the massive weight of the structure and the neighboring prison were inadequate, given the soil composition of New Orleans. The city was and remains under sea level. The city engineer raised other issues during construction, though he and the contractor, M. A. Orlopp, were able to settle most disputes. Nevertheless, within a matter of a few years of its opening, the courthouse began to show signs of sinking in places, causing some interior and exterior walls to crack. In one area, shifting walls caused one part of the courthouse to separate from the other. Orlopp later admitted that his choice of West Texas sandstone was wrong, as it could not withstand the rigors of the humid New Orleans climate. The prison also showed some evidence of paint and plaster cracking, with a few deeper cracks discovered in some walls, though Orlopp attributed that to ordinary settlement, not to a lack of pilings or a faulty foundation design.

Adding to the overall safety concerns, by late 1901, the bridge connecting the courthouse and prison was deemed structurally unsound. It was subsequently demolished and rebuilt after the underlying problems within the courthouse and prison were corrected. The connecting bridge reopened in November 1903.

Located in the middle of the Franklin Street block between the courthouse and prison was a fifty- by fifty-foot building divided in two sections, which constituted the engine house or boiler and the city morgue. Fronting Franklin Street, the engine house generated steam power for heating, running the various elevators, and operating the machinery that pumped out raw sewage from the complex into large, underground pipes that emptied into the Mississippi River. The morgue and a dissecting room were located in the rear of the building, strategically placed a short distance from the coroner's office. The entire judicial complex's lighting apparatus was electrical.

Adjacent to the courthouse, but fronting Saratoga Street in the middle of the block, was the First Precinct Station. (The previous station, which faced Tulane Avenue at the corner of Saratoga, was torn down to accommodate the new courthouse.) The first floor contained a space for the assigned desk clerk and had ample space for two wagons and a stable to accommodate up to thirty horses. Connected to the first floor was a loading dock, conveniently located near the First Recorder's Court and used to usher prisoners in and out of the two buildings.

Initially the second floor contained the offices of the police captain, his clerk, the matron of the station and prison, and up to three additional rooms used for conducting various police business. On the third floor above the open stable floor, but separated from view by a brick wall, were twenty "holdover" cells for prisoners awaiting trial or various court appearances. The floor also contained a fifty- by fifty-two-foot drill room for exercising the inmates. When the decision was made to relocate the First City Criminal Court to the second floor, the drill room was converted to accommodate the offices of the police captain and his subordinates.

Orleans Parish Prison was situated on Gravier Street directly behind the courthouse. Surrounded by a twenty-foot wall, the structure was made of stone, brick and mortar, concrete, and steel and iron but no wood, rendering it essentially fireproof. It was accessed through a wide, arched corridor, sealed off from the outside by an imposing iron gate that led directly into a small two-story, twin-towered administrative section.

On the right side of the first floor were the jailer's room, bath, and search rooms, along with a room for storing the prisoners' property at check-in.

Orleans Parish Judicial Complex, view from Saratoga Street, now Loyola Avenue (circa 1902)
From left to right, with the ground floor blocked from view:
Orleans Parish Prison, showing the five-story square, its dormers and cupola, a side view of the front administration section, and east and north prisoner wings
The three-story First Precinct Police Station and Orleans Parish Courthouse with clock tower, corner of Saratoga Street and Tulane Avenue. (Courtesy Miscellaneous Images, Southeastern Architectural Archive, Special Collections Division, Tulane University Libraries)

To the left of the main entrance was the office of the criminal sheriff, a spacious room initially carpeted, with papering on the walls and ceiling, fine engravings on the walls, and lace curtains in the windows. Besides the office furniture, described as "pretty," the room accommodated a bed covered by a lace bedspread. (Presumably sometime after the opening, the prison warden occupied or shared the office with the sheriff.) The left side of the corridor also housed the prison armory and the reception hall where visitors waited before being escorted to the rear. (Visitation days were Monday, Wednesday, and Friday from 9:00 A.M. until 3:30 P.M., which was amended by 1898 to include Sunday visits. By then, the hours had changed to 10:00 A.M. until 4:00 P.M.) Sleeping quarters for guards and jailers were on the second floor and extended into the second floor of the main jail building. Both sections of the prison directly connected with each other.

Once out of the two-story administrative section, the building widened to a seventy-five-foot square-shaped, five-story structure, with three three-story prisoner wings radiating from its right, left, and rear walls, or east, west, and north wings, respectively. Accessing the ground floor of the square required passing the stairway at the end of the administrative corridor and walking through two iron gratings and a heavy iron door to the guard's hall, or "bullring," as it was called, where the visitors' room was also located. With a stone floor and protected by iron bars with an interior octagon-shaped design, the bullring extended to the building's third-floor steel rafters. From this vantage point, watchmen could easily observe activities in all three prisoner wings, regardless of the floor.

The entrance into each wing was separated from the bullring by a locked, steel door with a head-size opening at man's height. The hole was encased by a grated, dome-shaped basket projecting into the wing. This provided the guards with a 360-degree visual field before opening the door. In addition, on each floor, the cells were locked by means of a manual lever. Each lever was encased in a closed, iron box and dual-locked. Access to the lever required a key to the box and knowing the combination of a separate lock.

Each floor of a wing contained nine cells, and each cell could accommodate up to six prisoners comfortably, or eight if necessity warranted. (In spite of the design, prison officials tried to limit each cell to four prisoners, with each inmate provided a canvas hammock to sleep in, without benefit of a mosquito bar.) Seven cells on the first floor (dispersed among the three wings) were constructed of two layers of steel and three layers of iron, a so-called "Stetson" bar, and reserved for the most hardened criminals. All other cells (often referred to as cages) were made completely of iron bars. In addition, each wing had a communal tub, sink, and toilet.

Along the front of each cell ran a corridor enclosed by iron and steel bars that afforded the prisoners some degree of freedom when allowed out of their cells. Prisoners were usually released from their cells at seven o'clock for breakfast and required to return to their cages after supper, which was served about four o'clock. Surrounding the cells and corridor was a second passageway for guards, who could scrutinize the prisoners' quarters without direct contact with the inmates.

Murderers' row (prisoners spared a death sentence or convicted murderers awaiting transfer to the state penitentiary in Baton Rouge) and/or death row (prisoners awaiting a formal sentence of death) were initially located on the first floor in the east wing. Its capacity was forty prisoners. By November 1903, the location was moved to the second floor in the north wing. Once a prisoner was formally sentenced to death, the inmate was usually transferred to "the tower" or the upper floor of the square to await execution.

Located along the periphery of the exterior prison walls in each quadrant were exercise yards, called "great yards," though some were further subdivided according to the gender or age of the prisoners. (Not long after the prison's opening, it was deemed prudent to isolate juvenile minor offenders from adult hardened criminals.) Two of the four enclosures were segregated by race and designated as the White Yard and Colored Yard. The former was located at the corner of Gravier and Franklin streets and lay in the shadow of the west wing, which usually housed white prisoners only. The latter yard, reserved for African-American prisoners, was located at the corner of Gravier and Saratoga streets. A sentry tower was constructed in each yard, at the two street corners, in the fall of 1897. This allowed sentries to observe activity inside the great yards as well as on the street outside.

On the third floor where the three wings met at the octagon's center were five rooms located along the periphery that were reserved for special prisoners. Situated one floor above the sleeping quarters for guards and jailers, these rooms were set aside for inmates who could afford to pay a weekly fee in order to receive better accommodations. The third-floor north wing also connected to the third floor of the courthouse by way of an iron gate and bridge, but this access was eventually sealed off several years before the overpass was demolished. The new overpass design only allowed a second-floor connection between the two buildings.

On the fourth floor above the special prisoners' rooms were four hospital rooms, two reserved for whites and two for African-Americans, with an interracial chapel located in the center, atop the bullring. Catholic and Protestant services were held each Sunday, though religious services might be offered on any given day, especially Friday-morning Mass for a professed Catholic on his execution day. Hangings were always conducted on Friday afternoons. The floor extended over the north wing where a storage area and large kitchen were located. Two dumbwaiters transported meals to the first floor, where meals were served initially in the great yards.

The fifth floor of the square constituted the tower, located directly above the chapel. The upper floor's ceiling was part of the building's crown, a hip-roof design with dormers projecting out of its four sides. Each dormer had three side-by-side vertical windows, which allowed some sunlight to filter down onto the floor. Entry to the tower from the fourth floor required ascending a separate flight of curved, narrow stairs, which was protected by an iron banister. Accessing the upper floor required passing through a heavy iron door at the top of the stairs. Once atop, the tower consisted of three areas: a gallery, corridor, and four cells positioned along the north wall.

The gallery or entry point to the floor allowed a space for visitors or reporters to congregate prior to visits. The condemned cells, which were solid-wall constructed, were designated by numbers one through four. Between the gallery and cells ran a narrow corridor, isolated from the gallery by a barred wall and accessible by means of a locked, swinging, iron door. When the condemned prisoner was permitted out of his cell, this corridor allowed him some exercise space, the ability to converse with outsiders in the gallery, and access to the toilet, sink, and iron tub that were located next to Cell No. 1 on the Franklin Street side (or west end) of the building.

Along the cell-wall portion of the corridor, a horizontal, rectangular-shaped, barred window protruded into each cell. This opening allowed officials to inspect each cell prior to opening its two doors: a solid-steel entry door (located adjacent to the window) and an inner barred door. The solid door was usually kept open during the day when the cell was occupied and the inner barred door locked or unlocked depending upon the activity of the day. Each cell contained an iron bed, encapsulated within a mosquito bar and netting, mattress, pillow, and blanket. Located along the rear wall of each cell was a barred window, which provided some ventilation and a view to the outside world.

If a condemned prisoner ever thought of escaping the tower by way of the dormer windows, which surprisingly were designed without protective bars, it would have taken a herculean effort. This was assuming that the guards were sleeping at their posts and the prisoner was allowed to freely roam the corridor. The top of each cell was likely barred to allow sunlight to filter in from above. However, the top of the corridor was not, as its height extended to the rafters. Nevertheless, the northern dormer, the only dormer accessible to a condemned prisoner, was located high above the row of cells, projecting out of the exposed underbelly of the roof.

On top of the tower, but sealed off from the exposed steel rafters and dormers, was an octagon-shaped cupola with eight vertical windows. The cupola rose to a height of twenty feet and in the center a cone extended another thirty feet at its apex, the highest point in the prison.

When the prison opened, most officials assumed that the facility was escape proof, especially from the fifth-floor tower. But escape attempts were inevitable. One of the most interesting and daring breakouts occurred shortly before 4:00 P.M. on Wednesday, October 10, 1900. Matthew McCaffrey, a convicted burglar who had been elevated to a prison trustee, successfully escaped from the tower while it was unoccupied. McCaffrey never divulged how he managed to open the floor's locked entry door. In any event, he gained access to the tower, climbed up to the north dormer, broke one of the three glass panes, squeezed through the vertical window, and jumped ten feet onto the north wing's roofline. From there, he walked in the direction of the courthouse along the edge of the roof's broad gutter on the Saratoga Street side of the wing. McCaffrey managed to get as far as the roofline of the bridge before he was discovered by two deputy clerks. They saw the escapee from their third-floor window in the First Precinct Station.

McCaffrey based the timing of his escape on the belief that by that hour, police and courthouse personnel would not be in their offices. The business day usually ended between three and four o'clock. Thus, McCaffrey hoped to reach the prison's north wall undetected and then climb down to safety somewhere near the rear of the courthouse. He brought three blankets he planned to tie together to use as a rope.

Execution day dawned clear in New Orleans, with the temperature reaching seventy-five degrees. In the Colored Yard, last-minute preparations were under way for the early-afternoon hanging of Lewis W. Lyons, Jr. He and another prisoner were all who remained of five condemned men who were transferred to the tower in May 1904. Among the group, two of the men were executed in September and October, and, in January 1905, a third had his death sentence commuted to life imprisonment.

In July 1903, Lyons murdered John Ward Gurley, Jr., the district attorney of Orleans Parish. He then turned the weapon on himself, firing one shot in a failed attempt to commit suicide. Gurley's death sparked outrage throughout the city and across the nation. The crime was later recorded as the nation's first judicial murder of the twentieth century. Convicted of his crime in November 1903, Lyons languished in prison until this fateful day.

During the predawn hours, Deputy Barney Conniff, one of three watchmen assigned to the tower, told Lyons that he had read in the newspaper that he was losing his nerve as his execution drew near.

"I know, boys; it's a hard road to go," Lyons responded to Conniff, with a half-smile, "but I'll go it without faltering."

Lyons, who occupied Cell No. 1, hadn't attempted to bed down that night until 2:00 A.M. and then spent the next two and a half hours unable to fall asleep, thanks in part to Deputies Conniff, Joseph Cassard, and Henry Carroll. The watchmen spent the greater part of their eight-hour shift loudly discussing the Spanish-American War and Cassard's observations of the English army. Cassard had visited South Africa during the Second Boer War (1899-1902).

"Boys, if you stop talking now I'll try to get a little rest," Lyons finally requested.

The watchmen consented, but Lyons continued a restless sleep, unable to fully lapse into unconsciousness. The *Daily Picayune,* like other dailies, had planted a reporter near the tower's entrance door to observe the prisoner. Lyons's incessant "tossing about reflected the working of a disturbed mind," the *Daily Picayune* speculated, though he had some medical issues.

When at last Lyons gave up all attempts at sleep, he sat fully clothed on the edge of his bed. He had never completely undressed before retiring, except to remove his shoes and coat. As he sat with his elbows on his knees and his hands cupping his chin, a melancholy mood swept over him before he decided to walk to the sink and freshen up, never uttering a word during the activity. Returning to his cell, he quietly sat until shift change at six o'clock, at which time he bade farewell to the night watchmen.

Soon afterward, Capt. Richard "Dick" Meredith, the warden, arrived and mistakenly believed that Lyons had risen from a restful sleep and had dressed. Reporters who had been banned from the gallery the night before rushed in.

"How do you feel, Mr. Lyons?" Meredith inquired in a friendly tone.

"Oh, I'm feeling all right, only the rheumatism in my legs is bothering me a lot," Lyons responded in a cheerful way. He also suffered for years with lumbago, or lower back pain.

Meredith asked if he wanted anything to eat for breakfast, but Lyons wasn't hungry. Instead, he requested a pint of hot milk, which was brought up from the kitchen a few minutes later. He seemed to relish the drink, according to one reporter. In addition, the criminal sheriff of Orleans Parish, Matthew Long, Sr., who was in the yard below overseeing last-minute preparations, had a glass of rye whiskey sent to him. He had authorized whiskey rations for Lyons in the past.

"Captain," said Lyons, as he savored the last drop of alcohol, "you've been very kind to me and I want to thank you for it."

Taken aback by Lyons's unsolicited expression of gratitude, Meredith told him it wasn't necessary to thank him.

The hot milk and whiskey had their desired effect, because shortly after Lyons finished drinking both beverages, he yawned, his eyes got heavy, and his body relaxed. At about 8:30, he informed Meredith that he was going to take a nap and requested to be awakened ninety minutes later.

Meanwhile, in the Colored Yard, the hangman was hard at work conducting last-minute checks of the wooden gallows, which included an examination of the platform's underside. Stacks of hay had been carefully placed below either side of the double trapdoor to retard its striking of the underside of the platform after the supporting rope was cut. The hangman didn't want the doors to rebound and strike Lyons as he hanged.

The executioner, Francis "Frank" Elsworth Johnston, alias "Jack Ketch," was a well-known figure in the city. Standing at five feet, eleven inches tall, with thick, black hair and dark, blue eyes, Johnston was a handsome gentleman who looked more the part of a mild-mannered store clerk than a hangman. Currently living in Waveland, Mississippi, Johnston was born in neighboring Bay St. Louis on December 14, 1874. The son of George Washington Johnston and Victoria Virginia Caldwell, natives of London, England, Johnston had officiated at a number of executions prior to this time, though that was not his original calling.

At a young age, Johnston chose the priesthood as his vocation and at eighteen enrolled in a Catholic seminary in Baltimore, Maryland. But after two years of study and devoid of his religious collar, he returned home. Shortly thereafter he received his first contract as a hangman from Joseph

Frank Johnston (circa 1895). (Courtesy Colin O'Key)

F. Cazeneuve, sheriff and tax collector of Hancock County, Mississippi. His father had served in that capacity some years before.

"I officiated at my first hanging," Johnston told a reporter several years after Lyons's execution, "because another man lost his nerve."

Sheriff Cazeneuve had heard of Johnston's Christian views for a more humane way to hang a man. Johnston believed that the prisoner should be afforded a painless death. He had witnessed or heard of botched executions and thought he could do a better job. The sheriff agreed.

A contractor, farmer, and later game warden by profession, Johnston was never employed full time as a hangman. Through trial and error he perfected his skills over the years at various prisons in Louisiana, Mississippi, and Florida. In addition, though not the executioner, he set the trapdoor for convicted murderer William Henry Theodore Durrant, hanged on January 7, 1898, at San Quentin State Prison in California. Paid between $100 and $500 per hanging, his final price depended on the distance he traveled, the number of days required to do the job, and whether he constructed the gallows. When he was not employed as a hangman or engaged in his normal livelihood, Johnston found employment as a bounty hunter for the state of Louisiana.

In spite of his religious upbringing, Johnston had his fair share of brushes with the law. At the time of the Lyons hanging, he had been granted an early release from a sixty-day sentence in the parish prison. On January 31, 1905, he pled guilty to petty larceny for stealing less than one hundred dollars worth of jewelry. His release didn't end his troubles with the law, however. Over the next seven years he saw the inside of additional prisons, though ultimately he was adjudicated not guilty in each case, including a charge of grand larceny for cow stealing.

"What drop are you going to give him?" Sheriff Long inquired of Johnston, who by then was standing alone on the gallows' platform. This was Johnston's third execution at the prison, having hanged two of Lyons's former inmates the previous year.

"Just nine feet," Johnston answered, smoking his cigar as he went about his business.

"Isn't that a long fall?"

"No, sir, he's a light man," he said, looking up at the tower where Lyons slept, "and nine feet will just crack his neck nice."

In both of Johnston's previous executions, the fall had broken their necks, but he thought he could do a better job at rendering Lyons unconscious and motionless prior to his death.

Johnston finished placing the rope on the gallows and descended the platform's seventeen steps to the yard, where he described to the sheriff his newest strategy for terminating life.

"You see, I gave that noose three twists," Johnston explained, pointing up to the rope, "and I think it'll be just fine."

Johnston spoke about executing a man with the same ease that a butcher might discuss the slaughter of a cow. He continued to enlighten the sheriff and a nearby *Daily Picayune* reporter by explaining that two twists of the rope ran the risk of tearing the prisoner's head from his body, "as if I'd [used] a thin clothes line," Johnston said. (Ironically, months earlier he admitted to using a thin rope at some past hanging, with horrific consequences.) "Four twists would be bulky, and the noose wouldn't split the neck bone, but would do a strangling job." As he continued puffing on his cigar, he confidently added, "That's the science of my business, knowing how to fix the noose."

Knowing Lyons's body type—Johnston had visited the tower in the past—

and the depth of the descent that was required, he calculated that three twists of the knot would crush his spinal cord at the snap of the rope. This would render Lyons immediately unconscious prior to his painless death, Johnston's ultimate goal.

After explaining his plan to Sheriff Long, Johnston retired to one of the special rooms on the third floor until called on to cut the supporting rope that kept the platform's swinging trapdoor in place.

As promised, Lyons was awakened at ten o'clock, took his bath, groomed himself, and dressed in his burial clothes—a black alpaca coat, black trousers, white shirt with downturned collar, black tie, and slippers. Described as blue eyed, though blind in his left eye, Lyons had grown a snowy-white mustache and full beard, matching the long, thinning, snowy-white hair that ran around his otherwise bald head.

After dressing, Lyons sat in the doorway of his cell and talked nonchalantly to his day watchmen and fellow inmate, Samuel Sparo. The *Daily Picayune* described Sparo, a Sicilian native, as a member of the city's "dread Mafia Society."

At eleven o'clock, Lyons was visited by Rev. John O. Miller, the curate of Trinity Episcopal Church on Jackson Avenue. They had met one another for the first time the previous day. Lyons greeted him respectfully, but his mood soured at the prospect of having to engage in further spiritual talk with the minister, who came dressed in his white, priestly robe. Nevertheless, he knelt down for a short prayer and seemed relieved only when the final "amen" was uttered.

By then, the prison was buzzing with chatter from prisoners confined to their cells and workers making last-minute preparations in the yard. In spite of this, Lyons remained composed and collected, calmly talking to his keepers and unmoved by the racket that reverberated up from the yard.

As noon approached, Sheriff Long, Chief Deputy Patrick King, and Chief Deputy Criminal Clerk Charles Reilly, who were authorized witnesses to the execution, Captain Meredith, and six reporters gathered in the tower's gallery. Lyons continued to show no fear as he was about to be escorted out of the corridor.

"Gooda-bye, Meester Lyons, be brav now," Sparo said, speaking in broken English, as he rushed up and warmly grasped his hand.

Lyons turned, looked at his fellow condemned inmate, and with a faint smile said, "There's no dunghill in me; I'll walk to that gallows as easily as I'll walk through this door." Lyons had consigned himself to death long before that day.

Sparo retreated to his cell, fell to his knees, and prayed earnestly for the repose of the soul of his fellow prisoner. But Sparo knew his time was coming, when he would also have to take the long walk to death.

Lyons stood in the gallery with Reverend Miller at his side as Deputy King slowly unfolded and read the official death warrant. His "voice trembled once or twice as he read the baleful words contained in the warrant," the *Daily Picayune* reported.

"Have you anything to say, Mr. Lyons?" Sheriff Long asked at the conclusion of King's official duties.

"Nothing at all," he responded, nodding his head.

Instinctually, Sheriff Long and the guards gathered around Lyons as they bade him goodbye and shook his hand.

"God bless you, Lyons," the sheriff proclaimed, as he released the prisoner's hand and began to lead the slow march to the gallows. As the procession commenced, a universal chorus of goodbyes echoed through the gallery. It was a remarkable show of respect towards a man who had cold-bloodedly murdered the parish's beloved district attorney two years before.

Lyons followed Sheriff Long with Reverend Miller on one side, Captain Meredith on the other, and the rest of the men forming the rear. No one spoke as they slowly descended the narrow stairway to the fourth floor and then down three additional flights of stairs to the ground floor. Out of the building, the procession passed through an iron gate that led into Yard No. 7, where some tools and heavy materials were stored, and then through another entranceway into the Colored Yard.

As Sheriff Long ascended the gallows' steps, Lyons stood at the foot for a moment to briefly study the death machine before joining the sheriff atop. Reverend Miller, following Lyons up the stairs, placed a reassuring hand on his shoulder, though Lyons didn't appear to need the emotional support. Captain Meredith also took a spot on the platform, along with Deputy Jack Spellman and Charles Brainey, who were already in the yard when the procession arrived. The remaining members of the party stood in front of the gallows and were joined by other official witnesses. There were no other spectators allowed in the yard except the executioner.

Delayed by a few moments, Johnston arrived disguised in a long, black robe, with his head completely covered by a black hood. Lyons turned and stared at the cloaked face, not realizing who the man was, though he had first laid eyes on him the previous September.

"Try to make a clean job out of it," Lyons instructed Johnston, with a slight sneer in his voice.

Johnston gave an affirmative nod and then pulled out several strands of ropes from beneath his robe. Deputy Spellman and Brainey, along with Captain Meredith, extended their hands to Lyons in a farewell shake and goodbye.

"I thank you again, Captain," Lyons said. He then extended his hand to Sheriff Long.

"I held to my word, didn't I, Mr. Lyons?" Sheriff Long asked, as he grabbed his hand. "Are you satisfied?" The sheriff had promised no unauthorized persons and no mass of spectators would be allowed in the yard, as had been the case during the previous year's hangings.

"Yes, I am," Lyons replied. "You certainly kept your word, and you have my thanks for it and for the other favors and kindnesses you extended to me."

Reverend Miller then offered his hand and bade Lyons a final goodbye. Soon after, Johnston bound Lyons's hands behind his back and then bent down and wrapped several yards of rope around Lyons's legs near his ankles. While Lyons was being tied, he looked down into the yard one last time to survey the witnesses, pleased that his execution was devoid of a circuslike atmosphere.

"Do you have anything you would like to say, Lyons?" the sheriff asked, as Johnston, standing to the rear of Lyons, brought the noose to his head. Lyons, the taller of the two men, bowed his head a little so Johnston could properly place the noose.

"No, nothing at all," Lyons steadfastly replied. They were his last words.

Johnston pulled the noose snug, causing some folds of skin to lap over the tightening snare. Positioned in the center of the trapdoor, Lyons closed his eyes and stood like a statue as Johnston placed a black hood designed with tightening strings over his head. Unbeknownst to the executioner, a portion of the hood had caught Lyons's chin, which required Johnston to loosen the strings and reposition it. Reverend Miller began to recite the prayer for the dying, as Lyons remained motionless, moments from death.

Johnston retreated to the rear of the platform and knelt down near a paper-wrapped package that contained a steel cleaver. The taut cord supporting the trapdoor was inches from his reach. Retrieving the hatchet and raising it above his head, Johnston waited for Reverend Miller to finish his prayer.

At 12:14 P.M., scarcely a second after the final "amen" was uttered, Johnston severed the rope, causing the trapdoor to swing down and strike the stacks of hay beneath the platform. Lyons's descent was terminated by a quick snap of the rope, his feet only six inches from the pavement. His neck stretched a bit from the sudden deceleration, as his head tilted towards his right shoulder and his chin slightly rose. The noose's knot sank deeply into the flesh of his left jaw. The death scene caused a momentary gasp from the witnesses. Thereafter, no movement of the body was observed. Lyons was rendered instantaneously unconscious and paralyzed, with only part of his autonomic nervous system functioning for a brief period.

Lyons hanged for ten minutes before Dr. Joseph A. O'Hara, the parish coroner, and his chief assistant, Dr. Sidney Mioton, pronounced him dead. His stubborn heart, its pulsating chambers barely audible to the ear, refused to stop beating. His body was allowed to hang for another eleven minutes before it was cut down and placed on a table beneath the gallows for an autopsy.

Drs. O'Hara and Mioton discovered that not only had the neck been broken, but the spinal cord had been completely severed. Lyons's face was also badly cyanotic "from the congealed blood trapped beneath the noose and his lower jaw dropped almost to the throat when the noose was cut off," the *Daily Picayune* reported.

After the autopsy, Lyons's sagging jaw was bound and his body placed in a rosewood coffin with a silver plate on top that bore the inscription *At Rest.* Thomas Doyle, an undertaker, whose parlor was located at 625 Elysian Fields Avenue, took charge of the body. At 5:00 P.M., a graveside service was held at Carrollton Cemetery, where Lyons had requested to be buried. Officiated by Reverend Miller, the service was attended only by Lyons's estranged wife and five children.

For his crime of murder, an act that could only be described as senseless, Lewis Lyons suffered the ultimate penalty with the forfeiture of his life. For eight long years he was able to suppress the pent-up frustration and rage he harbored towards the local judiciary. But by the summer of 1903, he could no longer control himself. What motivated him to commit murder was easily determined, but why he chose to direct his rage only towards the district attorney was baffling for some.

Chapter Two

THE DIAMOND STUD

Carroll, you well know that I had nothing to do with the stealing of your stud.
Lewis W. Lyons

On a cloudy Monday morning, July 20, 1903, Lewis Lyons was seen standing in front of the Macheca Building. The edifice was a newly constructed seven-story office complex located at 828 Canal Street, near the corner of Baronne Street.

"Is Mr. Gurley in his office?" Lyons asked Dr. Charles Buck, who approached the building's entrance. The time was approximately 9:45.

Dr. Buck, a dentist whose office was located on the third floor, was a casual acquaintance of Lyons. In the past, he had frequently seen him at the law office of his friends, J. Ward Gurley, Jr., and Delos Mellen, when both men rented space in the New Orleans National Bank Building on Camp Street. When they dissolved their firm in the fall of 1902, Mellen and Gurley relocated to the third and fourth floor of the Macheca Building, respectively.

"I guess he ought to be by now," Dr. Buck responded, but he wasn't sure.

Leaving Lyons on the street, Dr. Buck ventured to Mellen's office before attending to his first appointment. He had no idea what was in store that morning. For his part, Lyons stood for a few moments before entering the front lobby and taking the elevator to the fourth floor. Thirty minutes later, shots rang out. A murder and attempted suicide had occurred, and the citizens of New Orleans were in shock.

⌖⌖⌖

Lewis Williams Lyons, Jr., was born in New Orleans on August 14, 1858, the second of five children of Lewis W. Lyons, a native of Kentucky, and Charity R. Wilson from Selma, Alabama. What year his parents arrived in the city is uncertain, but by the time of their marriage on December 5, 1854,

Lyons Sr. was an established clothing entrepreneur who sold adults' and later children's attire. Two months before his marriage, he opened his first store at the corner of Canal and Camp streets. Four years later he relocated to a larger and more profitable location on St. Charles. The business occupied a huge four-story building at the corner of Common Street, with *L. W. Lyons & Company* prominently displayed atop the upper-floor façade.

Lyons's father and his business survived the Union occupation of New Orleans during the Civil War. But his life was cut short on April 17, 1867, when he died of an unknown cause at age thirty-eight. His wife continued to run the business and later went into partnership with businessman H. B. Stevens. Their collaboration lasted until about 1871, when Stevens became the sole proprietor.

Lewis W. Lyons, Jr. (July 1903). (Courtesy Colin O'Key)

During Lyons's formative years, he attended Magnolia School on Carondelet Street, between Jackson and Philip streets, two blocks from his parents' home. At that time, the family resided at the corner of Jackson and Prytania streets, the home where his father passed away. Several years after the patriarch's death, the family relocated to the corner of St. Charles and St. Mary and, by 1876, moved again to 91 (now in the 1600 block of) Prytania, at the corner of Terpsichore Street.

Over the years, Lyons had an assortment of jobs. Leaving school in his early teens, he worked for a short time on a sugar plantation. His older brother, Wilson, was employed there and got him the job. Returning to the city, he worked at Maginnis Cotton Mill on Magazine Street as a clerk, press operator, and night watchman during his seventeen-year tenure, which ended around 1887-88. On April 4, 1885, Lyons married twenty-eight-year-old Clara Smyth Wootan, a native New Orleanian, and the couple had six children over a nine-year period. Their first child, Lewis Williams Lyons III, was born seven months after their marriage.

After leaving the cotton mill, Lyons worked as a clerk at another Maginnis family business, Lafayette Warehouse Company. While employed there in late 1892, he opened a saloon at the corner of Dryades (now Oretha Castle Haley Boulevard) and Felicity streets, selling it four or five months later. During that time he also speculated on horses, bred racing dogs, and sold poultry for a living. After leaving the warehouse, he found seasonal work as a cotton clerk at the Port of Chalmette and later was employed at the Union Oil Company, selling cottonseed meal and hulls before being laid off during the summer of 1895. While steadily employed, Lyons purchased several rental properties in town. Among his holdings, located in the Carrollton neighborhood, was a New Orleans-style double cottage (a duplex) at 931-33 Hillary Street, where his family resided beginning in the early 1890s.

On Monday evening, July 8, 1895, Lyons ventured out for a few hours of social drinking, leaving his wife and six children at home. He had a history of frequenting various saloons in the city, so it wasn't an unusual occurrence, though he was unemployed at the time.

Sometime that night, Lyons entered the Smile Saloon, located at 113 Baronne Street, near the corner of Canal. (Walgreens, its entrance on Canal, now occupies the property.) There he encountered Daniel Carroll, an acquaintance of his. Prior to Lyons's arrival, Carroll had been drinking with his friends, Charles Lebanno, William Leonard, Dan Hickey, and William McGrath. At about eleven o'clock, Carroll left the saloon with Lebanno and

Leonard but returned alone a short time later to resume his revelry with the others.

At midnight, Lyons departed the saloon, boarded one of the streetcars running along Baronne Street, and headed home. Meanwhile, Carroll, Hickey, and McGrath continued their merriment before relocating a short distance to the French Quarter at the Little Diamond Saloon, 741 Customhouse (now Iberville) Street at the corner of Bourbon. (The property is now occupied by Jester Mardi Gras Daiquiris and Pizza and has a Bourbon Street address.) There they were joined by a fourth man, James Howell, alias Kid Murphy. (His forename was also listed in the newspaper as *Henry.*) Howell was a dubious character from Toronto, Canada, who had recently come to the city by way of Florida. At three o'clock, when the merriment ended, Carroll discovered that his diamond stud had been stolen off the front of his shirt.

Carroll was employed as a general auditor for the Great Southern Telephone and Telegraph Company. His tenuous association with Lyons dated back several years when he had business dealings with the Union Oil Company. As a member of the upper class, Carroll cherished his valuable keepsake and wore it proudly, if not recklessly, for all to see. Unbeknownst to Carroll, his diamond stud caught the attention of Howell.

In an inebriated state, Carroll reported the theft to the police. His drinking companions had long ago vacated the premises. Summoned to the scene were Detectives Richard Kirwin and Fernand DeRancé, along with Sgt. Richard Walsh, a friend of Carroll. Leading the investigation, Kirwin and DeRancé were given the names of the other gentlemen with whom Carroll associated during the night, including Lewis Lyons, who had no connection to the continued revelry at the Little Diamond Saloon.

With Carroll intoxicated, the detectives had no choice but to jail him, at the Third Precinct Station in the historic Cabildo building on Jackson Square. (The incident occurred within that precinct's domain.) He would remain jailed until he sobered up. In the meantime, the police investigation was put on hold.

On the morning of July 9, patrolman Samuel P. Simone brought Carroll before Judge A. M. Aucoin of the Second Recorder's Court (also located in the Cabildo). It was hoped that Carroll was sober enough to swear out a criminal complaint, but Judge Aucoin refused to allow it, believing he was still too intoxicated. What transpired next lit a fuse to a powder keg that would explode eight years later.

Mortified by his actions the previous night, Carroll wanted to drop the whole matter and pocket his losses, but Judge Aucoin pressed on. A theft had occurred, the law broken, and justice had to be pursued. Judge Aucoin directed Simone to write the affidavit for Carroll, believing he had been given the facts pertaining to the theft. Simone wrote it, but his information later contradicted Carroll's sworn testimony in court.

The prime suspects listed on the affidavit were James Howell and William McGrath, with the Latin addendum *et al.* tacked on to the list, implying anyone who had shared a drink with Carroll, including Lewis Lyons. Hence, Lyons became a prime suspect by virtue of his proximity to Carroll that night. The fact that his name was never listed in the affidavit was highly unorthodox according to the Louisiana Supreme Court, which later opined on the matter. Nevertheless, the criminal matter went forward, though no arrest warrant for Lewis Lyons was ever issued by Judge Aucoin.

Later that afternoon, pursuant to the arrest warrants issued for Howell and McGrath, Kirwin and DeRancé went looking for the pair. The detectives soon realized that Howell had skipped town. Having problems locating their remaining suspect, the detectives sought the help of Lyons, whom they tracked down at the front entrance of the Smile Saloon. He agreed to take the officers to Hickey's residence at 129 North Rampart Street, where McGrath lived, but when the party arrived, only Hickey was home. (For reasons unknown, Hickey was never a suspect.) Later, while Lyons and the two detectives were standing in front of the Grand Opera House at 919 Canal Street, Carroll walked up. The facts concerning what transpired next split into two versions of the truth.

Lyons's account of the story began on July 9 at 6:00 P.M., as he stood in front of the opera house with the two detectives. By that hour, Carroll, who arrived shortly afterwards, was sufficiently sober to exonerate him had he been so inclined; he was not, according to Lyons. Detective Kirwin asked Carroll if he suspected that Lyons had anything to do with the theft.

"Yes," Carroll replied without hesitation, according to Lyons.

"Carroll, you well know that I had nothing to do with the stealing of your stud and that I was not with you when the theft was committed," Lyons responded, dumbfounded by Carroll's answer.

"Never mind. I will fix you tomorrow," he retorted.

Carroll then walked away. Soon after, the detectives arrested Lyons.

To Lyons's thinking, the "tomorrow" reference meant that when he was arrested, he wouldn't be arraigned until the next day, given the late hour. It was then that Carroll expected to get his satisfaction regarding the theft of his diamond stud. But Carroll later testified that he never spoke those exact words to Lyons, and the arresting officers never corroborated Lyons's version of the incident. In addition, Carroll unequivocally denied that he had anything to do with Lyons's arrest, in spite of the *Daily Picayune* reporting on July 11 that Carroll had pointed an accusatory finger at Lyons.

Not surprisingly, Carroll and the two detectives gave a different version of the incident. Acting under the assumption that Lyons had been in the company of Carroll when the theft occurred, and unable to locate the two prime suspects, the detectives arrested Lyons. It's conceivable that Lyons provoked the peace officers with some verbal irregularities after their unsuccessful hunt for McGrath. According to the detectives' version, Lyons was arrested before Carroll arrived in front of the opera house. Carroll later claimed that he had no knowledge of why Lyons had just been arrested; he barely knew the man. When the detectives asked Carroll if Lyons was in his company the previous night, Carroll said yes. Whatever response Lyons had after that point, Carroll ended the conversation with: "I'll see you tomorrow in court." Lyons was shortly afterwards booked and jailed until his court appearance the following day; Carroll did not attend.

Meanwhile, McGrath was located and arrested by patrolman Simone. But the whereabouts of Howell remained a mystery. His involvement in the jewel heist didn't come to light until the closing days of July.

On Wednesday, July 10, 1895, Lyons and McGrath appeared before Judge Aucoin. They were charged with robbery and placed under a $500 appearance bond. When the case was finally adjudicated on July 18, it was determined that Howell had acted alone. The barkeeper at the Little Diamond Saloon had seen Howell hovering over Carroll and eyeing his jewelry. He warned Howell to keep his hands off Carroll, who by then was fully intoxicated. Howell responded that he would give the barkeeper "a piece of the swag," or a share of the diamond prize, but the barkeeper refused. When the barkeeper turned his head, Howell snatched the diamond stud off the front of Carroll's shirt and disappeared.

Later that morning, at four o'clock, Howell attempted to sell the diamond stud for twenty dollars to a patron at the Referee Saloon, located at 130 Royal Street. He informed the gentleman that he and his mistress were leaving the city in a few hours and if he didn't buy it someone else would, given the bargain price. Suspecting the item was stolen, the gentleman refused.

On July 11, the *Daily Picayune* reported that the day after Detectives Kirwin and DeRancé arrested Lyons, they were aware of Howell's sole involvement in the theft. By then, they had interviewed the barkeeper. Why the detectives didn't inform the court and have the charges dismissed against the two men is uncertain. What happened instead was that both men languished in legal limbo for eight days until they were finally cleared—but not before Lyons's good name was splashed all over the newspapers in connection with the tawdry affair.

Meanwhile, the whereabouts of James Howell were at last discovered by July 26. Knowing that the suspect had fled the city, Dexter Gaster, superintendent of police, sent telegrams to various police departments across Louisiana asking them to be on the lookout for Howell. Acting on this information, the sheriff of Rapides Parish arrested the suspect in Alexandria. Fortunately for the sheriff, but ironically for Howell, Howell claimed that he was a victim of a robbery. Howell told the sheriff that he had been robbed by two strangers who were later apprehended, though the diamond stud was not found among their possessions.

After being transported back to New Orleans, Howell told police that he bought the diamond stud from an unknown party the night it went missing. However, he failed to mention his visit to the Referee Saloon or why he suddenly departed New Orleans for Alexandria after his so-called purchase.

Howell stated that upon reaching Alexandria, he was strapped for cash and pawned the jewelry for thirty dollars. He then used the money to gamble, winning fifty dollars. With part of that, he bought back the diamond stud, which he claimed was later stolen. He was eventually charged with grand larceny.

Though the mystery surrounding the theft of the diamond stud was later solved, the ramifications of the crime and its effect on Lewis Lyons lingered for years. It's not known if William McGrath sought legal retribution for his troubles, but Lyons did. After stewing over the matter for a year, he consulted the law firm of Gurley and Mellen. Their law partnership began on January 16, 1889, three days after the death of Mellen's father.

Mellen's parents, William Francis Mellen and Helen E. Carpenter, were natives of Mississippi who married in 1855 in Natchez, where Delos Mellen, their only child, was born on August 3, 1859. The family relocated to New Orleans in 1860, a year after William Mellen earned his law license. During the Civil War he served in the Twenty-Fifth Louisiana Infantry and was severely wounded during the Battle of Perryville in October 1862. His wound disqualified him from further battlefield service and he was eventually assigned as a legal advisor for Gen. E. Kirby Smith, until he resigned on August 22, 1864.

After the war, Mellen returned to Natchez, where he built up an extensive and lucrative law practice before relocating his family to St. Louis, Missouri, in 1874. Three years later, he moved back to New Orleans. At the time of his death at age fifty-two from kidney failure, William Mellen was one of the most respected attorneys in the city.

Receiving his rudimentary education in Natchez, Delos Mellen enrolled at Cornell University in Ithaca, New York, during the mid- to late 1870s, where he graduated with honors. Furthering his education, he traveled to France and then Germany before returning to New Orleans, where he enrolled at the University of Louisiana (beginning in 1884, Tulane University) law school. Mellen graduated in 1881, then went into partnership with his father. On November 23, 1887, he married twenty-seven-year-old Marie Corinne Castellanos, a native New Orleanian whose father was a prominent physician, and from that union had three children. After his father's death, Mellen went into partnership with Gurley, his senior by eight years.

Both men prospered as attorneys, becoming prominent figures in the city. From their exposure they were able to amass considerable political connections that served them well over the years. In May 1896, Pres. Grover Cleveland appointed Gurley, and in July, Mellen, as the United States district attorney and assistant district attorney for the Eastern District of Louisiana, respectively; their offices were relocated in the United States Custom House. It was after their federal appointments that Lyons sought their services. In spite of their federal positions, Gurley and Mellen had continued their private law practice.

Lyons knew Gurley, who was an early schoolmate of his brother, Wilson, though they were not close friends. Gurley was indisposed when Lyons sought the firm's assistance, so Mellen agreed to represent him in Civil District Court. The lawsuit was filed on July 8, 1896, with Lyons seeking $5,000 in damages for false imprisonment, plus $40 in court fees.

In his lawsuit, Lyons claimed that Carroll knew he was innocent of the crime and conspired with Detectives Kirwin and DeRancé, resulting in his arrest and the physical and mental anguish he suffered. He also claimed that he was placed in a filthy cell with a mixture of drunks and African-Americans of both sexes, a motley crew he described as "dirty." Having to share a cell with the latter group was especially unpardonable, to Lyons's thinking. Lyons

Delos Mellen (1896). (Courtesy NOLA.com/The *Times-Picayune*)

sought financial compensation from Carroll and the arresting officers for this and for having his good name dragged through the mud from the notoriety he received from the press.

In spite of being exonerated for the crime, Lyons found it difficult to secure steady employment. Adding to his woes, the country was in the throes of a crippling depression that lasted until 1897. Nevertheless, Lyons believed that the principal reason for his unemployment was his arrest. He felt ostracized by the business community. Lyons tried operating another saloon but was forced to sell it seven months later. Eventually he secured work with the Illinois Central Railroad as a freight receiver clerk, though he was let go. He later found work as a public weigher, his last known position, until he was dismissed in 1902. During this time he was constantly short of cash and forced to borrow against his property holdings, even going so far as to apply to charitable organizations for help when his children got sick.

Sometime after Carroll and the detectives were served their papers, the three defendants countersued Lyons, asking the judge to dismiss the suit. They were seeking "exceptions of no cause of action" or claiming no legal validity to Lyons's allegation. The Honorable Thomas C. W. Ellis, judge of the Civil District Court for Orleans Parish, Division A, was allotted by ballot the lawsuit and countersuit. He sustained Kirwin's and DeRancé's objections but overruled Carroll. Lyons's lawsuit against Carroll was allowed to proceed.

Lyons requested that the case be decided in a bench trial, by Judge Ellis, rather than by jury. The added expense of a jury trial would be prohibitive for Lyons, who continued to struggle financially. Mellen agreed to take the case on a contingency fee, but Lyons was still responsible for paying the stenographer and other court costs.

It's not known when Judge Ellis decided the countersuits, but he didn't hear Lyons's lawsuit against Carroll for nearly two years. By early 1897, Gurley and Mellen were in the midst of prosecuting several important federal cases, some of which weren't decided until late spring. Judge Ellis took his summer holiday in early June and didn't reconvene his court until mid-October. By then, a city health crisis affecting Lyons's family delayed again the start of the trial.

Beginning the first week of September 1897, various New Orleans dailies printed stories about yellow fever spreading through coastal Alabama and Mississippi. The epidemic reached the city on September 6, with the death of a thirteen-year-old local boy who had visited Ocean Springs, Mississippi. His death was the first confirmed yellow-fever fatality in New Orleans since 1889 and put the public on edge. By mid-September, a total of twenty cases of yellow fever were confirmed in the city, though no additional deaths were reported.

At first, the city health department believed they were dealing with a milder form of yellow fever; they were wrong. By the end of the month, 228 cases, with 28 confirmed deaths, were reported. The numbers of new cases and deaths only escalated as October progressed. Among the new cases diagnosed were Lewis Lyons (on October 25) and three of his children. If Lyons's lawsuit was on the docket, it was quickly withdrawn as his oldest child, thirteen-year-old Lewis, was the most critically ill in his family.

By the end of October, a total of 1,510 cases of yellow fever were confirmed in the city, including 183 deaths. Among those who died was Lyons's oldest son, who passed away on October 30. Clara Lyons arranged for her son's burial at Carrollton Cemetery, as the city health department did not declare her husband cured of yellow fever until November 7. Fortunately, no other family members died.

In spite of cooler temperatures, the mosquito-spread virus continued unabated though November. A total of 1,873 cases of yellow fever were confirmed in New Orleans by November 22. By then, the death toll had risen to 281. On December 7, the city health department reported 14 additional deaths. By year's end, another 4 people were added to the mortality table from an estimated 1,900 cases of yellow fever.

Before it was over, the epidemic spread as far as Louisville, Kentucky and Memphis, Tennessee, though only a handful of cases were reported in those more northerly regions. The epidemic was concentrated on the Gulf Coast from Mobile, Alabama, to Galveston, Texas, with most of it occurring in coastal Mississippi and in New Orleans. When the epidemic ended, over five thousand cases of yellow fever were confirmed, with 10 percent of that number dying. Even with those numbers, the 1897 yellow-fever epidemic was later classified as a tamed plague. In contrast, in 1878 over four thousand people died in New Orleans alone. Prior to this latest epidemic, it had been years since the death rates from yellow fever had exceeded nineteen per year.

With the yellow-fever epidemic now history and the family's health restored by year's end, Lyons resumed his efforts to seek justice for the offenses committed against him during the summer of 1895. Undoubtedly, he believed that 1898 would be his year of vindication; he was wrong.

Chapter Three

JUSTICE DENIED

I never saw a man so worked up over a suit as he was over that one.

Delos C. Mellen

It wasn't until June 1898 that Lyons's lawsuit against Daniel Carroll was finally argued before Judge Ellis. Lyons contended that Carroll was the driving force behind his arrest and therefore should be held liable for the physical and psychological anguish he suffered. Thus, everything hinged on Delos Mellen proving that Carroll was the catalyst. This point was the sole reason for Judge Ellis's earlier decision to dismiss the lawsuits against Detectives Kirwin and DeRancé. After reading the plaintiff's brief, Judge Ellis believed that the arresting officers had acted on probable cause when they arrested Lyons, based on what Lyons declared was erroneous information given to them by Carroll.

Judge Ellis did not announce his verdict until the fall, finding in favor of the defendant, Daniel Carroll. He found no direct link that tied Carroll to Lyons's arrest. Rather, the evidence showed that the detectives had acted independently when they arrested Lyons. Also, the evidence showed that Carroll had originally wanted to drop the whole matter, humiliated by his drunkenness the night of the theft. This proved to Judge Ellis that Carroll harbored no malice towards the plaintiff. And then there was the original affidavit issued for the arrest of parties involved in the robbery in which Lyons's name did not specifically appear.

It would be an understatement to say that Lyons was disappointed with the ruling. But what disheartened him above all else was Judge Ellis's declaration that he was absolutely innocent of the crime. Lyons believed that if this was so, the judge should have ruled in his favor. But he had no one to blame but himself. In his lawsuit, Lyons had blamed Carroll alone for his arrest and then failed to prove it in court.

Almost immediately after the ruling, Lyons began to pressure Mellen to seek an appeal with the Louisiana Supreme Court. He wished for the High Court to set aside the lower court's decision. Months dragged on as Lyons became a frequent visitor at Mellen's office in the United States Custom House. But Mellen's duties as a federal prosecutor precluded him from taking swifter action. Likely his delay also stemmed from his belief that it was a waste of his time and resources. Besides, he wasn't going to work the appeal for free, and Lyons still owed him for some court costs that he had incurred, though Lyons later disputed that claim.

Meanwhile, Lyons scoured over the court transcript, looking for any inconsistencies in the testimonies that could be used at appeal. What he discovered instead were instances in the record where he alleged that the stenographer, Leslie Bobb, had changed words or totally misquoted sworn testimony to the benefit of the defendant. Though Mellen agreed that some minor transcription errors had occurred (which was common), he hardly believed that Bobb had deliberately altered the transcript. And he felt that the Louisiana Supreme Court would not set aside Judge Ellis's verdict based solely on that.

Over time, Lyons came to believe that Mellen, too, was responsible for the verdict and accused him of being negligent in his duties, being incompetent, and conspiring with Bobb to lose his case. Mellen told him that if he wasn't satisfied with how he was handling things, he was free to seek the advice and counsel of another attorney. By then, their professional relationship was nearing a boiling point. Ironically, it would be Mellen's partner who got burned when Lyons eventually switched attorneys.

J. Ward Gurley, Jr., was born in New Orleans on July 14, 1851, the eldest of six children of John Ward Gurley, Sr., and Rosamond Richards. His father was a prominent attorney in the city with a long and distinguished career serving as the clerk of the U.S. Circuit Court and later in the Confederate States District Court in New Orleans until Union forces occupied the city in May 1862. After the war, he served as the U.S. assistant district attorney for the Eastern District of Louisiana between 1869 and 1895. During part of that time, he also functioned as one of the masters in chancery of the U.S. Circuit Court. In poor health during the last year of his life, Gurley, Sr., died of "senile debility" on September 18, 1897, at age seventy-eight.

The younger Gurley was educated at public and private schools in New

Orleans before attending Washington College (now Washington and Lee University) in Lexington, Virginia, where he graduated in 1872. Upon his return to New Orleans, Gurley was admitted to the Louisiana bar in April 1873 and served in the office of the U.S. Register in Bankruptcy for the District of Louisiana between 1876 and 1880. On October 29, 1878, he married twenty-six-year-old Aurora Huntington Torrey, a native New Orleanian, and from that union had two daughters. Entering the local political arena, Gurley served as the assistant city attorney for New Orleans between 1880 and 1882 and thereafter went into private practice until partnering with Delos Mellen in January 1889.

Over the years, Gurley earned tremendous respect in the legal community for his mastery of lawyering inside the courtroom. But his conduct outside the courthouse garnered the most praise. Possessing "human kindness and a true sympathy for the weak and afflicted," according to the *Daily Picayune,* Gurley was a champion for the underprivileged, never turning away a person with a legitimate grievance, no matter their lack of stature in the community.

In addition, he dealt with his own tragedies privately. A courteous gentleman and a model family man, Gurley suffered the loss of his wife, Aurora, affectionately called Rosa, on April 12, 1892, when she died of nephritis at age thirty-nine. Gurley's youngest daughter was six years old at the time of her mother's death. Unquestionably, the family's heartache was profound. Gurley's restraint and patience, his inability to say no, and his kindness towards others appeared to have been his undoing when he finally agreed to become Lyons's attorney.

The exact date that Gurley filed his client's legal brief with the Louisiana Supreme Court is not known, but oral arguments were likely heard in early 1899. When Associate Justice Joseph Breaux rendered the court's opinion on June 12, 1899, it was yet another disappointment for Lyons. The Supreme Court upheld Judge Ellis's verdict, finding no evidence that Lyons's arrest was traceable to any actions taken by Daniel Carroll. Lyons's civil suit against Carroll was over. However, the jurist did find it "a little out of the ordinary" that Lyons's name never appeared on the affidavit and therefore his arrest should never have occurred.

With that opening, Lyons believed that the court might invalidate Judge Ellis's exclusion of Detectives Kirwin and DeRancé from the original lawsuit. If he could convince the Supreme Court to do so, Lyons would have another opportunity to sue for damages. Of course, he was wrong, as both things were mutually exclusive. Judge Ellis hadn't excluded the police officers from the lawsuit because he ruled the arrest was lawful. He excluded them because Lyons accused Carroll of conspiring with them to have him arrested. Since the conspiracy was never proven, Lyons lost his case.

As a purely procedural motion, Gurley sought an immediate rehearing of the appeal before the Louisiana Supreme Court, spurred by Lyons and the inferences he drew from Justice Breaux's comments. But on June 26 the Supreme Court denied the rehearing. The matter related to *Lyons v. Carroll* was settled.

If Lyons ever contemplated challenging Leslie Bobb in court, his hopes were dashed on February 9, 1899, when Bobb died of a stroke at age forty-six. Lyons's unluckiness with his adversaries continued eight months later when forty-one-year-old Daniel Carroll suffered a fatal heart attack at his farm near Covington, Louisiana. In spite of Carroll's death, his name appeared as the appellee when Gurley took Lyons's case again before the Louisiana Supreme Court and later when Lyons filed another lawsuit against the late Daniel Carroll.

In November 1899, Gurley was elected Orleans Parish district attorney, though he didn't take office until June 1900. His duties as a United States prosecutor and an important case pending in federal court precluded him from assuming his new position in January, as dictated by law. The outgoing district attorney, Robert Marr, Jr., remained in office temporarily. When Gurley was finally able to assume his elected office, the seat was declared vacant. By law, there was little anyone could do otherwise, given the six-month lapse from when he was to take office. To solve the problem, Gov. William Heard simply appointed Gurley to fill the vacancy.

Because Mellen was not retained by the newly appointed United States district attorney, he found himself working again full time in the private sector. In spite of Gurley's new position, with his office now located in the parish courthouse, Mellen and Gurley remained law partners and moved their private practice to the five-story New Orleans National Bank Building, at 201 Camp Street.

With 310 cases left on the dockets when District Attorney Gurley assumed his new position, including five ongoing murder or manslaughter investigations, he had no time to work on Lyons's behalf during the remainder of the year. Still, Lyons became a constant and bothersome visitor at both of Gurley's offices. In spite of the interruptions, Gurley remained courteous and attentive during these occasions. But Gurley began to think that Lyons was becoming unbalanced by all the stress; his law partner agreed.

"I never saw a man so worked up over a suit as he was over that one," Mellen later commented. "He brooded over it and never thought of anything else."

On February 18, 1901, Gurley finally appeared before the Louisiana Supreme Court, asking the jurists to compel Judge Ellis to include the detectives in Lyons's original lawsuit. But on March 17, 1902, the High Court reaffirmed the lower court's decision, based on Judge Ellis's pretrial assertions about the circumstances of the arrest. In retrospect, had Lyons instead sued the detectives for false arrest knowing that Carroll had not implicated him, and lost his case, the Supreme Court might have looked on his appeal more favorably. But Lyons never pursued that legal pathway.

Meanwhile, Lyons's mounting debt and inability to adequately maintain his standard of living caused him to devise a creative way to earn additional income to support his family. Sometime in early 1901, Lyons asked Zach Spearing, an attorney, if he was interested in renting to him his double cottage located across the street from his own duplex on Hillary Street. The property was vacant and in disrepair. Lyons offered eight dollars a month for both sides, even though Spearing was originally asking twelve dollars a month per unit. To sweeten the deal, Lyons offered to make any necessary repairs to the structure if he waived the first month's rent. Spearing finally agreed, and Lyons moved his family, renting out his old place for a greater monthly fee than he was paying to Spearing.

Things went well for Spearing until March 1902 when Lyons's monthly payments abruptly stopped. By then, Lyons might have been strapped for cash, as one of his tenants fell behind in his rent and was evicted.

In August, after he sent numerous notices to Lyons asking for back payments, Spearing went to his property only to discover that another family had moved in and was giving their monthly rent to Lyons. Lyons was nowhere to be found, having sold his duplex across the street months before. In the end, Spearing never received any of Lyons's back payments and only learned about his whereabouts after reading his name in the newspapers the following summer.

Having exhausted all legal avenues by the spring of 1902, Lyons asked Gurley to reimburse him for all the expenses he had incurred or at least to find him a job. There was even a rumor that he asked Gurley to assume the monthly note on his home. The original loan was $800, plus interest. Lyons agreed to relinquish ownership to Gurley, move out, and have Gurley rent out the property. Gurley could use whatever rental income he collected to pay off the loan, at which time Lyons expected Gurley to transfer ownership back to him. These proposals were occurring while Lyons was defrauding Spearing. Gurley refused.

In May 1902, without the means to satisfy his creditors, Lyons sold his Hillary Street property at a loss. By then, his family life was in shambles, as he separated from his wife, Clara, who took the children and moved to 1428 Joliet Street. Meanwhile, Lyons moved closer to downtown, where he found employment as a public weigher, though that position did not last for long.

With all that was going wrong in his life, Lyons blamed the only person he believed was responsible—J. Ward Gurley. Unbeknownst to Gurley, Lyons contemplated suing him for malpractice, but he never followed through because he knew that no attorney would take the case. This only added fuel to the rage he harbored towards Gurley.

For his part, Gurley did everything in his power to placate Lyons, going so far as to impanel a three-member commission at his expense with Lyons's approval. Their mission was to review all the court documents, testimonies, and opinions and decide if Lyons had been wronged during the various litigations, including those under the direction of Delos Mellen. The commission, all attorneys who would work independently, was composed of one member selected by Gurley, one by Lyons, and one by the other two members.

Lyons constantly annoyed his handpicked arbitrator, George Denegre, by showing up at his office unannounced to discuss some aspect of the case. In the end, the commission unanimously found no fault with either counselor, inside or outside the courtroom, believing that both men had done everything in their power to seek justice for their client.

Not surprisingly, Lyons disagreed with their findings and continued to harass Denegre after the fact. Denegre did whatever he could to avoid further contact with the man, including ducking out of his office when he came to visit. Meanwhile, Gurley attempted to pacify his client with reason and understanding, but his efforts were futile.

Shortly after the commission disbanded, Gurley received a letter from Lyons challenging him to a duel with pistols. Dueling was commonplace in New Orleans a century before and ironically involved Gurley's great-uncle, his and his father's namesake, John Ward Gurley, then the attorney general of the Territory of Orleans. He was killed in a duel in March 1808.

Annoyed by the challenge, Gurley sought the advice of four of his closest associates, including Delos Mellen and one of his assistant district attorneys, Samuel Montgomery. The gentlemen all agreed that Gurley should ignore the challenge but counseled him to be vigilant and arm himself, though Gurley didn't. They all concurred that Lyons was not of sound mind.

Late one Saturday afternoon, Lyons appeared at Gurley's office at the courthouse. Montgomery was sitting at his desk in Gurley's private office when he happened to see Lyons standing in the reception room.

"There's your friend, Lyons, outside," Montgomery jocularly remarked to Gurley.

When Gurley gave no response, Montgomery asked his boss if he wanted see him. He nodded, and Montgomery motioned Lyons in.

"Yes, but you remain in the office also," Gurley instructed Montgomery, as Lyons entered the room.

"You didn't answer my letter," Lyons said. "Why didn't you give me satisfaction?"

"I owe you no satisfaction," Gurley calmly answered. "I haven't ever harmed you, and why should I seek to harm you, or you me?"

Gurley tried to cajole Lyons but to no avail. After Lyons became verbally combative, Gurley ordered him out of his office. Montgomery remarked later that he never imagined that Lyons would make good on his threats of violence towards Gurley, much less murder him. But Gurley's law partner, Delos Mellen, did not share the sentiment.

"Up to two years ago, I would not have been surprised to hear that he had shot DeRancé, Kerwin [*sic*], Judge Ellis, or Mr. Gurley," Mellen admitted the day of Gurley's murder, "and I was especially fearful that he would attack me—more likely me."

Two or three months after this verbal altercation, Montgomery asked Gurley if he had seen or spoken to Lyons; he had not. It seemed that the matter of the duel had blown over.

Gurley delivered his last public address on Thursday evening, July 16, 1903, four days before his murder, when he was among a group of speakers advocating the passage of a curfew law in New Orleans.

Lyons spent a portion of the following day going from one saloon to another in the downtown area. On Canal Street he met William Price, a plumber he had known for three or four years, and asked him to join him for a drink. He had a business proposition to discuss with him. The pair walked a short distance to the Cosmopolitan Hotel at 123-25 Royal Street, where a

J. Ward Gurley, Jr. (1903). (Courtesy Colin O'Key)

saloon was located on the first floor. With their drinks in hand, Lyons began to spin an incredible tale about acquiring a contract to erect a waterworks project in Gulfport, Mississippi, costing between $150,000 and $200,000. Lyons wanted to know if Price was interested in partnering with him. The young man was suspicious from the outset and asked who was fronting the money, but Lyons was vague on the details. Nothing was settled when they parted company a short while later.

The following afternoon at three o'clock, Price passed Lyons on the street without as much as an acknowledgment from the man. Price found that odd, given that he hadn't committed to or rejected Lyons's proposal. It only confirmed what he originally thought about Lyons's state of mind and his plan—that he was losing it and it was fantasy.

Meanwhile, on Saturday, July 18, 1903, Gurley spent his last working day at the courthouse. Under normal circumstances he would have put in a full day's work, but for unknown reasons he decided to leave early and spend the remainder of the weekend with his two girls and thirty-seven-year-old bride, Marie Angela Homer Gurley. The couple married seven months before, on December 2, 1902, in Chicago, Illinois, at the home of Dr. J. W. Heatfield, a dentist, and his wife, Susan. Miss Homer, a native Louisianian, had been visiting the couple for several months prior to the wedding.

After snubbing Price on Canal Street, Lyons spent the afternoon drinking and playing card games and dominos at the Continental Saloon, located at 738 Gravier Street. At 4:30, he fell asleep on his chair, attracting the attention of Officer Albert Anderson, who was detailed to the establishment. Anderson calmly walked up to Lyons, tapped him awake, and told him that he couldn't sleep on the premises and had to leave.

"You're wrong. You're wrong," Lyons protested as the officer escorted him out of the building.

Since his July 1895 arrest, Lyons had acquired a quick temper when interacting with the police. He was arrested a second time in July 1896, the circumstances of which were highlighted during the closing days of his murder trial. Then there was the incident one evening in 1898 while Deputy Sheriff Fitz Pohlmann was refreshing himself at a local saloon. Lyons confronted the lawman, accusing his children of bullying his own. Lyons's harsh words quickly escalated to blows. Fortunately for Lyons, he wasn't arrested a third time. Pohlmann likely dismissed the incident was nonsense, chalking it up to parental instincts or just feeling pity for Lyons's plight. He might have also been clueless that his own children might have been guilty of bullying.

Back on the sidewalk in front of the Continental Saloon, Lyons met up with James Barry, an acquaintance, and Oscar Prados, an employee of the saloon, who took charge of the ousted patron and invited him back inside for a drink. Lyons, who was clearly inebriated, threatened to take the matter of his expulsion to the district attorney and grand jury and then go after the police officer. He ranted that he was a gentleman and would not stand to be treated like a criminal.

Prados likely convinced the lawman that Lyons was harmless, as the trio sat down for a social drink. When Lyons requested yet another shot, his companions refused. They felt that he had had enough alcohol by then, but Lyons thought otherwise. He spent the remainder of the day drinking alone, as Barry and Prados went their separate ways.

Beginning on September 22, 1902, until the day of the murder, Lyons rented an upstairs room at 1008 Gravier Street, a property owned by Lena

Heffner. His children often visited him there but never his wife, Clara. Prior to moving to Gravier Street, he had rented a room from Louise Durand, but after a month's stay, he had to go. Unlike Mrs. Heffner, Mrs. Durand found Lyons an unruly tenant, with his comings and goings at all hours of the day and night.

On Sunday, July 19, 1903, Lyons spent a quiet morning up in his room reading the newspaper. At 1:30, he ventured out for lunch, dining at the Hammond Dairy Café at 728 Gravier Street, just a few doors down from the Continental Saloon. As far as Mrs. Heffner remembered, her tenant returned to his room after his meal, though it's hard to imagine that Lyons didn't head back to the saloon for an afternoon drink.

The weather that weekend was beautiful with clear skies, though the temperature peaked at ninety-one degrees by late Sunday afternoon. It was summer after all, and this was New Orleans. On the last full day of J. Ward Gurley's life, he spent a relaxing Sunday with his wife and children. The thought that Mrs. Gurley would be a widow the following morning was an impossibility that no one ever pondered, no one but Lewis Lyons.

Chapter Four

The Assassination

Oh, my God, he's murdering me.

J. Ward Gurley

On Monday, July 20, 1903, the lead story in the morning *Daily Picayune* was the impending death of Pope Leo XIII. In Rome, all eyes were focused on the window of the pope's chamber, which overlooked St. Peter's Square. The pontiff lay in a coma, the culprit of his doom being generalized sepsis (blood poisoning) caused by kidney failure. He would meet his Maker at 4:04 P.M. that day, Rome time.

In New Orleans at 9:00 A.M., approximately the same time as the pope's death, J. Ward Gurley and his wife, Marie, walked a half-block from their home at 1570 Henry Clay Avenue to the intersection of St. Charles Avenue, where they boarded one of several streetcars that shuttled passengers to and from Canal Street, the city's major business artery. On the Canal and Tulane Avenue streetcar line, the so-called "Tulane Belt," they headed up St. Charles to Howard Avenue (Lee Circle), then onto Baronne Street to its intersection with Canal Street. Marie planned to run errands that morning, while Gurley's schedule included a stopover at his private law office in the Macheca Building before venturing to the courthouse four blocks away.

By the time the Gurleys boarded their streetcar, Lyons had arrived at Nelson's saloon at 943 Gravier, near the corner of Baronne. While he drank and socialized with a friend, Dr. Joseph Mentor V. Richard entered the establishment, holding a bunch of keys that he had found four blocks down the road on Magazine Street. (The doctor was always referred to as Mentor V. Richard in various newspapers and in *Soards' New Orleans City Directory*. His death certificate listed *Joseph* as his forename.)

"The fellow who lost these keys is in a bad fix," Dr. Richard explained to the barkeeper. "He has lost the key to his home, the key to his office, and the key to his desk."

The only identifiable marking on the latchkey was the inscription *H. Conrad*. Naturally, Dr. Richard assumed the keys belonged to someone named Conrad.

"No," Lyons replied, overhearing the conversation. "Conrad is a locksmith, and I guess he made the key."

With that information, determining the owner was just a matter of returning the keys to Henry Conrad, whose business was located at 819 Iberville Street. Dr. Richard, who didn't know Lyons at that time, soon departed the premises.

"Who was that?" Lyons's friend asked him, as the physician walked out.

"Why, that's Dr. Richard, the coroner," Lyons answered, soon departing the saloon himself to eat breakfast elsewhere.

At 9:30, Robert Robinson, J. Ward Gurley's fifteen-year-old office boy, stepped off the elevator on the fourth floor of the Macheca Building. Walking down the narrow corridor in the direction of Common Street, Robinson arrived at the private law office of his employer. Gurley's corner suite, number 416, was located at the end of the hallway on the right, or the side of the building closer to Baronne Street. Gurley's office space, like the others in the rear section of that floor, consisted of two rooms, one behind the other. The front space often served as the reception or waiting room and the rear as the private office or business space of the occupant, where a "toilet room" was also accessible. In Gurley's case, the restroom was located on the right wall, which paralleled Canal Street.

The rear office also had a second exit point that led to a smaller hallway that ran perpendicular to and connected with the main corridor. This smaller hallway, which was duplicated throughout the floor's design on both sides of the main corridor, afforded a tenant an alternative route to their rear office that bypassed their reception room.

The building was equipped with electricity and heating, but without the benefit of central air conditioning (it's possible the rooms had motorized ceiling fans), open windows were critical for ventilation, especially during the summer. Occupying a corner space, Gurley's suite had three large windows—one in the waiting room facing Common Street and two in his rear office, one overlooking Common and the other facing Baronne.

After Robinson arrived, he began to open windows and to clean and straighten the reception room. Lyons walked through the door five minutes later and asked if the district attorney was in. Robinson told him no, he usually didn't arrive until around ten o'clock. Rather than sitting in the

Macheca Building (circa 1902-10). (Courtesy Louisiana Division/City Archives, New Orleans Public Library)

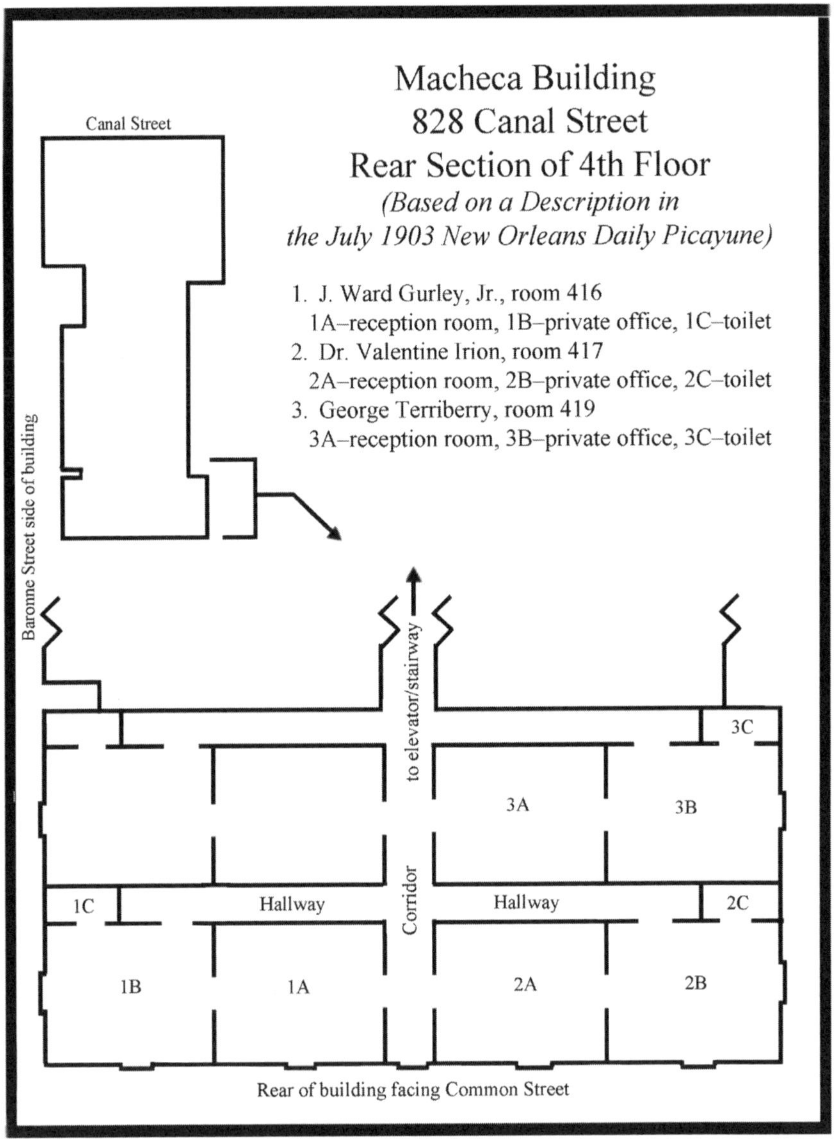
Macheca Building
828 Canal Street
Rear Section of 4th Floor
(Based on a Description in
the July 1903 New Orleans Daily Picayune)
1. J. Ward Gurley, Jr., room 416
1A–reception room, 1B–private office, 1C–toilet
2. Dr. Valentine Irion, room 417
2A–reception room, 2B–private office, 2C–toilet
3. George Terriberry, room 419
3A–reception room, 3B–private office, 3C–toilet
Canal Street
Baronne Street side of building
to elevator/stairway
Corridor
Hallway
Hallway
1A
1B
1C
2A
2B
2C
3A
3B
3C
Rear of building facing Common Street

reception room to wait, Lyons returned to the first floor and stood at the front entrance, where he later conversed with Dr. Buck. After Dr. Buck's departure and perhaps thinking that he had missed Gurley at the building's entrance, Lyons quickly returned upstairs, only to discover Gurley still hadn't arrived. He sat sideways on the windowsill in the reception room, looking at the skyline in the direction of Baronne Street. By then, Eugenie Rivero, a seamstress, was already sitting in Gurley's private office with the door open. The time was 9:55.

"Good morning, Robert," Gurley said in greeting as he entered his reception room five minutes later. He then turned to his other visitor, probably surprised to see him. "Good morning, Mr. Lyons."

"Gurley, I—," Lyons began, then checked himself when he saw Mrs. Rivero rise from her chair and approach the district attorney, who hadn't made it any farther into his suite than the reception room.

Mrs. Rivero and Gurley walked back into his office, where they conversed for a moment before Gurley reentered the reception room and called out to Lyons.

"I will see you first, Mr. Lyons," Gurley spoke. He must have wanted to get the unpleasantness behind him as quickly as possible.

"I am in no hurry. Get finished with the lady first."

Gurley conceded and returned to his office.

Meanwhile, Lyons continued to study the city's skyline from his window seat and asked the office boy what building was next door.

"It's the Medical Building," Robinson replied.

The building, located at 124 Baronne Street, was two stories shorter than the Macheca Building, though the façade of both places was similar. It was a curious thing that Lyons was interested in the building. At that very moment he was preparing to commit murder and suicide. Concealed in his coat pocket was a fully loaded .38-calibre, five-shot, long-barreled Smith &Wesson revolver, along with loose extra cartridges. He had placed a small packet of powdered cyanide in the sweatband of his straw hat and additional cyanide in a solid form in one of his trouser pockets.

Gurley and Mrs. Rivero conversed for about ten minutes before he bade her farewell.

"*Au revoir,* Mr. Gurley," Mrs. Rivero said in parting. "I will see you again."

Immediately afterwards, Mrs. Rivero turned and saw Lyons's face. She later claimed that woman's intuition caused her to fear the man, as he had a sinister smile. By the time of her departure, two additional visitors had arrived to conduct some business with the district attorney—John D. Doran, a clerk, and William L. Shepard, a real-estate and renting agent.

Once Mrs. Rivero left, Lyons quickly entered Gurley's office, slamming the door behind him. The door was composed of framed tinted glass on the top half and solid wood beneath, which made it impossible for anyone in the reception room to see with any clarity what transpired between the two men. They could only discern shadowy figures moving back and forth behind the closed door.

Gurley's furniture arrangement was familiar to Lyons. He had visited his office before, though not while the office boy was employed. Gurley's desk was pushed against the rear wall, with his chair in front, placing his back to visitors as they entered the room. A visitor's chair sat to the left of the desk, near the rear window. On the opposite side of the desk was a stack of books on the floor and a revolving bookcase located near the outer-right corner, by the door to the restroom. A washstand was located between the restroom and the exit door that led to the side hallway.

Two minutes after Lyons entered Gurley's office, Robinson heard Gurley cry out, "Oh, my God, don't do that." Two shots were then heard in rapid succession, followed by a scuffle, and then another shot before there was a pause in firing. Shepard later testified that during this interval, he heard Gurley say, "Oh, you're killing me!"

Panic ensued inside the reception room, with Doran the first person to bolt from the area, followed in short order by Shepard. Doran didn't stop running until he was safely on the ground floor, having taken the stairway in a mad dash to escape the bedlam.

The young office boy knew immediately that Lyons had shot the district attorney, though he didn't know his name at the time and later described him as a "rough fellow."

Robinson heard a fourth shot, but by then he was already in the corridor on the heels of Shepard, yelling at the top of his lungs that the district attorney was being murdered. He got as far as George Terriberry's office, room 419, one office up from Gurley's on the opposite side of the hall. Terriberry, an attorney, was stepping off the elevator when he heard the shots and hastened towards the rear of the building. Shepard informed Terriberry that the district attorney had been shot. Everyone, except Doran, returned to the scene of the crime, with Terriberry leading the way. Robinson later departed the building and ran to the courthouse to inform Henry Mooney, one of Gurley's assistant district attorneys.

As Terriberry entered the reception room, he saw Lyons half-pulling and half-dragging Gurley's bleeding body through the doorway between the rooms. Lyons was described as looking like "an apparition, staring wildly, first at his victim, then across the room." He momentarily pointed his weapon at Terriberry and Dr. Valentine Irion, another building occupant, before releasing his grip on Gurley and returning to the inner office, leaving the door ajar.

"Oh, my God, he's murdering me," Gurley cried out as he began to fall to his knees. "He's murdering me for nothing!" These were his last words.

Terriberry quickly grabbed hold of Gurley and gently guided him to the floor, putting a book under his head for support. Whispering to the dying man, Terriberry told him to have courage, and he was not going to be injured again. He added that perhaps the wounds were not as grave as they seemed, and he would be well cared for as soon as the doctor arrived. Ashen in color, with blood dripping from various wounds, the district attorney was moments from death. Dr. Irion took hold of his arm; he was pulseless. Gurley's soul had passed into eternity.

A feeling of shock and horror rolled over the witnesses like a tidal wave as they saw the lifeless body of the district attorney. With the office door still ajar, all Lyons needed to do to shoot another person was to aim his revolver and fire. No one was armed but the murderer. But Lyons alleviated their fears a minute or two later when he pulled the rear office door shut. The locking mechanism snapped into place, sealing the room off and preventing reentry from the reception room.

Directly across the corridor from Gurley's suite was room 417, the dental practice of Dr. Irion. He shared the suite with Dr. Leonard Chamberlain, a physician. At the precise time that Gurley entered his office, Irion was behind closed doors, attending to a patient. Miss Alice Watling, his stenographer who also worked for several other dentists in the building, passed in front of Gurley's office en route to see Dr. Chamberlain, who had yet to arrive. Hearing the first gunshots, Miss Watling looked directly into Gurley's office. Something was obviously amiss.

Hearing the same gunfire, Dr. Irion thought the noise had originated from the alleyway below. He was about to open his rear window and look down when he heard the young woman cry out.

"Oh, Mr. Gurley! Oh, Mr. Gurley!" Miss Watling screamed as she saw Lyons hauling Gurley through the doorway into the reception room. She exited the floor soon after.

Leaving his patient in the chair, Dr. Irion opened the door of his rear office and glanced directly into Gurley's reception room. He saw nothing until he entered the room and observed Gurley being dragged through the office doorway by Lyons, his weapon briefly pointed towards Terriberry, then himself, causing him to instinctually retreat from the room. He returned a moment later after Terriberry grabbed hold of the district attorney as he fell to his death. Dr. Irion recalled Gurley's dying words: "He's murdering me for nothing!" Dr. Irion unfastened Gurley's collar, opened his coat, and checked for a pulse.

Knowing that Lyons was still armed, Dr. Irion hurried to the cigar and tobacco shop located on the first floor, where a telephone was located. Dr. Irion summoned the police and an ambulance, then returned to the fourth floor, where he later recalled hearing two more shots, though it was only one, Lyons's suicide attempt.

Using his left hand, Lyons pointed the gun's muzzle at his left temple, with the intention of sending the bullet straight through the frontal lobe of his brain, just above the nose. Nerves or the awkwardness of the gun grip caused the gun barrel to veer at an outward angle when the trigger was pulled. The bullet penetrated only a small portion of the frontal lobe at a slant before exiting. Other than a lingering headache, some fever, an infection that lasted for weeks, and the total loss of vision in his left eye due to optic-nerve damage, Lyons survived his suicide attempt.

At approximately 10:15, Dr. Buck was visiting his friend, Delos Mellen, in his third-floor office suite, room 316, located directly beneath Gurley's office. Dr. Buck was sitting on the windowsill that overlooked Baronne Street when he distinctly heard a voice coming from above, then gunfire, a scuffle, and then more gunfire, though later at trial he testified that he couldn't remember the exact order.

"I am no North Rampart Street—," Dr. Buck recalled someone angrily saying, though he couldn't be sure it was Lyons, wasn't able to hear the entire sentence, and didn't know what it meant. Also, he couldn't remember if it was spoken before or after the initial shooting and scuffle.

By the time Dr. Buck arrived upstairs, Gurley was dead, with Mr. Terriberry and Dr. Irion at his side, along with one or two other individuals who had arrived. Dr. Buck attempted to open the rear office door, but it remained locked. Meanwhile, Henry G'sell, the building's engineer or supervisor, heard gunfire from his rear location on the ground floor and took the elevator to investigate. By then, there was utter pandemonium in the building. Men rushed about the floor's corridor hatless and coatless, women screamed, and the elevator bell rang nonstop, as tenants and guests desperately fled the building. Canal Street soon became thick with people, while lady shoppers dashed into neighboring stores such as D. H. Holmes, located at the corner of Canal and Bourbon streets. The women, fearing that the shooting would spill out onto the thoroughfare, took refuge where they could.

Like G'sell, Christopher Cain, a private detective whose office was located on the second floor in room 216, heard the gunfire and sprinted upstairs, arriving at the reception room at the same time as G'sell.

"He's in the private office with a revolver. Look out!" someone in the reception room told the men.

"The private office door is locked!" another person yelled.

As yet, no one knew that Lyons had turned the gun on himself.

G'sell and Cain, determined to gain access to the room no matter the danger, quickly ventured to the side hallway, where they encountered Ermano Brunner, the solicitor of the American Express Company. In order to see what was going on in Gurley's private office, G'sell climbed atop Brunner's broad shoulders and looked through the door's transom. G'sell observed Lyons, semiconscious, lying on his side in a pool of blood. Using a key and screwdriver, the engineer quickly pried open the hall door, gaining entrance to the rear room. Shortly afterwards, someone unlocked the reception room door.

The men discovered Gurley's office in a state of chaos, with the revolving bookcase turned over, books scattered, and chairs toppled. Gurley's spectacles were lying on the ground, along with the murder weapon. Lyons's hat was also displaced during the scuffle, buried under the debris and making it impossible for him to access the poison he had placed in its sweatband. Why he never reached for the poison stored in his pocket is a mystery. Perhaps he thought suicide by gunshot was a safer bet.

With an entry wound in his left temple, an exit wound over his right eye, and his skull cracked in both places, Lyons moaned in pain as the trio reached his side. Brunner quickly lifted him off the floor as Cain asked Lyons his name and why he had murdered Gurley. But Lyons only shook his head and made a nonsensible, guttural response.

⌖ ⌖ ⌖

Minutes after the shooting was reported, Capt. John Boyle, Sgt. Timothy Driscoll, and Cpl. Kosman Morgan, along with a wagonload of other police officers from the First Precinct Station, arrived at the scene, followed by an ambulance crew. (Cain also claimed to have notified the police after gaining entrance to the rear office.) Meanwhile, other police squads patrolling the Canal Street corridor arrived and quickly took charge, calming the anxious crowd who gathered in the street.

Captain Boyle and his men, along with Detectives Patrick Dale and Thomas J. Roche, entered Gurley's office and began to restore order to the chaos. The ambulance crew (medical students from Charity Hospital), who had been originally dispatched to assist the district attorney, now turned their attention to the care of Lyons. Concerned that someone might take revenge on him, Captain Boyle ordered a squad of policemen to surround his stretcher as he was transported to a waiting ambulance on Canal Street. Lyons was then taken to Charity Hospital.

"Keep everyone from the man," the captain commanded, as Lyons was placed on the stretcher.

Meanwhile, John Journée, the superintendent of police, ordered a twenty-four-hour police detail to guard the prisoner at Charity Hospital, with Officer Frank McDonald the first patrolman assigned to the unit. McDonald was instructed to remain at Lyons's side at all times until he was relieved that night.

Back at the murder scene, Captain Boyle and the two detectives began to piece together the murder and attempted suicide. Initially, everyone believed that Gurley had been shot three times, but that changed once the office was carefully inspected and the autopsy completed.

Retrieving the Smith & Wesson revolver, which lay near Lyons, the officers discovered that the gun's cylinder contained two shell casings and three cartridges. In addition, there were three shell casings and two discarded bullets on the floor. Given the revolver's five-shot capacity, the police surmised that Lyons fired three shots into Gurley, then, for whatever reason, the two remaining bullets failed to discharge. This prompted Lyons to remove and discard the unspent bullets and shell casings and reload with five additional bullets taken from his coat pocket. He fired a fourth time and then dragged Gurley to the reception room, where he left him to die. Lyons then reentered the rear office and reserved the fifth shot for himself.

The scenario fit young Robinson's version of events, though the order, particularly the number and timeframe of shots heard, did not correlate with all eyewitness accounts. Captain Boyle suspected that the brawl began with two rapid gunshots, followed by a struggle, then a third shot, followed by a longer pause, and then the *coup de grâce,* the apparent mortal wound from the fourth bullet. The fifth shot, the suicide attempt, came a few minutes later.

In addition, the police likely accounted for all of the bullets fired by Lyons. Four of them were later retrieved during the autopsy. But no information was disclosed in newspaper accounts about the location of the fifth bullet, which passed through Lyons's head, and the police report about the crime scene has long since vanished.

Meanwhile, Dr. Richard was notified and raced to the scene from his office in the courthouse, arriving about 10:30. He found Gurley's body lying supine, with his feet close to the door of his private office. Discovered nearby were a few private letters, which he handed to Mooney, who, by then, had arrived with the victim's younger brother, Walter Morgan Gurley (Everyone called him by his middle name.)

A cursory examination of the body by Dr. Richard revealed that Gurley had lost a great deal of blood; the front of his vest was saturated. Tearing open his shirt, Dr. Richard noted bullet holes on the right side of the chest and arm, but he was unable to determine the course of one of the bullets' trajectory without an autopsy. In his grief, Morgan protested Dr. Richard's plans to cut open his brother. Had Lyons expired, no autopsy would have been necessary.

With the city morgue having no means to refrigerate the body (a cooler was not installed until July 1904), the autopsy had to be performed that day, but Morgan protested the location. Out of respect for the family, Dr. Richard agreed that the autopsy could be performed at the funeral home of the family's choosing: Johnson's funeral parlor, 800 Magazine Street. The establishment was quickly notified and a wagon dispatched.

In the interim, Dr. Richard impaneled a coroner's jury composed of five men, including George Terriberry. Also present at the time of the autopsy was Capt. Aubrey J. Parody, the coroner's secretary or clerk. Parody's rank was related to his service in the Louisiana State National Guard, not the New Orleans Police Department.

After a quick examination of the clothing, Dr. Richard found no firearm, only Gurley's watch, a knife, keys, and some loose change in his pockets. The autopsy revealed that Gurley died from internal hemorrhage caused by multiple gunshot wounds. Though Dr. Richard could not determine the order of the wounds, he did conclude that at some point Gurley was standing when shot and Lyons was sitting, because two of the four wounds had an upwards trajectory, and Lyons was taller than Gurley.

Dr. Richard's report stated, "Wound No. 1, bullet made its entrance at the point eight and one half inches below the right arm pit and directly in [alignment with the mid] axillary line; it travelled from right to left and in an upward direction; in its course it perforated the liver and both cavities of the heart. Bullet was extracted at a point one half inch to the left and one half inch below the left nipple." (The midaxillary line is an imaginary line starting at the middle of the armpit and traveling down the side portion of the chest towards the pelvis or hip bone.)

Why Gurley didn't die instantaneously from this wound, especially when the bullet penetrated the ventricles (or lower chambers) of the heart, is a medical mystery. That said, Wound No. 1 was probably produced by the fourth and final shot. The remaining wounds may not have proved fatal.

The report went on: "Wound No. 2, bullet entered at a point located five and one half inches below the right arm pit and two inches posteriorly [rear] to the axillary line; it made its exit at a point immediately above the right clavicle [collarbone], and continued two inches to the right of [the] median line [mid-chest]. Wound No. 3, bullet entered the right forearm eight inches below the elbow, shattering the bone. Wound No. 4, bullet entered the right forearm, three and one half inches below elbow."

Dr. Richard placed the time of Gurley's death at 10:00 A.M., though based upon eyewitness accounts, death occurred approximately fifteen minutes later. With the autopsy completed and the coroner's report signed by Dr. Richard and his jurymen, the body was prepared by the undertaker and, later that afternoon, transported to the late district attorney's residence on Henry Clay Avenue. He was laid in state in the front parlor of the house until the funeral service and burial, scheduled for the following day.

Gurley's wife and two daughters were devastated by his death. Gurley's twenty-year-old daughter, Aurora, was shopping in the downtown area that day when a paperboy began yelling, "Extra, extra!" Aurora queried as to the lead story, saw the headline, and fainted. She was immediately taken home by carriage by a friend of the family. Notification of next of kin before a murder victim's name was released to the public was not the protocol in 1903.

Though the service and burial were to be private affairs, throngs of mourners began paying their respects at the Gurley residence by Monday evening. Marie and the girls, too grief stricken to greet the public, stayed in their upstairs rooms until a few hours before the start of the funeral service. Instead, Morgan, Hewes, and Edmund Randolph, three of Gurley's younger brothers, kept vigil over the body during the evening and night until exhaustion overwhelmed them. Friends took up the watch thereafter.

"Many gentlemen prominently connected with public affairs, and with the business life of this city, called during the [following] day and proffered most sympathetic words to the sorrowing household," the *Daily Picayune* reported. Among the visitors was Mayor Paul Capdevielle, Superintendent of Police Journée, and a host of federal, state, parish, and city officials, including members of the bar and judiciary.

Beginning on Monday afternoon and continuing the following day, countless floral tributes from numerous individuals and city organizations poured into the Gurley home as a small token of respect for a man that the general public had come to love and admire.

A few hours before the start of the funeral service on Tuesday afternoon, Mrs. Gurley and her two stepdaughters finally descended the stairs and took their seats at the head of the coffin, with their heads bowed in grief. By the time the service began at four o'clock, the front parlor, as well as the spacious yard in front of the house, was filled with several hundred friends and associates, "men and women representing the best blood and culture of the city" wishing to pay their last respects. Rev. Beverley Warner, the rector of the Trinity Episcopal Church, officiated at the service, which was later described as very simple. At the request of the family, no eulogy was said. Instead, Reverend Warner read a simple prayer in accordance with the rituals of the Episcopal Church, and then the coffin was carried by eight pallbearers, including George Terriberry, to a waiting hearse for transport to Metairie Cemetery. Among fourteen additional pallbearers were Delos Mellen and Judge Frank D. Chretien; the latter would preside over the murder trial of Lewis Lyons.

Under a clear sky and an emerging array of thousands of stars, the funeral procession arrived at the cemetery just before twilight. Reverend Warner spoke a few appropriate words to family members who stood beside the Gurley family tomb. He reminded them that from the corruption of death new life sprang eternal and that they would all be reunited in the afterlife.

John Ward Gurley was fifty-two years old at the time of his death, having celebrated his last birthday just six days before his murder. At City Hall, Mayor Capdevielle ordered the city flag flown at half-staff in respect for the community's fallen brother.

In the days that followed, scores of people paid tribute to the slain leader in the *Daily Picayune*. But no person paid greater homage to the district attorney than Alfred. His last name was never printed. All that is known about the gentleman was that he was an African-American messenger who worked for a federal marshal at the United States Custom House.

"I am so sorry Mr. Gurley died," Alfred told a reporter, with tears streaming down his cheeks. "He was such a kind man. I will never forget his generosity towards me." At some earlier time, Alfred's son had passed away and he was feeling distraught when Gurley approached him on the street and asked what was troubling him. "He said he was sorry for me," Alfred continued, "and as I was leaving he called me back and silently put a five-dollar bill into my hand. He did not say anything, but his looks and his action showed he had a heart."

This was the caliber of man that Lewis Lyons had murdered. And for that hideous crime, there would be justice paid.

Chapter Five

AT CHARITY

Maybe a good many people don't think lead hurts. Well, let them try it.
Lewis Lyons

After the press announced the death of District Attorney Gurley, Wilson Lyons walked into the First Precinct Station on Saratoga Street and asked the desk clerk if it was true that Lewis Lyons was responsible for the murder. When the officer responded in the affirmative, Wilson introduced himself as his older brother and voiced deep regret for his brother's actions. He added that he hadn't spoken to Lewis in years and had no information about what led up to the shooting. He suspected that someone in law enforcement or the press would eventually seek him out for questioning, so he wanted to make known immediately his noninvolvement in the matter. He requested that this information be forwarded to the appropriate people. At some point during their conversation, the officer informed Wilson that his brother had been taken to Charity Hospital.

Charity Hospital was a massive three-story building complex located on Tulane Avenue, between Howard (now La Salle) and South Robertson streets. The hospital was seven blocks from the Macheca Building. Patrolman Frank McDonald was waiting at Charity as Lyons arrived and was transported to Ward 10 to recuperate from his head wound. Lyons shared the ward with as many as sixteen other patients and was placed under constant surveillance by the police.

Meanwhile, his estranged wife, Clara, was notified. Because of the uncertainty of Lyons's prognosis, Clara was told that if she wanted to see her husband before his passing, she needed to get to the hospital as quickly as possible. She complied, taking one of her daughters along with her—likely Chattie, the oldest—while presumably dropping off her remaining four children at her mother-in-law's, which was en route to the hospital.

After Gurley's autopsy was complete and at the behest of Dr. Richard,

Charity Hospital (circa 1890-1910). (Courtesy Louisiana Division/City Archives, New Orleans Public Library)

the coroner's jury was escorted back to the Macheca Building, where they surveyed the murder scene. George Terriberry soon discovered the small packet of cyanide in Lyons's hat, though no one at the time knew what the substance was or that the hat belonged to Lyons. Both items were wrapped in a newspaper and delivered to the coroner's office the following day.

In the interim, Detective Thomas Roche retrieved several items found in Lyons's trousers after he was admitted to the hospital. These objects included two handkerchiefs, numerous postcards and bullet cartridges, four keys, a one-dollar and five-dollar bill, some coins, a streetcar ticket, and an unidentified solid, white substance the size of a pigeon egg wrapped in a small bundle. (Later, it was discovered that this package, which wasn't leak proof, contained a sizable dose of cyanide.) Viewed as potential evidence, these items were turned over to Captain Boyle, who then delivered them to James Schillin, the clerk of the First City Criminal Court. Schillin wrapped everything in one of Lyons's handkerchiefs. The items were later placed in the safe in the property clerk's office in the courthouse.

On Tuesday morning at the coroner's office, Captain Parody's first impression after examining the small packet of cyanide retrieved from Lyons's hat was that it was morphine powder. But unsure, he had Dr. Allan Eustis, the acting city chemist, analyze it. (Morphine, which is derived from opium, was a much-abused curative agent at the time. Some people speculated that Lyons was a hop fiend, or opium addict.)

That morning at the hospital, Dr. James Batchelor, first assistant house surgeon who was placed in charge of Lyons's medical needs, declared his wounds survivable, though there was always the chance an infection could kill him at some later date. When Mrs. Lyons and her daughter (again, presumably Chattie) returned to the hospital that morning, the news must have been met with mixed emotions. Yes, Mrs. Lyons was thankful he would survive, if only for the sake of her children. But what lay ahead for her husband and the family?

Dr. Batchelor's initial examination of Lyons revealed that his face was edematous with both eyelids grossly swollen, which prevented Lyons from opening his eyelids without the use of his fingers. The eyes were badly bloodshot, with extensive damage noted to the left eye due to the bullet's trajectory from left to right. The left optic nerve (or disc) was probably irreparably damaged, which meant total loss of vision in that eye, though it was too early at that stage to state it as a foregone conclusion. Making matters worse, his right vision was very blurry, and he ran a slight fever. Icepacks applied to his face kept down both the fever and swelling.

The entry and exit wounds oozed blood-tinged fluid. The leakage, especially from the entry wound, likely decreased intracranial pressure and saved his life. After the wounds were cleaned, a bulky head dressing was applied, leaving only the right orbital region exposed in order for Lyons to see, once the swelling in his eyelids subsided.

Fully awake, coherent, and expressing less discomfort twenty-four hours after his attempted suicide, Lyons asked Clara to speak to his landlady, Mrs. Heffner, about not allowing anyone to take his personal belongings away. Mrs. Heffner promised to do so, though all he had in his upstairs room was some "fine clothing," according to her. Mrs. Heffner told reporters that "Lyons was a neat dresser and kept his clothes in good order." She also expressed shock that he had committed such a terrible crime, being such a polite renter.

Already there was gossip that Lyons was insane, the possible catalyst being an opium addiction. Mrs. Heffner thought that idea was absurd. As far as she knew, he was perfectly sane, and rumors that he had smoked opium and was addicted to the habit were ludicrous. The substance's unique odor would have clung to his clothing and his actions and mannerisms would have given him away, according Mrs. Heffner. She even claimed that he didn't drink excessively, though that was a stretch of the truth.

During Clara's visit, Captain Boyle arrived. He was hoping that Lyons was ready to make a statement now that he was fully conscious and feeling better, but Lyons preferred to hold his tongue. Nevertheless, he sensed that Captain Boyle was disappointed by his refusal to say anything about the crime.

"I have a statement written out and I will give this to you later on, but not now," Lyons informed him. "When I do make the statement, I want every word of it published."

The reporters who were present must have been delighted to hear that news, but not Captain Boyle. He asked Lyons what the subject of his statement was. But Lyons remained vague, only inferring that it dealt with the circumstances that led to the day of reckoning, without discussing the shooting per se. If nothing else, the fact that Lyons had prepared a statement before the murder—he was in no shape to write one afterwards—proved that his crime was premediated. But in spite of his blustering announcement, no such document was ever produced by Lyons. It never existed, except in his mind.

Though Lyons refused to discuss the shooting, he didn't mince words about what he thought about his victim. Lyons felt that Gurley had "thrown him down," related to his lawsuit. And he didn't consider him an exemplary man, as did the general public, though he admitted that Gurley wasn't all bad. Nonetheless, Lyons thought he deserved what he got.

Unable to see the entry and exit wounds beneath the bandages, reporters pressed Lyons to point to their locations, which he did. By then, Captain Boyle had seen enough. Appearing before Judge Thomas M. Gill, Jr., who presided over the First City Criminal Court, Boyle swore out an affidavit against Lewis W. Lyons, charging him with "the willful and malicious murder of J. Ward Gurley." (Lyons's crime did not normally fall under the dominion of this minor court. Captain Boyle likely sought Judge Gill's warrant because his courtroom was conveniently located on the second floor of the First Precinct Station.) As soon as Lyons sufficiently recovered from his wounds, he would be brought before Judge Gill and arraigned.

On Wednesday morning, when Dr. Richard and Captain Parody arrived at the hospital in the company of reporters from the *Daily Picayune, New Orleans Item,* and *New Orleans Daily News,* they discovered that Lyons was experiencing greater pain than the previous day. In spite of that, everyone hoped that he would finally discuss the circumstances of the murder. But Lyons remained defensive, aware that anything he said could later be used against him at trial.

Dr. Richard reminded him that they had spoken to one another at Nelson's saloon on the day of the murder. Lyons smiled, probably thinking about the irony of their meeting.

"Now, when you recognized me in the saloon that morning, did not the thought flash through your mind that I would soon have a duty to perform, or, in other words, that you would have a job for me?" Dr. Richard asked. "Didn't you think that probably I would soon be called upon to hold an autopsy?"

"Well, I know you have assistant coroners and you might have assigned one of them," Lyons acknowledged.

Dr. Richard remembered that Lyons was coherent that morning and recalled that Lyons's friend asked him if he wanted another drink before leaving.

"No," replied Lyons, according to Dr. Richard's recollection. "I will drink no more, for I have very important business to transact."

"Where did you go after you left the barroom?" Dr. Richard asked Lyons.

"To breakfast."

"And after that?"

"To the Macheca Building—to Mr. Gurley's office."

"Whom did you meet when you entered the office?"

Lyons paused for a second or two.

"I saw the office boy and a lady, and afterwards Willie Shepard entered the office." The two men had attended the same Sunday school as boys. "After the lady left I entered Mr. Gurley's office."

"What happened then?" Dr. Richard asked.

Lyons knew what he was up to.

"Doctor, don't try to lead me. I will make a statement at the proper time. This affair is a personal matter of my own. It doesn't concern anyone."

"You owe the public a full explanation for your deed," Dr. Richard countered.

Lyons wasn't buying it.

"I owe no one an explanation," he emphatically said, then added, "I demanded full satisfaction for the misdeed which had been done me. I was not given that satisfaction and I took it."

Dr. Richard quickly changed the subject, though he was far from ending his inquiry into the murder. He asked Lyons how his eyes were doing. No appreciable change had occurred since Dr. Batchelor's initial examination. But Lyons added that he had passed a bad night, his head hurt, and therefore his mind wasn't clear that morning. Dr. Richard didn't seem to care about his complaints and asked his opinion of Delos Mellen.

"Mr. Mellen did not conduct my case properly and I went to Mr. Gurley and demanded satisfaction," Lyons informed him. "I insisted that Gurley take the matter out of his hands and handle the case thereafter for me. I told him that Mellen was a crook, and I wanted him to take over my case and expose Mellen."

Lyons explained to Dr. Richard that Gurley assumed his case but never pursued legal action against his law partner (for obvious reasons). He believed that Gurley did everything in his power to shield his partner from any civil or criminal liability. And it was only when all appeals were exhausted that he demanded compensation from Gurley.

"I went to Mr. Gurley's office and asked him to reimburse me for the money I had lost through Mellen's practice and his own neglect, and he refused to reimburse me," Lyons explained. "If he had given me the money I would have walked off and would never have spoken to him about the matter again."

He told Dr. Richard that he had written letters to Gurley and Mellen asking them for his money back, and he assured the coroner that Mellen still had a copy of his letter. But Dr. Richard didn't seem interested in that part of his story.

"When you entered Mr. Gurley's office did you strike or attempt to strike him?"

"No."

"Were you seated or standing when you fired?"

Dr. Richard was trying to corroborate his autopsy findings and to get Lyons to admit that he had shot Gurley, but Lyons was too shrewd to fall into that trap just yet.

"Now, you're trying to lead me," Lyons warned. "I don't propose to answer all those questions."

Dr. Richard continued his fishing expedition, but Lyons wasn't taking the bait and changed the subject.

"Doctor, I'm not well," Lyons remarked. "I do not sleep at all. Come some other time alone and I will tell you everything."

"I would not do you an injustice," Dr. Richard clarified.

He informed Lyons that his inquiries were only in an official capacity as coroner. But Lyons suspected that anything he told him, including what had already been spoken, would be printed in the newspaper. He was right, because the reporters were taking notes.

"I don't believe you would do me an injustice, Doctor," Lyons confirmed, "but I have bosom friends—I have friends—whom I trust more than you. You see, it is only natural that I should."

But Dr. Richard persisted.

"Did you know Mr. Gurley long?"

"Yes," Lyons responded, "ever since we were boys together."

"How old are you?"

"Forty-four last birthday."

"Did you ever [hold] anything against Mr. Gurley?"

"Not up to the time of my case," Lyons confessed. "I always regarded him as an honest and upright gentleman."

"And—?"

"Don't, Doctor." The subject was getting stale. "I will tell you everything when you see me alone and when I am better," Lyons reiterated.

"How long were you in the office before you shot him?"

"About twenty minutes," Lyons blurted, not realizing he had just incriminated himself.

"What happened when you saw Mr. Gurley? Did you again ask him for satisfaction?"

"Oh, he always tried to smooth the matter over with sweet talk," Lyons replied.

"Did he talk sweetly to you Monday?"

"Yes."

"And you—"

"Now, please don't ask me anything more," Lyons demanded, cutting him off.

Undeterred, the doctor changed his line of questioning. "Did you want to die?" he asked bluntly.

"Yes."

He had nothing to live for, and his prospects were poor. But he added that he expected to survive the gunshot wound.

"What possessed you to shoot Mr. Gurley?"

"I told you that I demanded satisfaction from him and he refused," Lyons reminded Dr. Richard. "Now, no more questions."

"Well," Dr. Richard commented, "I care nothing for your personal grievances with Mr. Gurley and his partner. My duty is to ascertain the nature of the wounds and how the district attorney met death. Won't you tell me whether you were seating or standing?"

Their conversation was over. Clara and Chattie arrived shortly afterwards and stayed at his bedside for nearly the entire day.

In the meantime, Dr. Richard received the preliminary analysis done by Dr. Eustis on the white powder found in the sweatband of Lyons's hat. The substance was cyanide. Dr. Eustis's final report, issued on August 1, showed the concentration of poison to be 88 percent.

During the afternoon, reporters returned to the ward.

"How did you receive the wound in your head?" one reporter asked.

"I really can't say," Lyons responded. "Everything seems dim about that part of the matter."

"Didn't you tell Dr. Richard that you shot yourself in the head, using your left hand?" The reporter was trying to confirm the obvious, though he knew that Lyons hadn't said any such thing.

"I don't recollect telling him that, but I do remember saying that my right arm had been twice broken, and while it was [healing] I was compelled to use my left hand, so that I became ambidextrous from practice, and I now use my left hand as well as my right." This was information that the reporters had not heard before. "I can recollect but little of what happened in the office, and everything seems faint and dim to me," Lyons added.

"What kind of poison was that you had in the sweatband of your hat?" the reporter asked, aware of Dr. Eustis's report.

"I don't know anything about any poison or about anything being in the band of my hat," Lyons declared. With his wife and daughter at his bedside, he wasn't going to admit that he possessed poison. "I am sure that I did not place it there."

On Thursday, July 23, an inquest into the murder of J. Ward Gurley was held by Dr. Richard in his office at the courthouse. A total of ten witnesses were called to testify, including Terriberry, who also sat on the jury. The coroner's findings were never in doubt, and Dr. Richard forwarded his report to the newly appointed district attorney.

Meanwhile, Lyons woke on Thursday having spent a restful night with appreciably less pain and then passed a quiet day with only one official visitor. Cpl. Kosman Morgan with the police inquired if Lyons was ready to make a statement, and again, Lyons said that he would do so at the proper time. In addition, he felt confident that he would be discharged from the hospital by the early part of the next week. When Clara and Chattie returned to the hospital, they had a pleasant visit, spending the greater part of the day at his bedside.

Lyons's recurring headaches erupted again on Thursday night and lingered into Friday. Nonetheless, he sent for Captain Boyle, who assumed that he was ready to make a statement. But he was disappointed when all Lyons wanted was his postcards and money taken from his clothes. He needed to write someone and wanted his wife to dictate his words. Boyle agreed to retrieve the items and return the following day. As usual, Mrs. Lyons and Chattie visited under the careful watch of Officer McDonald.

On Saturday, July 25, when Dr. Joseph Danna, Dr. Batchelor's assistant, performed his rounds he decided that Lyons's bulky head dressing was no longer necessary. Instead, he placed a simple cotton gauze over the entry and exit wounds after cleaning them, noting that the entry wound now drained purulent fluid, a clear sign that it had become infected. Dr. Danna wasn't unduly alarmed, as it was a common clinical finding in those days. He also believed that Lyons's facial swelling had subsided enough that he looked as though he had been severely beaten, rather than shot in the head, though it begged the question, what did that matter?

After the head dressing was removed, reporters had their first opportunity to see the entirety of Lyons's battered face and his damaged left eye. By then, the puffiness of his eyelids had reduced, though both eyes remained profoundly bloodshot.

Mrs. Lyons and Chattie's visit was cut short after Lyons informed them it wasn't necessary to come to the hospital every day. He was feeling better and had spent a restful night, and the hospital was no place for his wife and child to visit now that he was out of danger.

Meanwhile, Captain Boyle ventured to the property clerk's office to reclaim Lyons's postcards and money. However, while unfolding the handkerchief, he discovered that the inside of the cloth, the postcards, and the currency were discolored by a slight yellowish fluid that gave off a faint, unrecognizable odor. The solid, white mass encapsulated within the handkerchief had partially melted, staining the objects. Captain Boyle carefully took the items to Dr. Danna, but he hadn't a clue what had produced the stain and odor. He suggested that Walter Taylor, the druggist at the hospital, examine it. Taylor immediately recognized the bitter almond odor of cyanide and indicated it was enough poison to kill a regiment of men.

When Captain Boyle informed Lyons that his postcards and greenbacks were unusable, Lyons didn't seem surprised and asked how the contamination occurred, since he had placed the cyanide in a different pocket from the postcards and money. When he was told, he asked if the bills could be exchanged at the sub-treasury at the United States Custom House, though it's not known if they were. Captain Boyle asked him if the cyanide was the same as that found in his hat, but Lyons refused to say. It's possible that Lyons carried around the egg-shaped cyanide to treat rodent problems.

In spite of the press clamoring to know every detail of Lyons's life, other organizations in the city spent the preceding week hosting scores of memorial services and tributes for the slain district attorney. But as the city continued to mourn his loss over the weekend, Lyons spent his Sunday venting his frustration over his own suffering, self-inflicted as it was.

"Maybe a good many people don't think lead hurts," Lyons explained to the press. "Well, let them try it. I don't want any more of it in [my head]."

Lyons had spent another restless night complaining of a severe headache, as his fever waxed and waned.

"No, I don't sleep much," Lyons said when asked. "I do all of my sleeping in the daytime."

But some reporters were skeptical of his answer, believing that he feigned sleep during the day to avoid their questions. But in spite of his complaints, Lyons admitted that he was seeing progress in his health, though he hated being confined to bed.

"I don't like to stay in bed a bit—never did like it," Lyons remarked, as he pulled at his clothes and tossed off the bag of ice placed on his head to keep his fever down. The bag's coldness was especially uncomfortable.

The reporters, delighted that Lyons was so talkative that day, hounded him for more details about the murder.

"Mr. Lyons, a report is being circulated that the killing of Mr. Gurley was the result of his refusing to release a note on your house in payment of his fee for representing you in a lawsuit," one reporter told him.

"I want that rumor refuted," Lyons forcefully replied, "and will be obliged to you if you'll do so. There's no truth in it." He suspected who was stirring the pot. "No such transaction was involved. Mr. Mellen knows better than that."

He then thanked them for their kindness. The interview was over.

Lyons had a number of visitors that day. Mrs. Lyons returned, along with two small girls who were his neighbors while he rented from Mrs. Heffner. Later in the afternoon he met with George Stevens, a trusted friend, about securing the services of an attorney. He also asked him to keep all newspaper clippings pertaining to his case. Thus far, he'd been unable to read and was anxious to do so, assuming that the blurriness in his right eye would resolve.

Meanwhile, Officer McDonald continued to closely observe his prisoner, looking for anything unusual in his behavior. Another suicide attempt was always possible. Thankfully, McDonald expected to be relieved of his duties soon, as he predicted that Lyons would be well enough in a day or two to be transferred to prison. He was excited at the prospect of returning to his foot patrol.

"I can't get used to the atmosphere here," McDonald said, referring to the hospital. "There's too much medicine, and it make a fellow lose his appetite."

In spite of McDonald's rosy predictions, Lyons remained hospitalized for a while.

On Tuesday, July 28, after a week at Charity Hospital, Lyons was finally seen by Dr. Edward W. Jones, an oculist, about his badly damaged left eye. Surprisingly, Dr. Jones believed that Lyons might recover sight in the eye. But aside from the eye drops he prescribed, no other treatment options were available to him.

Lyons received no other visitors on Tuesday, except for a reporter who sought his permission to formulate his own statement about the crime, based on information supplied by Captain Boyle. Lyons told him no and reiterated that he would make his own statement in due time.

On Wednesday when Dr. Jones returned to the hospital, he was less optimistic about the prospects of Lyons seeing out of his left eye. Naturally, Lyons became despondent over the news and believed (wrongly) that if the oculist had been consulted earlier, his left vision could have been saved.

"It don't make much difference, however," Lyons admitted, "as I have mighty little to hope for."

Dr. Jones also discovered that Lyons's right eyelid was now affected by some degree of paralysis attributed to nerve damage, though he believed that this new clinical finding would eventually resolve itself.

Sometime that same day, Mrs. Lyons received a gentleman caller at her home who was seeking information about her husband's crime. She knew nothing about the murder, and Lyons was outraged by the incident when later informed. It was another example of the public's insatiable appetite for news about the murder—or of one man's quest for fame.

Thursday saw no dramatic change in Lyons's health status, though his fever persisted. Nonetheless, Lyons felt that the physicians would consent to his transfer to prison by the beginning of the week.

Meanwhile, Judge Thomas Gill announced that he was leaving on Friday for a short holiday and wouldn't return to New Orleans until Monday, August

10. So, depending on Lyons's release from Charity Hospital, his arraignment would have to wait until the second week of August, at the earliest. But plans were already afoot to expedite Lyons's case.

On Friday afternoon, July 31, the district attorney convened the Orleans Parish Grand Jury. By day's end, the jurors delivered to Judge Frank Chretien a true bill for murder against Lyons for the killing of J. Ward Gurley.

Lyons wasn't surprised or anxious when informed of the indictment, though he appeared not as eager to leave the hospital. It seemed that one of his visitors, likely George Stevens, told him not to be in such a hurry to leave. After all, he was going to be transferred to Orleans Parish Prison, with all its associated horrors.

After Lyons's indictment was read, Judge Chretien issued an arrest warrant, delivered to Chief Deputy Sheriff Patrick King for execution and duly served on Lyons later that day. Custody of the prisoner now fell under the jurisdiction of the Terrence Reilley, Sr., the sheriff of Orleans Parish. The official transfer from city to parish control occurred the following morning, on Saturday, August 1, much to the delight of police officer Frank McDonald.

At noon on Saturday, Lyons was taken to the anteroom or dressing room of the hospital to have his wounds cleansed and re-dressed. Dr. Batchelor, on duty that day, was pleased by Lyons's progress. The doctor concluded that Lyons's fever was down; the right eyelid paralysis was resolving; both eyes were less bloodshot, though he remained blind in the left eye and reported blurred vision in the other; and his head wounds were healing appropriately, though the entry wound continued to ooze a small amount of pus. Also, Lyons stated that he felt comfortable.

The only immediate concern for the sheriff's department after taking custody of Lyons was that he might attempt to commit suicide again now that he was feeling better. Two days before the city-to-parish transfer, Mrs. Lyons brought her husband some home-cooked food. Drs. Batchelor and Danna had no problem with the gesture, but Officer McDonald expressly forbade outside nourishment. His superiors feared that the food might be tainted with a poison similar to that found in Lyons's possessions. Mrs. Lyons would hardly have consented to being party to such a fiendish act, but no one was willing to take a chance.

On Sunday morning, August 2, nearly two weeks after the murder, Lyons, in the company of Capt. Archibald Rennyson, the warden, was transported by ambulance to Orleans Parish Prison. Because of the notoriety of the case and his suicide attempt, Lyons was placed in one of the reserved rooms on the third floor, rather than upstairs in the hospital ward, until he was sufficiently recovered to be transferred to a cell.

His room, described as cool, spacious, and airy, had an electric light hanging from the center, wrapped in paper in an effort to shield his eyes from the glare. Provided with a bedside chair, Lyons slept on a comfortable iron cot encased by a mosquito bar suspended from the ceiling. Placed next to his bed (doctor's orders) were a saucer of crushed ice and a cloth he could moisten and bathe his forehead with when he complained of a headache or felt feverish. And to assist Lyons with his personal care (he was unable to walk due to vertigo), he was assigned a nurse (a fellow prisoner), with a guard keeping both men under constant surveillance.

Once settled into his new room, Lyons rethought his prior opposition to relocating to the prison.

"I'd rather be here than at the Charity Hospital," Lyons admitted to reporters who gathered at his bedside. "I can say that I'm very satisfied with my new quarters and am glad they moved me here. I'm quiet and free from all interruptions now."

The constant stream of visitors through his ward and the nauseating smells of medicines were two things he wouldn't miss about the hospital, though he praised the care and kindness he received from the Sisters of Charity. He admitted that he had lost twenty-five pounds since the murder, but the likely culprit was a loss of appetite caused by fluctuating pain.

After Lyons's arrival at the prison, as a precautionary move that first day only, a physician examined him on three occasions. The physician noted no changes from what Dr. Batchelor had observed the previous day. In the meantime, reporters continued to pressure Lyons to make a statement.

"No, I'm not ready to give out a statement just yet, but you can depend upon me giving you all a square deal," Lyons assured the press. Of course, he was lying. "All I ask of you is fair treatment."

He imagined that the newspapers had distorted some facts surrounding the murder. With his continued blurred vision, he was unable to read anything about his case and only knew what had been told to him by friends and family. In addition, he had not as yet engaged counsel.

Lyons spent Sunday afternoon visiting with his wife, Clara, his children, and his brother, Wilson, who finally came to see him. No other visitors intruded on their privacy.

Chandler Luzenberg (1903). (Courtesy Colin O'Key)

Chapter Six

Arraignment and Representation

Are you guilty or not guilty?

Arthur Desmond

With a vacancy created by the death of J. Ward Gurley, filling the late district attorney's unexpired term became an urgent matter for Gov. William Heard. Within two days of the murder, the governor sought the advice of Samuel Gilmore, the New Orleans city attorney. From among various candidates submitted, Chandler Luzenberg garnered the most support from members of the New Orleans bar. The governor agreed, though Luzenberg was initially reluctant to accept the appointment. However, he consented and promised to prosecute to the fullest extent of the law those charged with crimes and to bring the accused to trial in a swift and judicious manner.

Chandler Clement Luzenberg was born in the city on April 10, 1867, the second of four children, to Charles Henry Luzenberg and Anna Rebecca Chandler. His mother died when Chandler was a toddler, so the responsibility of raising him fell to his father. Charles Luzenberg was described as a loving and devoted parent and an exceptional litigator and jurist, who had a long and distinguished career as an attorney, district attorney, and criminal district court judge. As the district attorney, he had twice prosecuted Etienne Deschamps.

Receiving his rudimentary education in New Orleans, Chandler graduated from Louisiana State University before enrolling at Tulane University in New Orleans, where he received a law degree in the spring of 1890. He married Jennie McMain of Baton Rouge two years later and, from that union, had three children.

Prior to his appointment as district attorney, Luzenberg spent the preceding thirteen years honing his skills as an effective defense attorney, including successfully arguing before the Louisiana Supreme Court. He built a huge and lucrative practice over the years. In addition, he aided city and parish prosecutors, including J. Ward Gurley, on several major criminal cases, his last corroboration with Gurley occurring about a month before his murder.

When Luzenberg was sworn in on Monday, July 27, 1903, his first order of business was to retain the services of two of Gurley's assistant prosecutors, Montgomery and Mooney, and to appoint two new ones, St. Clair Adams and Philip Gilmore. Each of these attorneys was allotted cases assigned to one of the city's four criminal courts: Criminal District Court, Section A or Section B, or the First or Second City Criminal Courts. This added manpower allowed Luzenberg ample opportunity to review all criminal cases that came before the upper and lower courts and to devote his energies to the most pressing ones. But no criminal case was of more importance at the beginning of Luzenberg's tenure than the prosecution of Lewis Lyons.

Four days after assuming his office, Luzenberg convened the grand jury, presented his findings based on the coroner's report and the work summarized by Montgomery and Mooney, and secured a bill of indictment. Judge Thomas Gill's involvement in the murder case now became moot, as his duties in the lesser court only extended to conducting preliminary examinations of cases liable to be sent to the higher district court.

On Monday, August 3, Lyons's murder trial was allotted by ballot to Judge Chretien, who presided over Criminal District Court, Section B. Luzenberg immediately called upon the judge to determine when Lyons might be arraigned, now that he was out of the hospital. According to state law, after a trial was allotted to a judge, the court had to wait three days before the accused could appear. This allowed the individual time to summon potential witness on his behalf. Luzenberg discovered that Lyons would be brought to Charity Hospital for a follow-up visit on Wednesday, so the attorney and judge agreed that Lyons could be arraigned on Thursday.

When to start the jury trial was another matter. Luzenberg was informed that Section B had only six jury days in August and all had been fixed for trial. With Judge Chretien scheduled to take a three-month recess beginning on September 1, the prospects of trying the case before December were remote. Even then, Mondays were reserved for appeal cases and Fridays for arguments on motions, writs, rules, and other matters. The murder trial would have to be squeezed into a Tuesday-through-Thursday timeslot, with each day's session extending beyond the normal 5:30 P.M. adjournment, if necessary.

Meanwhile, during Lyons's first full day in prison, he spent a painful day in bed, following the cessation of atropine sulfate droplets that Dr. Jones had applied to his eyes while he was hospitalized. Besides dilating the pupils, atropine had some anti-inflammatory benefits. In spite of the pain and his continued complaint of vertigo, Lyons pronounced that he was slowly improving and was pleased with his accommodations.

Later that Monday, Lyons freely answered reporters' questions on any subject but his crime or the circumstances that led to it, and he continued to insist that he would make a statement in due time. He expressed satisfaction when informed that his trial had been allotted to Judge Chretien, though he wasn't opposed to Section A, with Judge Joshua Baker presiding. He knew that a guilty verdict and sentence of death were forgone conclusions.

It soon became apparent that Lyons's medical needs far exceeded the capacities of the prison hospital. For the foreseeable future, Lyons would need to be escorted to Charity Hospital, where his wounds could be properly cleansed and his vision monitored. Beginning on Wednesday, August 5, and scheduled for Mondays, Wednesdays, and Fridays thereafter, Captain Rennyson took Lyons to the facility three blocks away. Lyons, still suffering from vertigo, kept his eyes closed as he walked and leaned on Rennyson for support and guidance.

By the time Judge Chretien's chambers opened on Thursday morning, a large group of people had gathered near the base of the grand stairway. Expecting the first order of business to be the arraignment of Lewis W. Lyons, everyone wanted to see the murderer as he entered the main corridor of the courthouse. Some of the spectators were friends or past associates of his, but a majority of the group was just curiosity seekers. There hadn't been a murder case of this magnitude in the city in years.

As Judge Chretien sat in his private office to await the start of the proceedings, Captain Rennyson escorted his prisoner to the courthouse, walking down Saratoga Street towards the building's entrance on Tulane Avenue. As Lyons had done the day before, he leaned on his escort while keeping his eyes closed. Vertigo was still a problem when he opened his right eye.

For those people familiar with Lyons's appearance before the murder, he looked unrecognizable as he entered the courthouse. His excessive weight loss had thinned his face, and he wore a stubby beard that had not been cut or trimmed since his days at Charity Hospital. His thin mustache had grown in length, its edges drooping around the corners of his mouth, and a few white, straggling hairs along the side of his head poked out beneath his hat.

A crush of people gathered around the stooped and frail Lyons as he and Captain Rennyson walked towards the elevator and the lift operator, who transported them to the second floor. Meanwhile, the crowd made a mad dash to the grand stairway, hoping to arrive upstairs before the elevator door swung open. The scene that morning resembled children watching a circus act. The excitement was electrifying.

Arriving on the second floor, Captain Rennyson escorted his prisoner to the private office of the chief deputy sheriff, Patrick King, where Lyons took a seat to await his summons before Judge Chretien. He was exhausted from his one-block walk, more so than from his longer journey to the hospital the previous day. Only after he had recovered his breath did he open his good eye, look around the room, and speak a few words to one of the bystanders. Shortly afterwards, he was summoned.

Flanked by numerous deputies, who attempted to keep the crowd at bay, Lyons entered the packed courtroom and was escorted to the bar. District Attorney Luzenberg and two of his assistant prosecutors, Adams and Gilmore, were among the dignitaries in the courtroom.

Having arrived at his spot, Lyons listened to Minute Clerk Arthur Desmond read the indictment in a slow distinct voice.

"Are you guilty or not guilty?" Desmond asked Lyons, while folding up the true bill.

"Not guilty," Lyons immediately replied, his voice clear, but soft.

"Have you an attorney?" Judge Chretien asked.

"No, Your Honor," he responded after a short pause, "I expect to arrange to be represented."

Lyons had consulted with his brother, Wilson, and other family members to obtain the services of a defense attorney, though nothing had come of their efforts as yet. With no further business, Judge Chretien remanded Lyons to Orleans Parish Prison without benefit of bail. As Lyons was escorted out of the courtroom, a number of people asked him if he would care to make a statement.

"I have nothing more to say, except what I told the judge."

That afternoon, Luzenberg met with his assistant prosecutors to determine the feasibility of bringing Lyons to trial later that month. A court date had opened beginning on Tuesday, August 18, well in advance of Judge Chretien's scheduled vacation in September. Everyone at the meeting agreed to go to trial then, though the date didn't become official until August 11.

Luzenberg believed that the third week of August would provide Lyons plenty of time for his condition to significantly improve and also to secure the services of an attorney. Meanwhile, Lyons spent the following morning in consultation with his brother, discussing the prospects of obtaining a competent attorney. That afternoon, he returned to Charity Hospital for his scheduled dressing change.

Lyons's overall health continued to improve, though the entry wound still oozed pus. Some purulent drainage was also discovered in the left ear canal, a new finding, but the house surgeon wasn't especially concerned, other than to comment that it might take him longer to regain his strength. For countless decades, the general consensus among physicians was that the formation of pus in a wound was part of the normal healing process. Without targeted antibiotic therapy in those days, treatment options consisted of keeping the wound clean and wrapping or stuffing the site with gauze or absorbent cotton soaked in iodine.

Back in Lyons's room, reporters implored him to provide them with any new information about the murder, but he continued his relentless streak of silence. When told that he might go to trial on August 18, Lyons wistfully remarked, "Eleven days more."

Lyons did discuss with reporters his ongoing efforts to obtain an attorney and his hope that some money could be raised for his defense, though he hadn't solicited any contributions as yet. Until he could determine the exact cost, it was pointless to petition outsiders for funds. When asked to comment on his arraignment the day before, Lyons claimed he was weak and barely able to stand unsupported when he appeared before Judge Chretien. In retrospect, he believed it had been a mistake to go to court, though at the time he didn't object.

By Saturday morning, Lyons's recovery suffered a setback as he experienced a resurgence of severe head pain and fever that required some unspecified medication, probably morphine, to ease his discomfort. The drug rendered Lyons unconscious for the greater part of the day. When not asleep, he continuously asked his prisoner-nurse to apply an ice-cold cloth over his left eye to ease the throbbing, as his entry wound continued to drain. To prevent leakage, absorbent cotton was stuffed into the wound.

Lyons's setback didn't stop reporters from trying to interview him, though he wasn't very talkative for obvious reasons. When he was conscious he only repeated what he had spoken about before—his efforts to obtain an attorney. He had already sent word to friends, probably by way of Wilson, to endeavor to help him regarding his upcoming trial. With the court date scheduled in ten days, Lyons told reporters that he fully expected the district attorney to do everything in his power to see to it that he was brought to justice, though he was indifferent to the process. For now, all he wanted was to be left alone and undisturbed.

Sunday saw no improvement in Lyons's overall status, as he continued to complain of severe pain and remained under the influence of some form of opiate. One reporter noted, "He was unusually reticent, and his two or three monosyllables were spoken in a low, dejected tone."

With Lyons shunning reporters' questions, the press naturally (and wrongly) assumed that he was finally having some regret for what he had done and speculated that "he had the appearance of a man suffering from companionship with a horrible thought," as one article stated. "His brow was contracted in a troublous frown, and his face seemed to have a worried look."

Dressed in striped linen trousers and a loose-fitting shirt, Lyons spent most of his time in bed with a cold, wet towel covering his left eye. By then, the wound over his right eye was nearly healed, with only a small blemish noticeable where the bullet exited his skull and tore the flesh. Perhaps Lyons's only solace that day came when his wife and brother visited. But that may not have been enough to lift his spirits, one reporter surmised. "It seemed that the spirit of hopeless regret [was] gnawing at his heart strings, and he [dreaded] the gaze of the curious as if the eye could read his soul."

On the day before his scheduled murder trial was to begin, Lyons still hadn't secured the services of an attorney. The exorbitant fees that some of the men were asking made it impossible for him to hire anyone. Lyons realized that it was only a matter of time before he would have to plead *in forma pauperis,* or without the funds to pursue a criminal defense, though he wasn't giving up all hope of finding an attorney.

On Tuesday morning, August 18, when Lyons appeared in court, his physical condition had improved remarkably compared to his last visit, though he still had to lean on the arm of a deputy sheriff who escorted him into the courtroom. Soon afterwards, Crier George Conrad called for *State v. Lyons,* the first case on the docket that day. A call of prospective jurors revealed that all were present in the courtroom. Some of the witnesses were reportedly absent when their names were called, though no one believed that was a crisis. As expected, Lyons informed the court that he had not secured an attorney.

"How long will it take you to employ counsel?" Judge Chretien asked.

"About a week."

"That's too long."

Lyons explained that his triweekly visits to the hospital and the hours it took for him to recuperate his strength made it difficult for him to concentrate on matters related to securing an attorney or to withstand the rigors of any pretrial preparations after an attorney was hired. But the most important reason he gave for his inability to obtain legal representation was the enormous expense he foresaw. At that time, the average yearly income for a male laborer in New Orleans was $502.

"One lawyer asked my family for $4,500 to defend me," Lyons explained to the judge, "another $3,500."

Judge Chretien gave him until the following morning to secure representation or the court would appoint an attorney for him.

Early the next day, Judge Chretien summoned Lyons to his private office to ascertain if he had acquired a counselor, which he had not. Lyons paused for a moment when asked if he wished the court to appoint an attorney for him, and then indicated that he didn't object. After swearing in an affidavit that he had been unable to obtain counsel and formally requested that the court intervene in his behalf, Judge Chretien appointed the law firm of Generelly & Doyle, whom he had preselected, anticipating Lyons's response. Their office was located four blocks from the courthouse in the Hennen Building, 203 Carondelet Street, room 302.

Prior to their notification, Lyons informed Judge Chretien that there was still a small chance that his family could find a suitable attorney. The judge warned him that Generelly & Doyle would likely decline to take up the case if they believed for a moment that Lyons was contemplating switching to another counselor. In other words, Lyons could be squandering the services of two capable litigators on a chance he could find someone else. Lyons was sensible enough to understand that possibility and agreed not to do so.

Judge Chretien felt confident that he had selected the right team to defend Lyons. In the event that he was convicted, it wouldn't be because he had been underserved and misrepresented in court. The deputy clerk immediately notified Joseph Generelly and Warren Doyle were of their appointments.

Not long after Lyons's conference with Judge Chretien, Generelly made his initial contact with his client, who by then was back in his prison room. After their short conversation, Lyons felt confident about Judge Chretien's choice.

When the case would be brought to trial was another matter. After talking to Lyons and reviewing the merits of the case, Generelly returned to the courthouse and spoke to the judge, then later to the press.

"It is practically impossible for me to prepare a case of that magnitude within a month," Generelly told reporters. "There must be a delay."

He reminded everyone that the court could not force his client to trial, "as the Supreme Court decided that question before." Generelly was referring to the state's attempt in mid-1889 to bring Etienne Deschamps to trial two days after appointing him an attorney. His conviction was subsequently set aside by a majority of the High Court, who felt that the trial judge had not given the defense adequate time to prepare.

"I will fight the case to the best of my ability," Generelly informed the press.

With the original trial date now passed, Luzenberg decided not to reschedule it during the current term of the court. Lyons was still not completely recovered from his gunshot wounds. Though feeling stronger, he complained of headaches and dizziness, could not walk without support, and ran an intermittent fever due to the persistent infected drainage from his entry wound.

Given that Judge Chretien planned a three-month recess starting the first week of September, Lyons couldn't possibly stand trial until the end of the year. The only saving grace for Luzenberg was that the judge hinted he might delay his vacation until October, if Lyons could be tried in September, or reconvene his court a month earlier, in November. With Lyons's recovery timeline uncertain, the prospects for a September trial were remote. Luzenberg's only hope for a November trial date was if Judge Chretien agreed to amend his scheduled recess.

Chapter Seven

The Joys of Convalescence

I don't call that singing, do you?

Lewis W. Lyons

On Wednesday, August 26, 1903, for the first time since he began visiting Charity Hospital, Lyons refused to go for his checkup. He woke that morning complaining of lumbago, which prohibited him from walking to the hospital. Besides, he considered it nonsensical to trot him off to the hospital three times a week when the physicians could easily examine his eyes and clean and re-dress his wounds at the prison instead. Lyons didn't win the argument, and he continued to be escorted to the hospital as scheduled. But his routine Wednesday appointment that week was canceled.

Although his lower back pain had eased slightly by the following morning, Lyons complained of pleurisy. The possibility of this more serious respiratory complication necessitated a visit by Dr. Mioton, the assistant coroner and a leading ophthalmologist in the city. But after auscultating and percussing his chest and examining his nose and throat, Dr. Mioton diagnosed Lyons with a common cold, not evolving pneumonia. However, he confirmed Lyons's prior complaint of lumbago, though there were few treatment options available short of doping.

The chronic headaches and other generalized discomforts Lyons voiced since his suicide attempt were taking their toll on him, resulting in bouts of irritability. When deputies inadvertently touched a few of Lyons's personal belongings, he became incensed and barked his displeasure at them.

Exacerbating his discontent, Lyons hadn't eaten anything of sufficient quantity in days. The reasons had nothing to do with the taste or variety of the prison food; it simply hurt to eat. His wounds and their proximity to his jaws caused him pain when he chewed. Lyons also had extensive dental disease—bad teeth. As a result, his diet consisted of mostly soft, bland foods. He flippantly told reporters that his breakfast consisted of hominy and gravy.

He mockingly added that his supper consisted of gravy and hominy. In his opinion, it was hardly enough calories to sustain life. Lyons claimed that if it hadn't been for a quart of milk provided to him for breakfast and supper, he would starve to death. As a result, he had to create his own food at times just to maintain his strength.

"I make my own cream cheese," Lyons told reporters, laughing sarcastically. "I just drain the clabber and wait until the milk gets thick enough, and I have a fine cream cheese."

Though Dr. Mioton was sympathetic to Lyons's plight, there wasn't much he could do to solve this diet problem, short of extracting all of his teeth and miraculously healing his wounds. And there was still a ban on family members bringing outside food to the prison.

Lyons's aches and pains and his complaints about the food weren't the only things that aggravated him. He expressed no love for organized religion, either. One day, Mary O'Connor, the matron of the prison, informed a visiting Episcopal minister that "the old man," as she called Lyons (she was two years older than he), was in need of some spiritual uplifting. When the minister arrived unannounced, he did his best to comfort Lyons by citing passages from the Bible and singing songs of godly praise.

"If that psalm singer comes here again," Lyons informed the guard after the minister departed, "just tell him I'm asleep and can't see him."

In spite of his request, the minister returned with a lady friend, perhaps his wife. The couple took great pleasure in bellowing out various songs of worship. When they finally departed, Lyons looked at his jailer.

"I don't call that singing, do you?"

The jailer made no comment, likely thinking, oh, the joys of convalescence. By then, Lyons's religious jabs were grating on his prison guards.

Sometime afterwards, another Christian lady sought to comfort Lyons by reading him passages from the Bible. Lyons, who had heard enough religious talk by then, interrupted her midsentence.

"Oh, stop that," Lyons demanded, clearly irritated. "I don't want to hear [anymore] reading; my head bursts too much."

Unquestionably, the lady left his room feeling underappreciated and horrified that he had rejected God's words.

After Dr. Mioton's departure on Thursday, August 27, Lyons's defense team, Joseph Generelly and Warren Doyle, arrived at the prison in the company of Dr. Yves René LeMonnier, Jr., the former Orleans Parish coroner and a highly respected medical authority on mental illness. During the infamous Etienne Deschamps murder trial, he was a key State witness who testified that Deschamps was not criminally insane when he took the life of his young victim. Deschamps's conviction was largely based on Dr. LeMonnier's observations of the prisoner conducted over an extended time.

Prior to this visit, the defense had supplied Dr. LeMonnier with all pertinent documents about the case. The doctor may have also interviewed Lyons's family and known associates. The purpose of his visit was to initiate a dialogue with Lyons and begin the process of evaluating him for evidence of mental illness, something he might have already suspected after reviewing Lyons's casefile. Dr. LeMonnier was knowledgeable enough about the signs of mental illness that he could spot a ruse. The defense was confident that Lyons was actually insane, and not pretending, when he murdered the district attorney.

Even before Dr. LeMonnier's visit, there was talk among prison officials that Lyons was demented or becoming so, though he was also described in one newspaper as being exceedingly cunning. The defense wasn't worried about the latter claim and assumed that Dr. LeMonnier would get to the truth.

Joseph Generelly (1903). (Courtesy NOLA.com/The *Times-Picayune*)

Warren Doyle (1903). (Courtesy NOLA.com/The *Times-Picayune*)

Surprisingly, after his first visit, Dr. LeMonnier was convinced that Lyons suffered from a form of monomania that progressed over the years to delusions of persecution, followed by homicidal then suicidal mania. He agreed to be a witness for the defense and returned to the prison several more times over the course of several weeks. How many additional visits isn't known, but it couldn't have been more than a handful. Rather than conducting intensive person-to-person sessions with Lyons over a protracted period, Dr. LeMonnier relied heavily on Lyons's personal correspondences to formulate his opinion about the man.

The irony of this is striking. Years before, Dr. LeMonnier had chastised a group of physicians who examined Etienne Deschamps over the course of a week and came to the conclusion that he suffered a form of monomania, the same diagnosis he now pronounced about Lyons after his first session. Fortunately for the defense during the trial, the district attorney never questioned Dr. LeMonnier's inconsistent standard for rendering a diagnosis of mental illness. Instead, the State presented a rebuttal witness to counter Dr. LeMonnier's testimony.

Generelly and Doyle had only been law partners for about two years when they were appointed to defend Lyons. By then, Generelly had earned a reputation of being a skilled litigator.

Edward Joseph Generelly was born in New Orleans on December 29, 1874, the first of eight children born to Laurent Generelly and Marie Denise Villeré. His mother was the older sister of Gabriel Villeré, who served as the Orleans Parish sheriff during Etienne Deschamps's three-year incarceration and later execution at the old parish prison. Seldom using his first name, Generelly lived his entire life in New Orleans, where he received his early training at Jesuits' College, graduating in 1890. While holding down a clerical position, Generelly attended evening law lectures at Tulane University and earned his law degree in 1895. He married twenty-four-year-old Elise Sarpy in June 1897 and from that union had six children. The year following his marriage, he was appointed by Orleans Parish district attorney Robert Marr, Jr., as one of his assistant prosecutors, a position he held until Marr left office in June 1900.

John Warren Doyle, or Warren Doyle as he was called, was born on March 2, 1877, in Henry County, Kentucky, to James Francis Doyle and Catherine Montagnon. His father was a native of Ireland and his mother hailed from Ohio. One of nine children, Doyle was educated at various elementary and preparatory schools in Kentucky and Ohio before the family moved to New

Orleans when he was fifteen years old. Doyle attended Boys' High School in the city and thereafter enrolled at Tulane University, receiving his law degree in 1896. It's possible that Generelly and Doyle attended some of the same law classes at Tulane. Their school friendship possibly paved the way to their partnership.

The year after Doyle graduated, he married Viola C. Brown, but they would have no children. On July 28, 1902, five years after they wed, Viola died of tuberculosis, at the age of twenty-seven. She was patient at one of the sanatoriums in Colorado Springs, Colorado. The town had a number of sanatoriums and boardinghouses that cared for patients afflicted with that fatal, chronic, progressive pulmonary disease. With a cure for tuberculosis many decades away, the thinking in those days was that dry, cool, mountain air could stabilize or perhaps even drastically reduce the detrimental effects of the illness. The medical establishment was wrong. It is not known if Doyle took a sabbatical from his law practice while his wife was dying, but sometime during the last year of Viola's life, he entered into a partnership with Joseph Generelly.

⌖⌖⌖

Lyons resumed his triweekly visits to Charity Hospital on Monday, August 31. By then, both his lumbago and vertigo had eased to the point that he no longer required manual support from Captain Rennyson, who always accompanied him.

Dr. Jones again examined his eyes and questioned Lyons as to how he was getting along. He still complained of a great deal of head pain, though his left wound and ear no longer drained. Nevertheless, the doctor wasn't satisfied with his patient's progress. He suggested he get more fresh air and recommended that he go to one of the exercise yards at least daily. Lyons wanted to do nothing of the sort. He was quite content to remain within his secluded third-floor room and felt he could stretch his legs just as easily there as downstairs in the yard.

As was becoming all too familiar to reporters, prison officials continued to portray Lyons as a cranky and dissatisfied man who only spoke when necessary. Lyons's chronic headache was clearly the root of his longstanding irritability. Officials may have misconstrued his unpleasantness as an early sign of psychosis, based on Dr. LeMonnier's confirmation of Lyons's mental peculiarities.

If ever there was a suitable time for Lyons to feign madness, which he didn't, the sighting of a ghost near his bed one night was an ideal opportunity to do so. On the night of September 9, 1903, Joe Horn, an inmate serving time for assault and battery, was assigned as Lyons's nurse. At about midnight, while Horn lay awake in a neighboring cot reading the newspaper, he saw an apparition of a man standing at the foot of Lyons's bed.

"Ai-yi-yi-yi!" Horn bellowed when he caught sight of the ghostly, white figure.

To Horn's recollection, his guttural shout caused the thing to turn and wave his long, white hands at him. Horn suddenly found himself the object of the ghost's wrath, as the spirit walked towards him and attempted to touch the top of his head. At that point, Horn scampered from the room, yelling at full volume. His shouting didn't stop until he ran upstairs and sought shelter in the prison chapel. Fortunately for the terrified prisoner, the phantom chose not to follow him.

Rushing to the fourth floor in search of Horn, two deputies found him in the sanctuary.

"What's the matter?" one of the deputies asked Horn, who by then was trembling in fear for his life.

"I s-s-saw er ghost," he said.

"Where?"

"In Lyons's room."

Later, Capt. Meyer Dreifus, the night clerk, questioned Horn, who repeated his story about his ghastly encounter. Horn claimed that he didn't recover from his fright for several hours, and he continued to insist that what he saw was real.

Meanwhile, Lyons heard Horn scream and saw his quick departure from the room, but he maintained that he saw nothing that resembled a ghost. Lyons believed that if anything manifested itself that night in his room, it was in Horn's vivid imagination only.

"That fellow's crazy," Lyons declared. "There has been nothing here. Ghost—I don't believe in such nonsense."

⊕⊕⊕

On Monday, October 5, 1903, while still on holiday, Judge Chretien met with Luzenberg at the courthouse to discuss the prospects of bringing Lyons and another accused murderer to trial before Christmas. Prior to taking his recess, Judge Chretien was allotted three murder cases, with more possible, if new cases were added to the docket. Nothing was agreed upon that day, but Judge Chretien anticipated having to reconvene his court earlier than December 1, if he ever wished to conclude the trials before the end of the year. Meanwhile, Generelly and Doyle informed the press that they hoped to bring their client's case to court at the earliest possible time, though they probably weren't thinking about October as a start date.

As Judge Chretien and Luzenberg met at the courthouse to discuss their options, Lyons returned to Charity Hospital for his routine visit, escorted by Captain Rennyson. Sporting a full beard, Lyons walked in a stooped position and appeared weak, emaciated, and generally broken down. His lumbago had flared up again, wearing him down and preventing him from walking completely upright.

On Tuesday morning, after weighing the pros and cons of reconvening his court early, Judge Chretien announced that the murder trial of Louis W. Lyons would begin on Monday, November 2. He planned to impanel a group of prospective jurors on that date and then wait three days, as prescribed by law, before he called the trial to order. He also expected that Monday would be filled with various preliminary procedures. In any event, with the regular pool of talesmen (prospective jurors) selected on Monday, Judge Chretien anticipated that jury selection would begin in earnest no later than Thursday, November 5.

Because of the high-profile nature of the case, Judge Chretien expected the court to exhaust the regular jury pool by Saturday, November 7, assuming jury selection began as scheduled. If that was the case, he planned to create a special venire of talesmen over the weekend.

In a separate matter, Judge Chretien decided it was necessary to establish new classifications of crimes for court allotment. Clearly something had to be done differently in the future so as not to burden one criminal court judge over the other. The current system in place, by luck of the draw, had allotted three capital murder cases to Judge Chretien, while Judge Baker received lesser cases to preside over. Judge Chretien decided that future casework would be divided into four new categories. Capital murder cases would now constitute the first category. Those crimes of murder or mayhem punishable by hard labor at the state penitentiary would constitute the second category. The third category of crimes would include those punishable by incarceration in either the state penitentiary or Orleans Parish Prison. And finally, the fourth category would involve lesser offenses where the guilty party was sentenced to the parish prison only. Both judges would be afforded the opportunity to pick an equal number of cases per category.

On Monday, November 2, 1903, Judge Chretien summoned the district attorney and Lyons's defense team to his courtroom and selected a jury pool of sixty-one men, who were subsequently issued subpoenas to appear in court at ten o'clock on Thursday morning. As was the case with the Etienne Deschamps murder trial, by law, women (lacking suffrage) were prohibited from serving on the jury.

Later that day, Generelly and Doyle filed with the docket clerk, Dan Malone, a list of potential witnesses, which included Lyons's mother, one of his sisters, his brother, Wilson, Dr. LeMonnier, and, surprisingly, Delos Mellen. Shortly after Gurley's murder, Mellen was quoted in the newspaper saying that he believed Lyons was "crazy." With Generelly and Doyle mounting an insanity defense, Mellen's testimony would be critical. His professional relationship with Lyons, coupled with his quote about his state of mind, caused the defense to believe that Mellen would help prove that their client was insane.

Meanwhile, during the month of October and early November, Lyons languished in Orleans Parish Prison. By the start of his trial, his self-inflicted gunshot wound had completely healed, though his headaches and lumbago persisted. He had been transferred to a regular prison cell by then, and his third-floor room reverted to an income source for the prison from any inmate willing to pay for more comfortable accommodations.

Lyons's relocation was unquestionably a welcome change for guards who had stood private watch and inmates who had been assigned as his nurse. Lyons never thanked anyone for the special attention he received. Why would he? He had failed to take his life and suffered miserably from his wounds. All he could hope for now were a speedy trial, a guilty verdict, and a timely execution.

Chapter Eight

A Tedious Process

Have you any conscientious scruples against the infliction of—
Chandler Luzenberg

On Thursday, November 5, 1903, under mostly cloudy skies with the temperature peaking at seventy-three degrees, the murder trial of Lewis Lyons began in Judge Chretien's courtroom. Though a practicing attorney for thirty years, Chretien had only assumed his judgeship less than three years before. The Lyons trial would be his first high-profile murder case to preside over.

François "Frank" D. Chretien, Jr. was born in St. Martinville, Louisiana, on April 19, 1849, to François Dazincourt Chretien, Sr., and Virginie Briant Fuselier, both natives of the state. This was his mother's second marriage. During the antebellum years, Chretien's father owned a sizable sugar plantation in St. Martin Parish. As a slave owner, he was spared the wrath of the Civil War when he died in 1858 at age sixty-eight. Chretien, his mother, an unknown number of siblings, and at least two stepbrothers lived with various family members during the war. He and his mother eventually relocated to New Orleans.

In spite of the hardships he encountered during the war, including the loss of his father's land, Chretien endeavored to make a better life for himself. Chretien received his early education in Louisiana, then traveled to Fordham, New York, where he graduated in 1868 from St. John's College (now Fordham University), a private, Catholic-founded, higher-learning institution. Returning to New Orleans, he worked as a clerk for a number of mercantile firms before setting his sights on the law. He may have been convinced to become an attorney by his older stepbrother, Fergus Fuselier, an attorney who practiced in the city. Fuselier may have even sponsored his apprenticeship, a process that spanned several years.

In June 1873, Chretien easily passed his bar examination when he appeared before the Louisiana Supreme Court. On July 21, he married Blanche Williams

Judge Frank Chretien (1903). (Courtesy NOLA.com/ The *Times-Picayune*)

of Opelousas and from that union had three daughters. The Chretiens soon moved to Lake Charles, Louisiana, where he opened a law practice. Why he relocated there is not known, but he quickly became a successful litigator and was elected district attorney of Calcasieu and Cameron parishes. He served until 1876, when he resumed his law practice.

Meanwhile, in April 1875, while shopping in the French Quarter, Fuselier died of a stroke at age forty-two. Chretien returned to New Orleans the following year to settle his stepbrother's affairs and decided to stay.

Chretien prospered in New Orleans, made a name for himself among the legal community, and was elected to the state legislature in December 1879, serving in that capacity for four years. After leaving the statehouse, he remained very active in politics, serving as a member of the state printing board. He was appointed to the Orleans Parish School Board during Gov. Francis T. Nicholls's second term (1888-92). Nicholls's successor, Gov.

Murphy J. Foster, appointed Chretien examiner of public records, a position he held until 1894. In January 1900, when a vacancy was created in the United States Bankruptcy Court in New Orleans, Chretien was appointed, serving until February 1901, when Governor Heard chose him to serve out the unexpired term of Judge James C. Moise, who died of a ruptured cerebral aneurysm.

Judge Chretien experienced his own tragedies over the years. Besides the passing of his father and his stepbrother, his mother died of a stroke on February 24, 1887, at age seventy and his wife, Blanche, passed away on January 18, 1903, at age forty-nine from peritonitis and septicemia, probably from a ruptured appendix. Chretien's responsibilities as a father and judge prevented him from mourning long. Chretien buried his wife in a private ceremony the day after her death and, by week's end, resumed his courtroom duties.

On the first day of the Lyons murder trial, District Attorney Luzenberg arrived early at his office in the courthouse, making last-minute preparations such as finalizing a series of questions he would ask potential jurymen. Meanwhile, Lyons's defense team arrived at the courthouse armed with a stack of law books and a determination to vigorously defend their client.

Shortly before the trial commenced, Judge Chretien reached his second-floor office, donned his judicial robe, and prepared for the momentous task before him. He speculated (wrongly) that the trial would last twenty days, given the large number of witnesses scheduled to testify.

By ten o'clock, minutes before the murder trial was to commence, the courtroom filled to capacity. Among the scores of spectators were a number of ladies who had ventured from their homes to see justice served. Murder trials generally drew very few, if any, female onlookers in that era. Like the Deschamps trial more than a dozen years before, Lyons's trial was the exception.

For the first time since Lyons was incarcerated, his trips to the courthouse didn't involve being paraded through the streets. A shorter walk could now be accomplished internally from building to building. On November 2, 1903, the newly constructed covered, steel bridge connecting the second floor of the prison and courthouse opened. Unfortunately, Lyons wasn't the first inmate to use the conduit. That distinction went to Samuel Sparo, another accused murderer whom Lyons would come to know. Criminal Sheriff Reilley dubbed the new passageway the "Sparo Bridge" in his honor, though other nicknames were used.

When Lyons was ushered into the courtroom, spectators saw a weathered man who had aged considerably since that fateful day four months earlier. His protruding cheekbones were flushed, and his face had wrinkled to such a degree that he appeared twenty years older than his forty-five years of age. His long, snowy-white beard and long, white, stringy, sparse hair only exacerbated his hoary look. Though Lyons's entry wound and damaged left eye had healed, the effects of the injury continued to haunt the man with pain. His suicide attempt appeared to have hardened his soul, and the lingering discomfort turned Lyons bitter towards life, more so than he had been before his crime.

Taking a seat at the defense table alongside his attorneys, Lyons showed very little emotion or interest as everyone else around him busied themselves before the call to order. By then, District Attorney Luzenberg and two of his assistants, Samuel Montgomery and Henry Mooney, had arrived in the courtroom and sat at the prosecutor's table.

Judge Chretien entered, and the murder trial of Lewis Lyons began. The first order of business, after determining that both sides were ready to proceed, was to establish if all witnesses for the State and the defense were present. A call of State witnesses revealed that all were present or accounted for. But when the defense called their witnesses, it was discovered that Delos Mellen was the only person absent. (Delos was also a State witness, but his absence was not a concern for Luzenberg at this early stage of the trial.) Aware that he was critical to the defense, Generelly wanted to know why he hadn't arrived. Generelly informed the court that Luzenberg had told him the day before that Mellen would be there, having already spoken to him. Luzenberg denied having any such conversation with the defense. It soon became apparent to all that this trial was going to turn into contentious brawl, with both sides determined to win. In the end, Luzenberg assured the court that Mellen would appear when summoned by the defense.

With that portion of the preliminaries concluded, the State witnesses were dismissed until 10:30 the following morning. Luzenberg assumed that impaneling an impartial jury would only consume a single day and that the State could call their first witness shortly afterwards; he was wrong. The defense witnesses were given greater latitude prior to their dismissals. They weren't required in court until the following Monday morning.

With that matter concluded, the process of impaneling a jury commenced. The first name called was Albert G. Winn, a clerk who worked for a dry-goods store at the corner of Canal and Carondelet streets. His workplace was several doors down from the Macheca Building. When

Luzenberg asked Winn if he opposed capital punishment, he answered no. He added that he wouldn't oppose convicting Lyons on circumstantial evidence, would decide the case based on the law and the evidence submitted, and would not be swayed by any sentiment.

Luzenberg believed one factor that might play on the emotions of the jury was Lyons's weathered look. Knowing Lyons was in his mid-forties but appeared decades older, the district attorney asked Winn if it was proven that Lyons had committed a "brutal murder," would he consider the accused's age while deliberating.

Even before Winn could answer the question, Generelly objected to the word "brutal." He reminded the court that the State had not presented its case and clearly no witnesses had testified as to the nature of the crime. Judge Chretien sustained the objection.

Winn responded that the defendant's age would play no factor in his verdict. And he assured the court that the evidence presented would have to be "strong" in order for him to convict and that he would give capital punishment "serious consideration."

Lastly, Luzenberg asked Winn about his opinion on proving insanity. Would he convict if the defense proved by a preponderance of the evidence that Lyons was insane at the time of the murder? (Based on the law, the defense had to prove insanity by a preponderance of the evidence, not beyond all reasonable doubt.) Winn stated that he would give the accused the benefit of the doubt if the defense proved he was insane. The district attorney appeared satisfied with his answer and then tendered the witness.

"Did you read the newspaper accounts of the affair?" Generelly asked.

"Yes sir," Winn responded. "I read the *Picayune* and the [*New Orleans Daily*] *States.*"

"Did you form an opinion based on what you read?"

"Yes sir, and I still have that opinion but have never expressed it," Winn replied.

Winn was one of hundreds of New Orleanians who quickly gathered on Canal Street that fateful morning. Though he admitted that he had formed an opinion about the case, Winn assured the court that his view of the murder did not rely on the mental state of the accused. He would be guided only by the evidence submitted.

"If one witness should testify in accordance with the opinion you say you formed, and another against that opinion, how would you decide?" Generelly continued.

"I would divide them up," Winn answered. And then he contradicted himself. "I have formed an opinion as to the sanity of the accused and still hold that opinion." But he clarified, "I know Mr. Gurley by reputation only. My opinion is not fixed and would give way to evidence."

When pressed by Generelly, Winn admitted that he would not convict if the accused was proven insane, but it would have to be strong evidence to sway him from his original opinion of Lyons. In other words, based on what Winn had read in the newspapers, he believed that Lyons was sane and criminally responsible for his actions. Winn also believed that Lyons would have to prove his innocence.

Of course, the defense asked that the witness be challenged for cause, but Judge Chretien refused at first. Luzenberg reminded Winn that the defendant did not have to prove his innocence. It was the duty of the State to prove his guilt beyond a reasonable doubt.

"On the question of insanity, however," Luzenberg explained, "he [Lyons] has to prove he was insane. The State does not have to prove that he was sane."

"But apart from the matter of insanity," Generelly probed, "you say you have an opinion?"

"Yes sir," Winn responded.

"If taken as a juror, you would go into the box with that opinion?"

"Yes."

By that point, Judge Chretien had no choice but to dismiss Winn.

And so began the tedious process of selecting a jury. When court recessed at five o'clock that afternoon, only three men had been picked (a cashier, a clerk, and a real-estate agent) out of forty-two men questioned. With the vast amount of pretrial publicity, selecting an uninformed and unbiased jury would be a monumental task.

⌖⌖⌖

Judge Chretien realized after the first day that the original jury pool of 61 talesmen would be exhausted by the following morning. Thus, as soon as court adjourned, the jury wheel was brought into his office, and a special venire of 100 talesmen were selected. Deputies spent that evening and early the next day attempting to notify each man of his legal obligation to appear in Judge Chretien's chambers on Friday morning.

By the time court reconvened, not every talesman had been notified, and of those who had, some failed to appear. Nonetheless, thirty men were questioned, with only one additional juror, a clerk, seated by the recess for lunch.

Some of the disqualified men claimed that they personally knew Gurley or that they opposed capital punishment. Others would not sentence to death a man convicted based solely on circumstantial evidence. Still others had already formed a fixed opinion of the defendant, based on what they read in the newspapers. At least one person knew Lyons when he was a boy and was currently acquainted with one of his sisters. Two gentlemen were too deaf and two more were too sick to serve on a jury. One prospective juror believed that he would have to participate in the hanging if a guilty verdict was reached. Lyons, who was apathetic throughout the jury-selection process, smiled for the first time at that point. Even he seemed to realize how ignorant the man was regarding the duties of a juryman.

Before the day's end, one newspaper called into question the patriotism of businessmen who seemed to be shirking their civic duty, saying anything necessary to avoid their obligation to serve as jurors. Their potential loss of income seemed to be the overriding reason why many merchants and "the better class of citizens" wanted no part of the criminal proceedings, especially when the trial was scheduled to last several weeks.

The report that many of the potential jurymen were shirking their obligations may have been right. When court adjourned late that afternoon, only 4 jurors had been seated out of 161 talesmen summoned thus far, though 10 men had failed to appear when called. These absentees were ordered to be rounded up and forced to appear in court the next day. In the meantime, Judge Chretien ordered a second special venire, this time consisting of 150 talesmen. The court would reconvene at 10:00 A.M. on Saturday.

With Saturday's court legislated a half-day session (the law stipulated that Saturday afternoon in Orleans Parish was *dies non juridicum,* day without judiciary), Judge Chretien didn't expect to complete the jury selection by the noon deadline to adjourn. Nevertheless, he would try, though he expressed disappointment in the process thus far. He indicated that if a jury was still not secured from the second special venire, he would order as many venires as it would take to select a jury.

When Lyons walked into the courtroom on Saturday morning, he looked to be in considerable pain. His lumbago had apparently flared up again, because he stooped as he approached the defense table and took his seat. The *Daily Picayune* wrote that he seemed to age ten years in one day, "and his face betrayed more anxiety than it had done since the trial commenced."

In spite of the tiresome ordeal of selecting a jury, interest in the murder trial hadn't waned on this third day—in fact, just the opposite. The courtroom was now filled to overflowing, with every seat taken, the aisles and gallery full, and the space between the rear seats and back wall overcrowded with spectators. During the two-hour court session, a total of nineteen talesmen were questioned. With the original special venire dispensed with, prospective jurors from the second special venire were examined. Most of the talesmen were excused due to either their opposition to capital punishment or their insistence on eyewitness testimony. Others had already formed an opinion of Lyons based on what they had read in the newspapers.

When one gentleman was asked if he could convict based only on circumstantial evidence, he responded, "It depends on the circumstances entirely." This caused the courtroom to erupt into laughter. The deputy was forced to bellow out "order in the court" to silence the crowd. One prospective juror was so eager to be excused from duty that, after taking the stand, he interrupted Luzenberg in midsentence.

"Have you any conscientious scruples against the infliction of—"

"Yes sir," he responded, as he jumped from his seat in order to head for the exit. He was ultimately released.

The *Item* reported that several talesmen also indicated they would have to carefully study the evidence against Lyons. It would have to be compelling in order for them "to render a verdict against one so old." Everyone assumed that Lyons was ancient. Besides his facial features that painted him years older than he was, Lyons's limp and stooped shoulders added to the perception that he was not in his mid-forties.

Only one juror even came close to being selected on Saturday morning. He informed the court that he did not oppose capital punishment or convicting someone based solely on circumstantial evidence, if such circumstantial evidence was compelling. He admitted that he had read about the murder and in July had formed an opinion about the guilt or innocence of the defendant. But he stressed that his opinion would carry no weight when he deliberated.

Both sides thought that they had secured their fifth juror, until the gentleman was warned not to openly express his opinion about Lyons. Of course, this caused him to inadvertently blurt it out, bringing another outburst of laughter from the spectators. The man was excused.

At noon, Judge Chretien adjourned his court until Monday morning, forcing one prospective juror in the middle of his questioning to return after the weekend. Generelly then moved that the four jurors selected thus far be allowed to read the daily newspapers after all mentions of the trial had been removed from their pages. Judge Chretien consented, with Luzenberg agreeing. The jurors were then escorted to their third-floor rooms in the courthouse.

On Monday, November 9, jury selection resumed at ten o'clock, with the four impaneled jurors brought downstairs. Lyons's attitude about the legal proceedings had not changed since his first appearance before the bench the previous Thursday. "His countenance [did] not [betray] any signs of interest, or of either hope or fear," the *Daily Picayune* reported. He remained apathetic, or he wished the audience to think him so. Before court resumed, Lyons's wife visited but left before the proceedings.

By the time the lunch recess was called at 12:30, 32 talesmen had taken the stand, including the gentleman who had been interrupted the previous Saturday. Only 1 additional juror was chosen, a clerk who fortuitously had been out of town on the day of the murder, had not heard the case discussed, and had not formed an opinion about the defendant. Reconvening at 1:45, and holding session until 5:00, the court heard from scores of other talesmen. Fortunately, 3 additional jurors were selected: a coffee and tea dealer, a salesman, and a proprietor of a grocery store. Only 4 more jurors were required, but the current pool was nearly exhausted. Before court adjourned, Judge Chretien ordered a third special venire of 100 talesmen.

As was becoming a familiar scene, on Tuesday, November 10, the fifth day of jury selection, the courtroom was crowded with spectators, as two more jurors, a salesman and collector, were chosen by the lunch recess. Forty jurors from the third special venire of talesmen had been examined that morning, leaving sixty men from which to choose the remaining two jurors. There was every expectation that the selection process would be completed when court adjourned, as the State and defense had but one peremptory challenge left.

When court reconvened at 1:30, the ten jurors chosen thus far were brought downstairs, having consumed a tasty lunch. After his meal, Lyons was seen walking briskly back into the courtroom, though his shoulders remained stooped. His gait suggested that he was feeling little or no pain from his lumbago.

The first man called to the stand that afternoon, a store dealer, was ultimately chosen as the eleventh juror, after both sides sought clarification regarding what he believed to be the standard of proof to convict. Twenty-five talesmen later, the last juryman picked was Henry Gehbauer, an employee of the Craft Tobacco Company. But his selection ran counter to the wishes of the State. During questioning, Luzenberg believed that Gehbauer "entertained false ideas of capital punishment and circumstantial evidence," the *Daily Picayune* reported. Nevertheless, the district attorney was powerless to stop the defense, who easily accepted the man. Luzenberg had exhausted his legal limit of challenges by then.

At 3:30, with the jury selection now complete, Gehbauer took his seat among the other jurors. Judge Chretien discharged the remaining candidates, who left the courtroom much pleased at their good fortune.

After a short recess, the jurors were brought downstairs and sworn in by Minute Clerk Arthur Desmond. He then read the murder charge against Lewis Lyons, the bill of indictment, and Lyons's plea of not guilty. Given the lateness of the day, it was mutually agreed that testimony would commence the following morning. Court adjourned.

Judge Chretien had ruled out a night session for that day, but he made it clear that future court sessions might extend past the usual 5:00 P.M. adjournment. Those days, however, would be announced beforehand. And to accommodate those longer days, the court would not convene until 10:30, and adequate time would be provided for lunch and supper. He also announced that henceforth, barring a night session, the trial day would begin at 9:30 A.M. and last until 6:00 P.M., with an hour lunch break.

On Wednesday, November 11, 1903, the first day of witness testimony, the *Daily Picayune* printed a disparaging editorial against the voting-age, literate, male population of New Orleans, the only portion of the populace who could serve as jurors. The editor believed that the main reason it took five days to secure a jury was not because the men had formed prejudices for or against the defendant. Rather, it was because a sizable portion of the male population had declared themselves absolutely unable to weigh the evidence in a capital murder trial.

Of the 311 talesmen who were questioned, 110 stated that they would never condemn a man to death under any circumstances. And another 56 talesmen made it clear they couldn't send Lyons to the gallows unless an eyewitness saw the defendant pull the trigger. All told, that constituted 53 percent of the men questioned.

But in a broader sense, based on what had occurred in Judge Chretien's chambers, the editor claimed that well over half of the 65,000 literate males in New Orleans (based on 1900 U.S. Census figures), or 34,371 men, "would be constitutionally unable or unwilling to punish with death a murderer or a ravisher." With the laws of Louisiana calling for the death penalty for certain crimes, the editor declared that over half of the eligible men in New Orleans couldn't be depended upon to vindicate state law if asked to serve on a jury, an appalling reality.

The *Daily Picayune* editor further believed that the greater danger in buckling under to conscientious objectors to capital punishment was that the truly guilty would escape the death sentence imposed by law. The ramifications of this were clear. He argued that this trend would spark vigilante justice next time around, when the public believed that it would be quicker and justice better served if the murderer was executed outside the bounds of established law. "There is no question that the growing prevalence of lynching arises from the increasing lack of confidence in the efficiency of judicial methods to punish criminals," the editorial concluded. "The people alone are responsible."

Chapter Nine

IT BEGINS

What do you expect to prove by this witness?

Judge Frank Chretien

On Wednesday morning, November 11, 1903, after five days of jury selection, testimony in the Lewis Lyons murder trial began. By the time Judge Chretien convened his courtroom at 9:30, his chamber was crowded with spectators eager to hear from the various witnesses.

The court determined that both sides were ready to proceed, then if all the witnesses were present or accounted for; they were. Perhaps anticipating a problem, Generelly requested that, per the current rules, all witnesses, except experts, be barred from the courtroom until called upon to testify. Generelly presumably had experienced such a breach of protocol during a previous trial. Because of the high-profile nature of this murder trial, he wanted to remind witnesses and enlighten the public that such infractions would not be tolerated; the court concurred. State witnesses were immediately relocated to the witness room. Defense witnesses were instructed to return to the courthouse at 2:00 P.M.

Before the first State witness was called, Luzenberg directed the court to delete several names from his witness list. Among the excluded names was Orleans Parish coroner Dr. Richard. His removal puzzled the defense, since he had performed the autopsy. His testimony as an expert witness was critical for the State in proving cause of death and the trajectory of each bullet fired. The State cited that Dr. Richard was unavailable as he was leaving town, though that was hardly a valid excuse to exclude him as a State witness.

In Dr. Richard's place, Captain Parody, the coroner's secretary, took the stand as the State's first witness. Parody testified that he knew Gurley and had seen his body in his outer office in the Macheca Building and then again at Johnson's funeral parlor, where the autopsy was performed. He then stood and pointed to his chest and right arm, indicating the sites of Gurley's various gunshot wounds. The defense objected when he began to use such medical terminology as "axillary line." Generelly wanted to know how Parody acquired such knowledge, given his lack of medical training or expertise. His objection was overruled.

When Parody began to explain the bullets' extraction points, Generelly objected again even before the witness could finish his sentence. Judge Chretien ordered the jury out of the courtroom and instructed both legal teams to approach the bench.

Generelly explained to the judge that Parody was not qualified as a medical expert and therefore shouldn't be allowed to discuss what transpired during the autopsy conducted by Dr. Richard. That was Dr. Richard's duty. Luzenberg believed otherwise, since Parody had witnessed the autopsy. In fact, Luzenberg stressed that everyone who saw the autopsy was qualified to testify to what they had seen.

Judge Chretien overruled Generelly's objection, though he stressed that the witness wouldn't be allowed to render an opinion about anything that required medical expertise. For instance, he could speak to the location of the wounds but not the trajectory of the bullets, since Parody had not performed the autopsy; Dr. Richard had. The defense reserved a bill of exception, one of many that occurred during the course of the trial. The jury was then brought back into the courtroom.

Captain Parody continued to regurgitate the facts documented by Dr. Richard on the day of the shooting concerning the exact location of each gunshot wound, especially the two in the chest.

"Did you see whether either of these bullets in its course had perforated any of the organs of the body?" Luzenberg asked.

"Objection," uttered Generelly.

"Overruled."

"Yes, one bullet perforated the liver and the heart, for I handled these organs after they were taken from the body," Parody replied. He then stated that he accompanied Dr. Richard to Charity Hospital and saw the defendant.

"Was anything said to him, or did you say anything to him, in his presence?" asked Luzenberg.

"I object," Generelly stated. "He was under arrest at the time."

Again, Judge Chretien overruled his objection.

"Yes, Dr. Richard spoke to him. He held out no promises, nor made any threats to the accused," Parody explained. "Dr. Richard was accompanied by [myself] and several reporters."

"Now, what did he say to Dr. Richard and what did Dr. Richard say to him?"

Generelly objected a third time, informing the court that Dr. Richard had gone to the hospital as a physician and that the accused was under arrest. Even if his client had spoken to a thousand people that day, his words were not admissible. Pending a ruling from Judge Chretien, the jury was retired a second time.

"What do you expect to prove by this witness?" Judge Chretien asked Luzenberg.

"I propose to prove that Dr. Richard went to the hospital and asked the accused what had taken place in the office of Mr. Gurley," the district attorney explained. "Lyons told him that he went to get satisfaction. That Dr. Richard had asked Lyons whether Mr. Gurley had made any demonstration against him, to which he answered no, but Mr. Gurley had given him no satisfaction, and he had shot him."

Generelly's objection stemmed from the fact that *if* his client uttered such words to the coroner on the day of the visit, he was suffering from his wounds and not of sound mind. Judge Chretien again overruled the counselor's objection, indicating that if there was any evidence as to the state of Lyons's mind, the defense could introduce that fact when they presented their side of the case. The jury was brought back into the courtroom.

Captain Parody resumed his testimony by retelling what had been printed in the newspapers about Dr. Richard's visit with Lyons two days after the murder. Parody had witnessed the conversation between the two men, along with three reporters. There appeared to be no inconsistencies in his testimony as earlier chronicled in the various New Orleans dailies. Finally, when asked if Gurley's body had been searched, Parody testified that Dr. Richard had done so, but he couldn't remember if any weapon had been found.

On cross-examination, the jury learned that Captain Parody had been affiliated with the coroner's office for the past two years, but he possessed no special knowledge of human anatomy or the various names of body parts and admitted he couldn't tell the difference between a calf's liver and a human liver if asked to do so. When asked how he came to articulate the details of the various wounds without notes, Parody admitted that he had reviewed the coroner's records the previous day in preparation for taking the stand. When pressed by the defense concerning the hospital visit, Parody stated that Dr. Richard didn't push Lyons to make a statement and that Lyons volunteered what he said. Finally, when pressed again, Parody couldn't say if Lyons was under the influence of opiates when he spoke to the coroner that day.

Morgan Gurley, J. Ward's younger brother, took the stand next. An attorney and notary public by profession, Gurley testified that he was the same height as his late brother, though J. Ward always insisted that he was slightly taller than Morgan. The relevance of that was to establish that the murder victim was shorter than the defendant, if the trajectory of the bullets ever became an issue with the defense; it did not. Morgan stated that he saw his brother's body, fully clothed, at the Macheca Building. He identified his late brother's clothing—a coat, pants, shirt, undershirt, collar, and so forth—after which these personal effects were offered into evidence. The defense chose not to cross-examine the witness.

Robert Robinson, the office boy, testified to what transpired the day in question and added that he never saw a weapon stored in the Gurley's office. Obviously, this implied that the district attorney was killed by Lyons's revolver. On cross-examination, Robinson went into greater detail concerning when Lyons arrived at the office and what occurred up to the time of the shooting, including facts about the aftermath. He stated that he never laid eyes on Lyons before that day.

Sgt. Timothy Driscoll testified that he saw Gurley lying in the reception room and Lyons on the floor in the private office. He recalled picking up one or two loaded cartridges off the floor, though there were other shell casings that someone else retrieved. He identified the murder weapon as a .38-calibre Smith & Wesson pistol and clarified that he had collected two empty shells and three loaded cartridges off the floor in Gurley's private office. His testimony ran counter to what the *Daily Picayune* printed the day following the murder: three empty shell casings and two cartridges were retrieved. This wasn't his only discrepancy.

During cross-examination, Driscoll couldn't remember if Lyons was conscious when he arrived, though he testified to seeing the revolver near Lyons's right hand, which was odd since Lyons had used his left hand to fire the weapon. Driscoll recalled taking possession of the pistol, but the defense forced him to admit that he couldn't remember the exact number of shell casings or loaded cartridges, two versus three, that were retrieved from the floor.

Generelly then showed Driscoll the murder weapon and asked if such a weapon ever became disabled, could the ejector dislodge all of the shells, spent or unspent. Driscoll's answered yes. He recalled the revolver had five shells in the cylinder and that he picked up five shells off the floor. But like before, Driscoll was forced to admit he couldn't remember if two or three of the cartridges in the revolver were loaded or spent. Obviously, the defense was trying to plant some doubt in the jurors' minds about how the police had handled the murder weapon, but to what end? The particular mechanism of the revolver and the number of shell casings and cartridges found on the floor and in the weapon were never again brought up by the defense.

After Driscoll's testimony, Dr. Valentine Irion took the stand, followed by William Shepard, before the court took a one-hour recess for lunch. Both men testified to what they had witnessed on that fateful day. Along with Robinson's testimony, the State believed it had begun to present a strong case that Lyons was the murderer, based on persuasive circumstantial evidence.

⌖⌖⌖

When court resumed at 1:30 P.M., Dr. Buck testified about his brief meeting with the defendant in front of the Macheca Building about thirty minutes before the shooting. He recalled hearing Gurley's voice, the ensuing scuffle, and shots fired as he visited with Delos Mellen, one floor below Gurley's suite. He remembered that when he arrived in Gurley's office, he saw the victim in the arms of Terriberry and later saw the defendant lying on the floor in a pool of blood in Gurley's private office. On cross-examination, he added some details but nothing problematic for the State or beneficial for the defense. On redirect, he admitted that he hadn't seen Lyons for about a year before the murder and that he heard the scuffle while sitting in Mellen's office, though at the time he wasn't sure where the noise originated from.

Henry G'sell, the engineer of the Macheca Building, testified to what he heard—the shots—and what transpired thereafter, including his seeing Lyons lying in a pool of blood in Gurley's rear office. During cross-examination, he revealed other minor details, though at times he seemed to contradict himself regarding the position of Lyons's weapon. But on balance, his testimony inferred that Lyons had fired the deadly shots and tried to take his own life.

Taking the stand, Detective Thomas Roche testified that after Lyons was admitted to Charity Hospital, he retrieved from his pockets several items, including some loose cartridges and a small bundle containing cyanide, though he didn't know it was cyanide at the time. But he admitted during cross-examination that he had found no "empty" cartridges in the pockets of the defendant, which implied that Lyons still had some unspent ammunition when he attempted to take his life.

Capt. John Boyle testified that Detectives Roche and Patrick Dale handed him Lyons's personal property, including the cyanide that he believed at the time resembled a clump of salt, all of which he carefully wrapped and turned

Dr. Charles Buck (1903). (Courtesy NOLA.com/The *Times-Picayune*)

over to Clerk James Schillin. During his cross-examination, Boyle testified that no empty cartridges were turned over to him, similar to Detective Roche's testimony. When Schillin testified, he confirmed Boyle's testimony.

Dr. Abraham Metz, the city chemist and a professor of chemistry at Tulane University, testified that the personal items retrieved from the defendant's pockets were tested on November 3 and found to be contaminated with potassium cyanide, from three to four grains, a sufficient quantity to produce death. (At the time of the murder, Dr. Metz was in California on city business, and therefore the task of analyzing the powder found in the sweatband of Lyons's hat fell to the acting city chemist, Dr. Allan Eustis. It wasn't until the first week of November that Dr. Metz tested the other objects retrieved from Lyons's pockets.) During cross-examination, he testified that cyanide was one of the deadliest poisons known to man. The defense was attempting to portray their client as a madman who, after murdering the district attorney, planned to kill himself one way or another.

The State then called George Terriberry, who testified to what had been previously reported in the New Orleans dailies. During his cross-examination, he shed additional light on events shortly after the shooting.

Frank Reitmeyer, a *New Orleans Daily States* reporter, took the stand and corroborated Captain Parody's testimony regarding Dr. Richard's hospital visit with the defendant. He added that Lyons admitted that Gurley had made no attempt to strike him, which meant that the first shot fired by the defendant was unprovoked. Reitmeyer also testified that Lyons refused to answer Dr. Richard's question about whether Gurley was sitting or standing when he was shot. His testimony (by inference) placed Lyons in the same room and at the same time when the fatal shots were heard.

On cross-examination, the witness stated he didn't know if Lyons was under the influence of opiates at the time of the interview, though he testified that Lyons seemed to "dodge" some questions. The court objected to the witness's choice of word and reminded the jury that what Reitmeyer had spoken "was a matter of opinion on the part of the witness, and not a matter of fact." With this minor setback, the reporter ended by stating, "Lyons appeared rational and answered questions intelligently."

John Doran testified to what he saw and heard while in the reception room. But during his cross-examination he admitted that he didn't know Shepard and never saw him in the office that day. He confirmed that he heard the first shot about two minutes after Lyons entered Gurley's office but couldn't remember who was in the reception room when he left, which was understandable given his panic at the time. It may also explain why he couldn't recall seeing Shepard in the room.

Eugenie Rivero testified that she reached Gurley's office about nine to ten minutes before his arrival and heard some shooting while she was still in the corridor after her departure, presumably waiting for the elevator to take her to the first floor. The defense saw no need to cross-examine her.

Randall H. Pickens, a real-estate agent, testified that he had known the defendant for about four to five years and, in May 1902, had transacted the sale of five of his properties. About two months before the murder, he ran into Lyons, who was standing in front of a saloon on Gravier Street. He said Lyons stopped him.

"Mr. Mellen and Mr. Gurley robbed me of my money, and I am going to get even with them," Pickens recalled Lyons telling him.

But after hearing the threat, Pickens admitted that he didn't bother to enquire as to the nature of Lyons's displeasure with the two attorneys. He backtracked during his cross-examination and confessed that he couldn't remember if Lyons specifically mentioned Mellen and Gurley. Instead, Lyons may have told him something along the lines of: "You know these people who had my case? They robbed me, and I am going to get even with them."

This admission or correction by Pickens was hardly a game changer for the defense. Though Lyons may not have mentioned Mellen and Gurley's names, the jury knew the party he was referring to.

After excusing Pickens, the State called Delos Mellen, their next logical witness to take the stand. Mellen began by recalling his partnership with Gurley and his association with Lyons beginning in the mid-1890s. He then discussed various court expenses incurred by the firm, which were not totally reimbursed by Lyons, including charges from the late Leslie Bobb, the stenographer.

The implications of these disclosures were clear. If anyone should be bitter about the unsuccessful outcome of Lyons's lawsuit, it should have been the witness and the late Gurley. Neither attorney ever received a dime for their services or the court expenses they incurred pursuing the case. In spite of that, neither attorney ever sought to sue Lyons for court costs he promised to pay.

Switching topics, Mellen went into some detail about the case being adjudicated by the Louisiana Supreme Court, another expense, though he didn't participate during that phase. By then, Gurley was representing Lyons before the High Court. The witness admitted that his only knowledge of what had transpired before the Supreme Court was taken from the *Louisiana Annual Report* about the case.

Warren Doyle conducted the cross-examination. Mellen recalled Lyons's lawsuit against Daniel Carroll and the two detectives, Lyons accusing him of being negligent and the source of his failure in court, and then Lyons cutting all ties with him and Gurley. Mellen was unapologetic about how he had handled Lyons's case.

After obtaining permission from the court, Doyle approached the witness and handed him various receipts for money paid by Lyons to Mellen and Gurley, including some court costs. Mellen was forced to admit that if Lyons had such receipts in his possession, then he surely gave his old law firm some money, contrary to what he had previously testified.

Having successfully impugned the witness regarding the money matter, Doyle turned his attention to what newspapers had printed about Mellen's description of Lyons. Mellen was quoted as saying Lyons was "crazy" over the lawsuit, was a monomaniac on the subject, and for the past three years had been acting irrationally.

Mellen admitted that he had been interviewed by several reporters but couldn't remember exactly what he said. If he used the term "crazy," he meant that Lyons had become cranky about his failure in court. While he couldn't remember the exact word he used to describe Lyons, he did recall that he was under a great deal of emotional stress when he was interviewed. His former law partner had just been murdered. On redirect, Mellen did his best to counter his prior testimony about having to shoulder the financial burdens of Lyons's lawsuit. He stated he simply didn't remember any money transactions.

Joseph Elsinger testified that he was a patron at Nelson's saloon on the morning of July 20. He knew Lyons by sight and had heard the conversation Lyons had with Dr. Richard about the coroner finding a bunch of keys. It was about nine o'clock that morning, as he recalled. On cross-examination, he confirmed that the conversation occurred on Monday, the day of the murder.

Clement Hearsey, a *Daily News* reporter, corroborated previous testimony related to Dr. Richard's conversation with Lyons at the hospital. On cross-examination, he couldn't say if Lyons was under the influence of opiates or not.

James Fitzsimmons, who was employed at the Continental Saloon on Gravier Street on the day in question, testified that he received a due bill from the defendant for ten dollars, which he identified. It was subsequently offered into evidence without objection from the defense. Obviously, the State wanted to illustrate to the jury that Lyons was mentally capable of conducting a business transaction prior to his premeditated act of murder, but there was more to come about this money transaction.

Paul Alpuente, a bartender at the Continental Saloon, affirmed that he transacted some business with the defendant on the Saturday before the murder. He was shown a thirty-five-dollar check that Lyons had written to himself, drawn from the Whitney National Bank in town and endorsed by the defendant. While at work, Alpuente cashed the check for Lyons, who pocketed the money. Lyons used part of the cash two days later to pay an old tab at the Continental Saloon, and therein lay a problem for the defense.

During cross-examination, it was revealed that the check was drawn on insufficient funds. In essence, Lyons cashed a worthless check at the Continental Saloon on Saturday and then paid an old tab there with a portion of the stolen money two days later. What he did with the balance of his cash is unknown. Undoubtedly, some of the stolen money was still in his pocket when he murdered Gurley.

Having cashed Lyons's worthless check over the weekend, the Continental Saloon wouldn't have discovered the fraud until the bank opened on Monday after the murder and Lyons's suicide, too late for the saloon to seek restitution. This evidence further illustrated that Lyons wasn't insane but rather a cunning thief. The defense may have been broadsided by this revelation.

Robert Robinson was recalled and testified that the hall door leading to Gurley's private office was kept locked. The State may have wanted to end any doubts in the jurors' minds as to why (prior to G'sell's arrival) none of the eyewitnesses had attempted to gain access to the private office by way of the side hallway.

Cullom W. Kay, a bookkeeper at the Whitney National Bank, was the last witness of the day. He testified that Lyons had an account at the bank but had drawn the last of his funds on July 1, almost three weeks before the murder. Again, this proved that Lyons had committed fraud when he cashed his worthless check at the saloon two days before the murder.

With the hour rapidly approaching six o'clock, court adjourned until the following morning, with the jury taken upstairs for supper and much-needed rest. Lewis Lyons was unceremoniously escorted back to his prison cell.

Unquestionably, the day ended well for Luzenberg, who felt confident that he had mounted a strong circumstantial case against Lyons. None of the State witnesses painted Lyons as crazed, irrational, or demented prior to the murder. If anything, Lyons came across as a vengeful person who sought satisfaction for the wrongs that he perceived were perpetrated against him by Mellen and Gurley.

If the defense was to win their argument, they would have to prove by a preponderance of the evidence that their client was insane at the moment he pulled the trigger. Though the defense's threshold for proving insanity was lower than the State's obligation to prove guilt beyond a reasonable doubt, Generelly and Doyle still had a mammoth task before them. It would take more than a single day to present their defense.

Chapter Ten

THE DEFENSE

If I have done any harm, I am sorry for it and did it innocently.

Henry Gehbauer

On Thursday morning, November 12, 1903, the courtroom was again awash with spectators, this time eagerly anticipating the start of the defense's side of the murder case. District Attorney Luzenberg had made it known the previous day that the State would rest its case in the morning. Everyone assumed that the court would be called to order at its usual 9:30 start time, but it didn't happen. By then, court observers were abuzz with gossip that a mistrial had been entered, with one rumor placing the blame on a lone juror who had become mentally imbalanced the evening before.

The rumor mill began as early as nine o'clock, when the district attorney, two of his assistants, and the defense team were called in to Judge Chretien's private office. Their meeting ended fifty minutes later when Crier Conrad called the court to order. By then, the counselors "wore looks of vexation and trouble" as they entered the courtroom, "and it was evident that something was brewing," the *Daily Picayune* reported.

George Terriberry was recalled to the stand. Luzenberg asked the witness, an attorney and member of the coroner's jury, about Gurley's wounds and cause of death. The defense objected on the same grounds as the previous day when Captain Parody testified. Generelly queried why the State was trying to prove the cause of death by relying upon non-expert witnesses, such as the coroner's secretary and now a member of the bar, rather than the sole testimony of Dr. Richard. Why wasn't he called?

"The coroner is not in town," Luzenberg explained.

"He is in town," challenged Generelly. "He was here in the courtroom all day yesterday."

But by Thursday, Dr. Richard had left the city for reasons unknown, and the court overruled Generelly's original objection. With that issue settled, though it was hardly satisfactory for the defense, Luzenberg produced the coroner's report that Terriberry had signed. Terriberry explained the various locations of bullet wounds, and Luzenberg followed by reading the coroner's report verbatim to the jury. By that time, it was pointless for Generelly to cross-examine, and Terriberry was excused.

When William O. Ramos was called, he corroborated the testimony heard the previous day. The check signed by Lewis Lyons on the Saturday before the murder and drawn from the Whitney National Bank was returned to the saloon with the notation "not sufficient funds." Again, the defense chose not to cross-examine.

Peter Roques (or Roach) testified that, at the behest of Dr. Richard, he escorted the coroner's jury to Gurley's office, where they found a small packet of cyanide tucked into the sweatband of Lyons's hat. The hat and packet were subsequently wrapped in newspaper and initially stored in the witness's desk overnight, until he delivered the items to the coroner's office the following day.

Dr. Allan Eustis testified that the substance found in the sweatband of the hat was cyanide. And regarding a minor manner, perhaps to tie up loose ends concerning Lyons cashing a fraudulent check, Detective Roche was recalled and testified that he retrieved $6.60 from Lyons's pocket after he was admitted to the hospital. After Roche's discharge, District Attorney Luzenberg reserved the right to call additional witnesses, especially on rebuttal. The State then rested.

The first defense witness to take the stand was William Price, who recalled his meeting with Lyons on the Friday before the murder, Lyons's flamboyant plans to erect a waterworks project in Mississippi, and Lyons's failure to recognize him the following day. Price believed that Lyons's behavior pointed to a diseased mind. The intent of his testimony was clear—to illustrate that Lyons was not of sound mind the weekend before the murder.

During cross-examination, the State inadvertently allowed Price to further explain why he believed Lyons was insane. Price wasn't an expert witness on mental illness—the State's saving grace—but it opened the door for other non-expert witnesses to express their opinion of Lyons's mental state. The witness was the defense's opening salvo for proving that Lewis Lyons manifested signs of insanity.

Oliver T. Nobles, an associate of Lyons for many years, testified to the defendant's good character and work habits prior to his arrest. But Nobles described Lyons in the years that followed as "morose, melancholy, and utterly the reverse of what he was before," the *Daily Picayune* reported. Lyons spoke so often about his legal problems that the witness admitted that he went out of his way to avoid the defendant whenever he saw him on the street.

"Did you consider Lyons insane from the conversations you had with him?" Generelly asked the witness.

The State immediately objected, as the witness's answer would be a matter of opinion and not established fact. Luzenberg quickly saw through the defense's strategy. That was: witness after witness telling the jury how the defendant had psychologically changed after his arrest. Judge Chretien overruled the State's objection. After all, the State had opened the door to this kind of questioning. Nobles testified that he believed that Lyons was insane at the time. Satisfied with his answer, the defense tendered the witness to the State.

On cross-examination, the witness was asked how long he had known Lyons and his family. Their history dated back for years, which prompted Luzenberg to ask about Kate Barringer, an associate of Lyons whose name would surface again during the rebuttal phase of the trial. The witness admitted that he had heard the name but couldn't recall when, where, or how. He never met the woman.

Letting that go for the time being, Luzenberg asked Nobles if he knew of any difficulties associated with the defendant and that Lyons frequented saloons. Other than the 1895 arrest, Nobles was ignorant of Lyons's 1896 arrest, couldn't recall any other problems, and expressed no knowledge of the defendant's drinking habits. Nobles resided for a time near Lyons's home on Hillary Street. When asked, he stated he never observed any marital difficulties, though he testified that he had only visited Lyons's home once.

Nobles admitted that he didn't believe that Lyons was insane when he began to voice his displeasure about his lawsuit. Only after Lyons's repeated and unrelenting rants about how unfairly he had been treated did the witness began to formulate his opinion that Lyons was insane. To illustrate the point, Nobles testified that he asked Lyons to manage a secondhand store he was about to open. But Lyons wasn't interested. The witness stressed that he based his belief in Lyons's insanity not on the defendant's reluctance to go into business with him but rather on his obsession with his lawsuit. Over the last year, the witness met with Lyons on at least five occasions, and each time Lyons fixated on his case.

"Did he ever tell you a single thing that a sane man would not tell you?" Luzenberg asked.

Nobles couldn't say. However, after Lyons lost his lawsuit and brooded over what he perceived to be unfair treatment, the witness thought that the defendant's mind had certainly been negatively affected.

Finally, Luzenberg asked the witness when was the last time the defendant had spoken to him about his case. Nobles responded, October 1902—in other words, nine months before the murder. Luzenberg was hoping that gap of time was long enough to illustrate that Nobles could not possibly know what was brewing in the defendant's mind on the day of the murder.

Dr. Marion Souchon was called. His office was down the hall from Generelly and Doyle's law practice in the Hennen Building. Apparently neither of Lyons's defense attorneys extensively interviewed the witness before he took the stand. He admitted that he had only a limited acquaintance with the defendant, having treated Lyons for minor health issues, and he described him as being "a very peculiar man," though he fell short of referring to him as insane. Referring to Lyons instead as "not ordinary," he put the defendant into a class of patients he described as coming to his office knowing what their ailment was, readily taking the prescribed medicine, but refusing to follow any additional professional advice.

On cross-examination, Dr. Souchon testified that he had numerous patients just as quirky as Lyons. He stated that he never questioned the mental state of the defendant.

At this juncture, the State was notified that Delos Mellen was in the courthouse and asked the court's indulgence to recall him to the stand, though his new testimony appeared to be pointless. He repeated what he had previously testified to—that his law firm had paid out money in Lyons's lawsuit that the defendant had failed to repay. In spite of evidence to the contrary, Mellen reiterated that the defendant was still indebted to his old law firm.

After Mellen stepped down, the defense called James Mott to the stand, an associate of Lyons for the past twenty-two years. Mott's testimony was similar to that of Nobles, describing Lyons's demeanor as pleasant and sociable prior to his arrest. However, it slowly devolved into a monomaniac personality, focused on the injustices and shame he had experienced thereafter. He testified that even Lyons's physical appearance changed after his arrest. Mott never doubted for a moment that everything that befell Lyons was "running the accused insane," the *Daily Picayune* reported.

On cross-examination, Mott testified that he told Lyons that he was becoming fixated on his failed lawsuit and was going crazy as a result. In other matters, when asked if Lyons frequented poolrooms and barrooms, the witness couldn't say but reiterated that Lyons's demeanor changed after his arrest. But because he didn't know Lyons's associates, being only a causal acquaintance of the defendant, he couldn't say if they had contributed in some way to his personality change. The witness admitted that he eventually shunned the defendant as Lyons became irrational over his troubles.

Luzenberg asked if he had ever heard of the defendant beating his wife or neglecting his children. Mott responded no. Surprisingly, the defense didn't object to the question. Perhaps they hoped such insinuations would further aid their insanity defense. Mott ended by stating he "never knew or heard of an instance where the loss of a case worked so heavily on one's mind as in Lyons's instance."

With the lunch-hour recess rapidly approaching, Judge Chretien suddenly ordered the courtroom cleared, except for the jury and the various reporters covering the trial. He then told the jury that one of their own had a statement to make. William C. Faust, Jr., Juror No. 1 and the selected spokesman, rose to his feet and said that he and other jurors overheard Gehbauer, Juror No. 12, the evening before remark that if the State couldn't present better evidence in the future, then he had already formed his opinion. After hearing those comments, Faust believed that Gehbauer couldn't consider the State's case fairly.

Gehbauer quickly rose to his feet and informed the court that his remarks were misconstrued. What he meant to convey was how quickly the trial was progressing and that they might be able to reach a verdict by Saturday, in time for everyone to go home for the weekend. He intended no harm by his comments. This was the first time he served on a jury, and he was unfamiliar with court protocol.

Judge Chretien remarked that he was extremely saddened by the comments and hoped that Gehbauer would refrain from uttering any such opinions in the future. That aside, the judge didn't feel it warranted a discharge of the jury.

"If I have done any harm," Gehbauer remarked, "I am sorry for it and did it innocently."

The jurors were escorted to their upstairs quarters for lunch, while Judge Chretien retired to his private office. He was soon joined by some friends and newspapermen, along with Luzenberg, Doyle, Generelly, and Hewes Gurley, another of the slain district attorney's brothers.

During the impromptu meeting, Luzenberg stated that he didn't believe Gehbauer had formed an opinion, though he indicated the man might be mentally unstable. Luzenberg still harbored some animosity towards the man. Had the State not exhausted its legal limit of challenges prior to his selection, he wouldn't have been a member of the jury. In any event, Luzenberg suggested that the jurors be called downstairs and individually polled to see if Gehbauer's remarks had exerted any unforeseen influence upon them. If they did, it could serve as grounds for a mistrial. But the matter was closed as far as Judge Chretien was concerned, except to ask the defense.

"If you gentlemen will have Lyons's consent to a new trial," Judge Chretien addressed the defense team, "why, then, it can be had."

"What, ask a crazy man for new trial? It's out of the question," Doyle responded. "We are conducting the case for him, and an insane man could not give consent." If a new trial was ordered, Doyle and Generelly pledged to resign. "We don't want to go through this thing again under any circumstances."

Nevertheless, Doyle stated that Gehbauer might be ostracized by the other jury members. Doyle believed that when it came time to reach a verdict, Gehbauer might vote against the others out of spite or prejudice, or he might vote with them in order to regain their good graces. In any event, his verdict might be tainted. If Judge Chretien sensed that Doyle was hinting for a mistrial, in spite of what he had previously said, he didn't accommodate him. The trial would go on.

The discussion ended shortly afterwards, with the attorneys rushing off for a quick lunch with instructions to return to the judge's office before the 1:30 reconvening. A formal meeting among the various parties was necessary. None of the statements from Faust and Gehbauer had been taken down by the court stenographer, Sturges Adams, as he left when the courtroom was cleared. He mistakenly believed that a formal recess had been called. Judge Chretien needed Adams to record what Faust and Gehbauer had stated, to the best of the attorneys' recollections.

After court resumed and these statements were entered into the record, presumably with Faust's and Gehbauer's approval, the judge addressed the entire jury. "After having listened to the statements made by Mr. Faust and Juror Gehbauer, the Court can see nothing in what has taken place which could possibly have prejudiced any member of the Jury." He then instructed the jury to erase from their minds the incident and to consider only the evidence presented when reaching their verdict. The defense took a bill of exception to the ruling of the court.

The defense then recalled William Price to the stand, apparently as a hostile witness. He was asked if he had held a conversation with a "Mr. Saunders." He admitted that while on a streetcar about two weeks after the murder, he may have discussed with Saunders something about Lyons's insanity.

"Did you not tell him that Lyons was of such a mean and vicious disposition that you had to dispose of a lot you owned next door to his?" the defense asked.

"I did not," Price responded, "because I still own that lot and have not disposed of it yet."

"Did you not say that you wanted to sell that lot on that account?"

"No sir. Mr. Lyons had already disposed of his lot at that time, and there was no occasion for me to make that remark."

The defense excused Price, having gained nothing of value by recalling him.

From the beginning of jury selection, Lyons had scarcely focused his attention on the judicial proceedings. He appeared fixed in one position, either looking down as he stooped forward in his chair or blankly looking to his front, his chin resting on the palm of his hand with his elbow planted atop the defense table. To break up the monotony, he occasionally shuffled his feet.

His demeanor changed when the next witness was called. Suddenly, he raised his head, his eyes following her as she took her place in the witness box. The woman was his sister, Chattie E. Lyons. Seven years Lyons's junior and the youngest of the siblings, "Miss Chattie," as she was often referred to, was "a very handsome and refined young lady," the *Daily Picayune* reported, who unbeknownst to the newspaper looked younger than her thirty-eight years of age.

Prior to his original arrest, Miss Chattie described her brother as a kind and sociable person, who was a good provider for his wife and six children. For a time she resided with the family. She never saw her brother quarrel with his wife, beat her, or maltreat her or the children. However, his disposition changed after his arrest. He appeared worried and miserable, and she often saw tears rolling down his cheeks. While she testified, Lyons occasionally sighed and looked rather affectionately upon her.

She recalled the yellow-fever epidemic and the toll it took on his family. She stated that her brother often blamed himself for the death of his oldest son, being unable to obtain what he needed because of the quarantine restrictions. She then described the effects of the lawsuit upon her brother's psyche and remembered how he blamed the attorneys and all connected to the case for his misfortunes.

Generelly showed Miss Chattie a bundle of letters and miscellaneous items that her brother had written. Two of the correspondences were addressed to the witness and dated November 1 and November 9, 1902, "the first being most kind and affectionate," the *Daily Picayune* reported, "and the last scolding her in very incoherent language." Miss Chattie testified that between the first and second letter, she hadn't spoken to her brother and nothing unusual had occurred between them. She couldn't remember a trigger that justified the anger he expressed towards her in his second letter.

The defense desired to enter all the papers into evidence, but Luzenberg wished to glace at the documents first, which was granted. Among the items were a number of architectural blueprints but nothing of consequence. From the pile, Generelly proceeded to read a long letter addressed to Gurley written by the defendant in 1901. The beginning sounded as though it had been written by a lucid man, but as Generelly continued, it began to sound more like the rantings of "a diseased mind," the *Daily Picayune* reported. A second letter that was read showed further proof that Lyons suffered from a mental defect, for it was "more wild and vague" than the first one. Miss Chattie identified the handwritten items stored in the box (letters, scratchpads, and documents) as having been written by her brother, and they were entered into evidence.

Continuing her testimony, Miss Chattie reiterated that her brother was very attached to his children, and they to him, but after his arrest and brief incarceration, "he lost much of his jovial disposition and seemed miserable." She explained that about a month after her brother wrote his second letter to her, he wrote to their mother. The content was just as foul, prompting their mother to burn the epistle after reading it.

For two hours the witness remained on the stand, discussing how their mother nurtured her children before sending them off to good schools or colleges (high schools). All of this was to illustrate that the family, including her brother, had been brought up to be honest, law-abiding citizens. She continued to emphasize that her brother changed for the worse after his arrest.

Sensing the strain under which Miss Chattie had testified, Luzenberg chose not to grill her "over the rack of cross-examination," the *Daily Picayune* commented. The witness was excused.

Lyons's seventy-one-year-old mother, Charity Lyons, followed. Sporting snow-white hair and clothed in a long, black dress and a black bonnet trimmed in subdued colors, she projected a "venerable and impressive" appearance but wore an "agitated" look, according to the *Daily Picayune*. Her voice trembled when she first spoke, and tears often came to her eyes during her testimony. Seeing his mother's anguish, Lyons could barely contain his own emotions, occasionally wiping away his tears with a handkerchief. However, his right tear duct continuously drained of late, another complication from his suicide attempt.

Like the testimony of her daughter, Mrs. Lyons indicated that her son had a kind and gentle disposition before his arrest. She couldn't say how he treated his wife, but she knew that her son adored his children. Everything changed after the arrest. Mrs. Lyons described her son's metamorphosis as "crying like a baby" when he discussed his arrest and his lawsuit that followed, then brooding after each legal setback. The stress even took a toll on his physical appearance. By then, their visits together were becoming infrequent.

She finally wrote a letter asking him why he wasn't taking better care of himself and, for that matter, of his children. He responded rather harshly, saying it was none of her business. The tone of his letter was so uncharacteristic that Mrs. Lyons burned it. By then, with her son seldom at home and separated from his wife for about a year, Mrs. Lyons believed that the whole ordeal had affected his mind. Out of respect, Luzenberg chose not to cross-examine.

⌖⌖⌖

Ambrose Smith, the counselor for the late Daniel Carroll, was called. He testified that he had known Lyons for seventeen years and that Lyons had sought his legal advice on other matters several years before his 1895 arrest. In fact, both men remained friends after Carroll hired the witness to defend him against Lyons's lawsuit. Smith remembered Lyons prior to his legal problems as "a bright, joyous man, a good conversationalist, intelligent, and interesting," the *Daily Picayune* reported.

Generelly asked him to tell all he knew about Lyons and his personality change after his arrest, but Smith preferred that he pose specific questions instead. He was a good friend of both the late Gurley and the defendant. Apparently understanding his predicament, Generelly complied.

Smith's answers were similar to those of other defense witnesses. In essence, Lyons's personality drastically changed after his arrest. Smith eventually warned Gurley to be cautious of Lyons, whom he believed was decidedly insane by that time.

At this juncture, Luzenberg interrupted. He surmised what Generelly's next question would be ("what was Mr. Gurley's reply to those concerns?") and didn't want it asked. He requested that Judge Chretien retire the jury, as he wished to conference. Giving Luzenberg some latitude, Judge Chretien excused the jury.

Luzenberg contended that only Gurley could answer such a question or describe how he reacted. But Generelly argued that Smith was present when Gurley replied, and what he said should be repeated as testimony. Luzenberg formally objected to this line of questioning, which Judge Chretien sustained.

With the jury back in the courtroom, Smith discussed his long friendship with the defendant. When asked if Lyons was ever intimate with a woman other than his wife, Smith answered that he had no such knowledge. Concerning Lyons's legal problems, Smith stated that he eventually tired of Lyons's obsessive behavior on the topic and did everything in his power to avoid him.

William J. Holden, another attorney, testified that he had known Lyons for five to six years. Like many of the prior defense witnesses, Holden repeatedly heard the defendant complain about how badly his attorneys and the judge had treated him. At some point, which was becoming a familiar theme to the jury, he told the defendant that he didn't want to hear anything else about his legal problems, but Lyons persisted. Holden also stated that he refused to act as his arbitrator when he asked. By then, Holden told Lyons that he thought he was crazy, though during his cross-examination, he admitted that the defendant was sane when discussing other matters.

Henry G. Thoele, a business owner who testified that he had known the defendant for over twenty years, described him as sociable and gentlemanly before his arrest and just the opposite afterwards. "He thought he was getting a little *off,* and thought he was getting insane on the subject of the suit," the *Daily Picayune* reported. But during the cross-examination, he admitted that he was no expert on insanity and couldn't definitely say that the defendant was insane. On the other hand, he heard Lyons threaten to kill Gurley, and he told him he thought he was insane.

"Was that the reason you thought him crazy, because he said he was going to kill Mr. Gurley?" Luzenberg asked.

"I would think any man crazy who went around telling people he was going to kill a man and talking about it," he replied, implying that a sane man wouldn't announce his intention to kill beforehand.

Thoele was asked about Lyons's social habits, particularly his drinking habits. Thoele never saw him intoxicated, if that was what the State was asking, though he saw him occasionally drink whiskey.

Oscar Pradat, an employee of the Illinois Central Railroad, testified that he had known the defendant for a number of years. Every time they met, Lyons discussed his legal problems and the fact that Gurley owed him a settlement, becoming excited on the subject when he talked about it. Pradat believed that Lyons was "a little off," obsessing over his lawsuit, though he could be perfectly rational when discussing other topics. When cross-examined, he reaffirmed that Lyons was cheerful and pleasant when he wasn't talking about his case.

Louise Durand, the elderly landlady who had rented an upstairs room to Lyons about a year before the murder, testified that her former tenant had a history of waking her up in the middle of the night when he moaned or walked around in his room. On cross-examination, she admitted that Lyons complained of back pain, which could easily account for his moaning. Nevertheless, his activities and his coming and going at all hours disturbed her sleep. She recalled that about two weeks before the murder, Lyons asked her for his old room. She told him no, as he disturbed her. It was clear what she meant. Lyons had a history of waking her up. It had nothing to do with him having a mental defect.

Steven Conway testified that he had known the defendant for twenty-five years, as they worked together years ago at the Maginnis Cotton Mill. He had also served as a character witness for Lyons during his civil trial. He described Lyons prior to his arrest as always pleasant and sociable, but that changed. Conway testified that when Lyons passed him on the street one day last December and failed to acknowledge him, he found it odd, given their work history and friendship. The witness came to believe that Lyons was crazy.

During cross-examination, Conway admitted that he had no idea what was on Lyons's mind when the two passed one another and that he could have been distracted at the time. However, when asked hypothetically if some party were to attempt to place Lyons into an insane asylum would he testify that Lyons was sane, Convey stated no.

Mary O'Connor, the matron of Orleans Parish Prison, testified that she noticed Lyons acting strange each time she saw him. She stated that some mornings, when he asked for his breakfast, he later refused it, saying he had already been served, while other mornings he was perfectly rational. She claimed that he didn't behave like an ordinary person and never obeyed the doctor, particularly when he refused to exercise in the yard. She just believed that Lyons wasn't "right in his head."

"Do you think his actions were for your special benefit, knowing that you were around and could see him all the time?" Luzenberg asked O'Connor.

"Poor me, what effect could I have on him?" she responded.

Luzenberg smiled, which triggered laughter among the spectators. Order was called to restore calm in the courtroom.

She also explained that Lyons wasn't a talkative person, and it was rare that he ever answered a question. Also, his appetite was never good, especially during the early days when he was sick and needed proper nourishment to recover. She admitted she didn't know Lyons prior to his arrest and couldn't swear that he wasn't shamming his psychological peculiarities. But she felt quite certain that Lyons wasn't putting anyone on. She had worked at the prison for eight years, dealing with a wide assortment of prisoners, and knew the idiosyncrasies of human behavior very well.

Dr. Edward Jones, Lyons's oculist, testified that he examined Lyons's left eye, which he found was clotted with blood and the vision gone. The right pupil was dilated with evidence of papilledema, swelling of the optic nerve or a "choked optic disc," as it was called at the time. Having diagnosed Lyons with this abnormality, he cited a number of etiologies, none of which Lyons had. He concluded that the choked disc had been caused by prolonged irritation to his brain, unrelated to the gunshot wound. In other words, Lyons's optic-nerve swelling predated the murder and was caused by the sustained mental anguish he suffered as a result of his failed lawsuit.

"Whenever you see a man with a choked optic nerve [disc], there is going to be an explosion sometime, and he is liable to be a dangerous person at any moment, and I don't want to be near him," Dr. Jones explained.

During the cross-examination, Dr. Jones stated that he conducted his examination of Lyons using the best available medical instruments and that alone proved his diagnosis was correct. Sensing that his testimony was medical quackery, Luzenberg got Dr. Jones to admit that he couldn't diagnose Lyons as insane but not for the reason Luzenberg expected—that he wasn't qualified. Rather, the witness believed that insanity couldn't be defined and therefore could not be diagnosed. He reiterated that Lyons's mental anguish triggered his optic-nerve disorder, which ultimately caused his violent behavior. In essence, Lyons was a bomb with a lit fuse. It was pointless at this juncture for Luzenberg to continue his cross-examination, and Dr. Jones was excused. Clearly, rebuttal witnesses would have to be called.

Generelly announced that the defense had one more witness to call before resting their case. But a more pressing matter lay ahead for the defense. In their possession were numerous letters and documents written by their client that hopefully proved he suffered from some form of mental sickness. As yet, the documents had not been shared with the State. Generelly suggested an early adjournment in order to allow the State ample time to examine the documents before reconvening the following morning. Judge Chretien agreed.

When court adjourned, the defense felt reasonably certain that they had proven their client had suffered a personality change after his arrest and failed lawsuit, and they believed that Dr. Jones had adequately explained the cause of Lyons's actions. But starting on Friday, they would have to prove that their client's altered personality led to his insane decision to end the life of J. Ward Gurley.

Chapter Eleven

Their Expert Witness

Will you let me go now?

Dr. Yves LeMonnier

Friday, November 13, 1903, was especially exciting for the throngs of spectators who crowded into the courtroom, for two reasons. First, Dr. Yves LeMonnier was expected to take the stand for the defense. But more titillating to the crowd was the defense's plan to introduce the content of scores of letters and documents written by Lyons. Everyone wanted to know what he had written. Some wanted another opportunity to see the murderer face to face when he was escorted into the courtroom, though there was no guarantee of that. Often on previous days, to frustrate the gawking public, Lyons held a handkerchief to the damaged left side of his face, especially his blinded eye. He rarely showed his face to the crowd, even while sitting at the defense table. On most occasions, all anyone ever saw was his back.

"Clear the way!" the deputy sheriff ordered, as he pulled the defendant through the mass of curious onlookers.

Doubled over, with his eyes looking downward, Lyons was escorted to his seat without anyone getting a good look at his face, in spite of their best efforts to do so. Soon the courtroom filled to capacity as people poured through the open doorway. Every seat on the floor and gallery and every imaginable spot in the aisles was occupied, including the space along the railing that surrounded the judge's bench. Everyone was eager to see what was to transpire on the third day of testimony.

With the court called to order, the mountain of personal correspondence written by Lyons was read and entered into evidence. The documents all contained the same theme. Lyons blamed everyone connected to his failed lawsuit, no matter how remotely. No one was left unscathed by Lyons, not even religious leaders. The progression of letters allegedly showed Lyons's slide into madness that culminated in the July 1903 murder. The defense never disputed that Lyons murdered the district attorney. In fact, they introduced little evidence touching upon the assassination. What they asserted instead was that their client was insane when he pulled the trigger that fateful Monday morning.

As Generelly read the various documents, Judge Thomas Ellis entered the courtroom, temporarily halting the proceedings so he could be sworn in as a defense witness. Many of Lyons's correspondences contained references to the judge and the late court stenographer, Leslie Bobb, especially how he had amended certain testimonies.

Judge Ellis testified that he remembered Lyons's bench trial, but he couldn't recall any evidence presented related to any impropriety or fraudulent undertakings by his late stenographer. He had nothing but praise for Bobb's work ethic, and he reiterated that he never heard any complaint by Lyons concerning his stenographer. And regarding the conduct of the attorneys during the trial, Judge Ellis distinctly remembered that both sides acted with the utmost professionalism and that Lyons could not have been better served by his counsel.

During the cross-examination, Judge Ellis admitted that from time to time, minor transcription errors occurred. This was the nature of the business, but it didn't imply that Bobb purposely changed words to suit one party over the other.

Luzenberg showed Judge Ellis one of Lyons's letters, where the judge referred to Lyons as "Old Dog Tray" when he announced his verdict. Lyons took it as an insult and believed it proved that the judge harbored prejudice against him. But Judge Ellis couldn't remember the exact phraseology he used to describe him. He explained that the expression was taken from an old fable about an innocent dog that often found himself in bad company. It was intended to refer to what had befallen Lyons. Judge Ellis never meant to imply he was no better than a dog. If anything, it was to show sympathy towards the defendant.

When re-cross-examining the judge, Generelly read another of his client's letters. Lyons accused Bobb of twisting his testimony when transcribing it and Judge Ellis of rendering his decision based on that altered version of the transcript.

"Do you think it possible that your stenographer could do such a thing?" Generelly asked.

"No," Judge Ellis responded, "I feel that Mr. Leslie Bobb was absolutely honest. I consider him a thorough gentleman at all times."

Patrick McMahon, an undertaker and a current councilman, testified that he knew Lyons for over twenty years and had bought Lyons's old saloon about twelve years ago. More recently, the witness noticed that the defendant stopped talking to him. Generelly asked if he thought Lyons was insane, to which he replied yes.

Luzenberg asked McMahon what circumstances led him to believe such a thing. He stated the defendant often passed him in the street without a word and on one occasion nearly ran him over. This change of behavior started about two years ago.

Luzenberg suggested that the defendant's silence might be based on a difference of politics, but the witness didn't know Lyons's political persuasion. Rather, he insisted that Lyons failing to recognize him constituted insanity.

The rest of the morning was spent with Generelly reading Lyons's litany of accusatory letters and documents. Members of the New Orleans police weren't spared, whom he accused of enriching themselves through their system of bribery and graft, particularly by their collection of "regular monthly assessments" from "houses of ill-fate" and other immoral establishments. He was referring to the District or Storyville, an area just above the French Quarter that operated in the city between 1897 and 1917. It was a city-sanctioned safe zone for prostitution and drugs, named after city alderman Sidney Story, who introduced the ordinance. Lyons alleged that some police officers were siphoning off a portion of Storyville's profits. He characterized the New Orleans Police Department as "an impure fountain [that] cannot bring forth pure water" when dealing with the public.

Generelly then read Lyons's account of his arrest and maltreatment by the police and of Mellen's mishandling of his lawsuit. Lyons also felt that Mellen had "invented stenographic notes of the trial." The letters and documents were a wholesale condemnation of the Orleans Parish justice system and the Flower administration. Mayor Walter Flower served between 1896 and 1900, the timeframe when much of Lyons's civil litigation was adjudicated and Storyville was first sanctioned.

In other letters, Lyons vented his anger towards organized religion. Though he may have been referring to all faiths, he was especially harsh towards the Catholic Church. He expressed the belief that the Church was stronger and more caring towards its flock when it was financially strapped than when its coffers overflowed with riches. He especially deplored wasting money on missionary work in foreign countries when "charity should begin at home first." This may explain why Lyons detested religion in general and shunned its leaders and laypersons when they visited him in prison. He probably believed that their prayers were empty gestures.

When the lunch recess was called at 12:30, Generelly still had an hour more of readings before calling Dr. LeMonnier to the stand. Generelly's purpose in flooding the court with Lyons's own words was self-evident—to lay the groundwork for the testimony of his expert witness.

When Dr. LeMonnier finally began his testimony at 2:30, he stated his credentials as a medical expert on insanity. Over the years, his studies in medicine also included an in-depth review of the diseases of the mind. Though currently in private practice and living with his wife on his farm near Amite City, Louisiana, LeMonnier served three terms as the Orleans Parish coroner and was a visiting physician at Charity Hospital. He also had served as a consultant to several state institutions that specialized in the care of the insane.

Dr. LeMonnier couldn't recall the exact number of insanity cases on which he consulted. Several prominent cases were brought up, including the Etienne Deschamps murder case, which the doctor had used to illustrate his unbiased view of the mentally ill. In Deschamps's case, he determined that

Dr. Yves R. LeMonnier (1903). (Courtesy NOLA.com/ The *Times-Picayune*)

the murderer was sane, contrary to the opinion of other medical experts. In other words, and adding credibility to his testimony, he wasn't exclusively a State or defense expert witness.

Explaining that in Lyons's case his insanity was a loss of free will, Dr. LeMonnier described the defendant's condition as belonging to a class of manias that fixated on one subject at the exclusion of everything else. In his opinion, Lyons had suffered from this form of mania for three to five years, with the genesis being his false imprisonment and later his inability to recover the damages he sued for. Luzenberg had barely begun his cross-examination when court adjourned at six o'clock.

Dr. LeMonnier's testimony completely occupied Saturday's abbreviated session. Meanwhile, Lyons sat with his left elbow on the table and his head resting on the palm of his hand, holding his handkerchief to his damaged eye. He barely moved the entire morning, watching the proceedings intently, though occasionally he closed his eyes, "as though he was weary," the *Daily Picayune* reported.

"Doctor, you were asked yesterday afternoon if, in all the complaints in the letters which were submitted to you, and on which you based your opinion as to Lyons's insanity, there was anything said about anything else except money, and not a word about honor," Luzenberg reminded the witness.

Many of Lyons's correspondences focused on the robbery perpetrated against him by his attorneys. Luzenberg believed that these facts spoke to motive. Insanity had nothing to do with why Lyons murdered Gurley. But Dr. LeMonnier wasn't taking the bait.

"You asked me yesterday about my diagnosis of the case, and I would like to answer that question first," Dr. LeMonnier replied. "You asked me about the delusions of persecution, homicidal mania, and suicidal mania."

"No sir," Luzenberg clarified. He wasn't going to allow the witness to change the subject. "There is no doubt in my mind as to these, but I wanted to know how you described the man as passing from monomania to delirium of persecution, from that to reasoning mania, and then to homicidal and finally suicidal mania."

Dr. LeMonnier opened one of the reference books he brought to the stand, citing various sources to confirm his diagnosis of insanity.

"Does not that authority say that all criminals are insane?" Luzenberg questioned.

"I don't know," Dr. LeMonnier admitted. Ironically, during the Etienne Deschamps murder trial, he concurred with the lead prosecutor, Charles

Luzenberg, Chandler Luzenberg's father, that all criminals were *not* insane. That said, Dr. LeMonnier proceeded to read from other experts who indicated that some forms of "insanity often led to a blind impulse to commit acts of violence."

"Is not that also the definition of moral insanity?" Luzenberg inquired.

"Explain what you mean by 'moral insanity'?" Dr. LeMonnier asked. He wasn't up to playing games.

The two adversaries spent the morning sparring over one another's definition of rational thought, perverted morals, reasoning mania, transitory insanity, and other obscure, psychological states of mind. Luzenberg did everything in his power to get the witness to say something that ran counter to a previously expressed opinion, but Dr. LeMonnier was too skilled a professional to fall into that trap.

"Is not your opinion as to Lyons's insanity based on the fact that he tried to commit suicide?" Luzenberg asked the witness. The district attorney was trying to get him to answer yes. Years earlier, Dr. LeMonnier opined that Etienne Deschamps had attempted suicide in order to escape the gallows. He believed that Deschamps' suicide attempt was a sham to paint him as insane.

"My opinion, or rather experience, is that all suicides who have recovered did not exhibit any signs of insanity except in rare instances," Dr. LeMonnier expressed.

His "rare instances" qualifier was an attempt to lump Lyons's failed suicide into that exclusionary category. Luzenberg then attempted to impugn the literature that LeMonnier cited. Some of the books were decades old.

"Is it not a fact that medical works of fifty years ago are of little practical use today?" Luzenberg asked.

"Don't believe that," Dr. LeMonnier hastily responded. "I have books in my library over a hundred years old, and in reading these I find many good things. The trouble with our modern profession is that there are too many fashions, which change as often as do the fashions of ladies in their dresses."

Luzenberg believed this line of questioning was going nowhere, so he redirected his queries towards suicide and its connection with insanity. Dr. LeMonnier admitted that his opinion regarding suicide changed over the years. For some time, he believed that suicide was an act of cowardice. But lately, and obviously post-Deschamps, he viewed it as an act of an insane mind.

Luzenberg cited several hypothetical cases and asked his opinion whether the person was sane or insane. Dr. LeMonnier refused to be pinned down and responded instead that he would have to examine the man in question and review his history before rendering a diagnosis. With Luzenberg's hypothetical cases going nowhere, he tried a different tactic with the witness.

In Dr. LeMonnier's prior testimony, he indicated that he had formulated his opinion of Lyons's insanity partially based on a letter he wrote to George Denegre, Lyons's handpicked arbitrator. In preparation for this review, Lyons wrote an epistle to Denegre that chronicled in great detail his legal problems with Gurley. The letter was written several years after Dr. LeMonnier asserted that Lyons had become insane. But to Luzenberg's thinking, Lyons's letter equaled the writing of a legal brief from a competent practicing attorney rather than the rantings of a crazy person.

"He might write a perfectly sensible letter one day, and the next day, under the influence of morphine or some drug, he would write a very irrational letter," Dr. LeMonnier responded.

"But if you did, I would not think you were insane," Luzenberg opined, implying that the drug would alter one's thought process, not insanity.

Luzenberg's cross-examination of the witness lasted until the court adjourned at noon.

On Monday, back on the witness stand—or "sweat box," as the *Daily Picayune* described it—Dr. LeMonnier resumed his testimony. For the better part of the morning, Luzenberg read to Dr. LeMonnier the defendant's letter to George Denegre, citing passages that sounded coherent. Dr. LeMonnier disagreed and stopped Luzenberg on several occasions to cite passages to the contrary.

It was Dr. LeMonnier's professional opinion that a person such as Lyons, who suffered from monomania, could be perfectly rational on all subjects but one—for instance, his perception that Gurley had done him wrong. Also, he testified that the mentally ill always behaved badly the day following a restless night and, conversely, less aggressively if afforded a good night's sleep. But he admitted that he couldn't say how Lyons had spent his night prior to the murder.

There was more. Dr. LeMonnier asserted that the insane could be easily influenced to do something else, rather than act upon their deadly impulses. But when Luzenberg pressed him to explain Lyons's actions at Nelson's saloon on the morning of the murder and his discussion with Dr. Richard, a logical distraction, Dr. LeMonnier replied that those influences weren't strong enough to divert him from his original obsession to commit murder.

"The man had been brooding on this for years," Dr. LeMonnier stated, "and it is not probable that his mind would be diverted from his purpose by these episodes."

And then there was the fact that Lyons carried poison on his person. Dr. LeMonnier testified that Lyons knew cyanide was deadly. It was his opinion that *if* Lyons was sane on the day of the murder, he would have logically prepared the poison beforehand and swallowed it immediately after he was convinced Gurley was dead. Since he didn't, he believed that Lyons *was* insane. Luzenberg tried in vain to get the doctor to admit that carrying around and/or not ingesting cyanide after committing murder didn't necessarily make a person insane.

Luzenberg then asked the witness to render his opinion whether an insane person would allow insignificant errors in a court transcript to oppress his mind. The district attorney was referring to Lyons's letter to George Denegre, where he asserted that Leslie Bobb had falsified testimony recorded during his bench trial.

Before Dr. LeMonnier could answer, the defense objected and argued that such inquiries deviated from the evidence, since no proof was presented that Bobb had fraudulently transcribed the court record. But the State disagreed, asserting that Judge Ellis had testified that demonstrated that the transcript *did* show errors, though they were inconsequential in nature.

Luzenberg contended that the defense had tried to prove unsuccessfully that there were no grounds for Lyons's delusions of persecutions (short of madness) to explain why he obsessed over the transcript. Now that Judge Ellis had acknowledged errors, Luzenberg believed that the defense wanted the subject to go away.

The jury was excused as both sides argued their points before Judge Chretien. The defense conceded that a sane man might construe negligible errors as immaterial, but Lyons didn't think so. Judge Chretien finally overruled the objection. It would be up to the jury to decide whether Lyons was delusional when he wrote the letter to Denegre.

With the jury back in their seats, both parties went back and forth over Lyons's allegations of wrongdoing on the part of Bobb. Did Lyons's obsession over the transcript errors equate to madness? Dr. LeMonnier certainly believed so, coupled with everything else that had happened to the defendant over the years. The prosecution thought otherwise. In spite of his best efforts, Luzenberg was never able to shake the doctor's opinion that Lyons was delusional and therefore insane.

The lunch recess temporarily halted the trial. With everyone rushing out to catch a bite to eat, the chamber soon filled with noise. In spite of that, Lyons had to be awakened, as he had spent the greater portion of the previous hour sleeping in a stooped position.

Rather than resuming at 1:30 P.M., Judge Chretien allowed a two-hour recess, out of respect for Joseph Generelly. His father-in-law, Dr. Emile Sarpy, a prominent physician in the city and seventy-three years old, died from bronchial pneumonia at nine o'clock that morning. As he had been ill for a number of months, his death was not unexpected. Generelly asked for an extension of the lunch hour in order to arrange for his father-in-law's funeral and burial, which was planned for the following morning.

When Luzenberg resumed his cross-examination, his initial focus was to determine what documents written by Lyons proved to the witness that he was insane.

"Now, tell me, Doctor, what there is in this paper that leads you to believe that it originated in a diseased mind and exactly what there is in it that cannot be the thoughts of a sane man?" Luzenberg asked, as he handed Dr. LeMonnier some of Lyons's correspondences.

"Why, all these writings, except one, might be the production of a healthy mind, but they are not," Dr. LeMonnier replied.

He admitted that some of the earlier correspondences appeared to be lucid. But as the years progressed and Lyons's mind became diseased, his later writings reflected his monomania and "his persecuted condition of the man's imagination." Dr. LeMonnier insisted that Lewis Lyons was insane on the day of the murder and "was insane many years previously to that." He concluded, "The bullet wound over the eye hastened the insanity and contributed to the weakness of his mind."

"Doctor, you seem to be guessing," Luzenberg proclaimed, fully aware that there was no way to know that for sure. Besides, Lyons shot himself after he murdered Gurley.

"No, I am not, but you are," Dr. LeMonnier responded. He could not be deterred.

Luzenberg then had the witness review the two letters Lyons wrote to his sister. It was discovered that the second letter, the one in which Lyons scolded her, was written on stationery from a local saloon and café.

"Now, don't you think that this letter might have been composed by a drunken man?" Luzenberg asked.

"No, I seriously doubt that that letter was written by a drunkard."

Dr. LeMonnier believed that the second letter and the one Lyons later wrote to his mother showed he had turned on both women, irrespective of alcohol influences.

Switching subjects, Luzenberg asked the witness to comment on the role of heredity in insanity. Was there such a thing? And if so, did Lyons's case show hereditary insanity? Luzenberg probably already knew the answer but wanted the witness to say it on record.

"If Adam and Eve had been subjected to all the diseases which the human race is heir to, I don't know what would become of us," Dr. LeMonnier responded. His answer to both questions was no.

Luzenberg then showed Dr. LeMonnier another letter that he had earlier stated proved Lyons was insane. He wanted to know how he reached that conclusion. The doctor pointed to numerous incomplete sentences, nonsensical phrases, and repeated letters that proved such notations originated from a diseased mind.

"If he were to die and an autopsy held on him, you would find in his skull an unsound mind, a brain that has been diseased for years," Dr. LeMonnier said, confident in his prediction, though no such autopsy of his brain was ever performed.

By this juncture in the trial, it was pointless for Luzenberg to continue. After three days, what more could be gained? On redirect, Generelly had only one question.

"In reaching a conclusion as to the sanity of the accused, you have to take all these things together upon which to base a correct diagnosis?" Generelly asked, knowing the answer.

Dr. LeMonnier responded yes and then stated that his diagnosis was based on his physical and mental examination of the defendant, along with knowing the defendant's history, habits, and disposition, what he had said to various people over the years, what he had written, and what the defendant had told him during their private sessions. There was no doubt in Dr. LeMonnier's mind that Lewis Lyons was insane when he murdered Gurley and had been insane for a number of years.

"Of this I am convinced," the witness concluded.

"That's all," Generelly said.

"Will you let me go now?"

"Yes," Generelly replied, amid a burst of laughter from the audience.

At 4:00 P.M., Dr. LeMonnier stepped out of the witness box, though it was too soon to celebrate the end of the trial. There were still two hours left until court adjourned, the defense had yet to rest its case, and there was still the matter of the State's rebuttal witnesses.

Chapter Twelve

THE VERDICT

That poor man there is subject for the lunatic asylum.

Joseph Generelly

After Dr. LeMonnier was finally excused from the stand, Delos Mellen was recalled. It was the first opportunity for the defense to directly question the witness. At first, an inordinate amount of time was spent quibbling over whether Mellen had paid Leslie Bobb for services rendered, what that cost was, and finally if Lyons had repaid all of his debt. Based on receipts in Lyons's possession, the defense claimed he had.

Likely puzzling the jury was why the defense was pursuing this line of questioning in the first place. Even if all the money questions were answered satisfactorily for the defense, what was the point? If anything, and contrary to the defense's aims, the money trail gave the State a possible motive for the murder. The defense's line of questioning revealed that Gurley and Mellen had lied about paying certain court costs. Lyons subsequently lost his lawsuit, felt cheated out of his money, and demanded satisfaction. If the defense was trying to prove that their client obsessed over money lost, and this was one of several factors that led to his insanity, the evidence seemed to weigh more heavily in favor of the State's contention that Lyons felt cheated and murdered out of revenge.

In closing, the defense asked Mellen if he was acquainted with Richard Lyons (no relation to the defendant) and remembered a conversation Mellen had in his presence with Ambrose Smith while the trio was on Chartres Street two years prior. Mellen was familiar with Lyons but couldn't recall the conversation with Smith. No new information was ascertained during the cross-examination.

Richard Lyons, an attorney, took the stand and was asked if he recalled a conversation he witnessed between Mellen and Smith. Luzenberg immediately objected and the jury was again excused from the courtroom.

The State contended that the defense could not place Lyons on the stand to contradict evidence brought out in the cross-examination of Mellen, a State witness. However, Generelly reminded the district attorney that Mellen was also a defense witness.

"But your witness said that he could not remember such a conversation," Luzenberg protested, "so, it is not in evidence that such a conversation had been held."

With the jury still out, Judge Chretien sustained the objection but wanted to hear Richard Lyons's story anyway. He told the judge that Smith conveyed to Mellen that Lewis Lyons was in a dangerous state of mind and had threatened violence against Gurley and himself. Mellen took the threat seriously but didn't think he would be targeted. Smith, who was in the courtroom, corroborated Richard Lyons's statement and added that he warned Gurley, something that he had previously testified to.

After both men spoke, Generelly announced that he would reserve a bill of exception. Luzenberg then withdrew his objection, believing that such testimony might further prove his case. If such a conversation occurred, why did it take the defendant, supposedly deranged by that time, two years to act upon his insanity? Luzenberg thought that the motive for murder sounded more like a longstanding grudge than insanity.

The jury was brought back into the courtroom and both men repeated their stories under oath. Afterwards, the defense announced they were resting their case, though they reserved the right to offer witnesses in surrebuttal.

The first rebuttal witness to take the stand was Dr. Joseph Danna, who had treated Lyons at Charity Hospital. When he was asked if Lyons's conversations were irrational in nature, the defense immediately objected.

"Unless the witness is ready to say whether or not this man is sane or insane, we must ask the Court for a ruling," Generelly demanded.

Luzenberg informed the judge that Dr. Danna would not be asked to prove or disprove insanity but rather his opinion if Lyons spoke irrationally or not. It was a fair question, given that defense witnesses had cited instances where they believed that Lyons acted illogically. The jury was excused again from the courtroom. While Dr. Danna remained on the stand, both sides argued their viewpoints for about an hour, before Judge Chretien adjourned without reaching a decision.

The funeral of Generelly's father-in-law, Dr. Emile Sarpy, was held the following morning. The trial didn't resume until 12:30 P.M., a fortunate turn of events. One of the jury members, Henry Gehbauer, was feeling ill that morning, which prompted a visit by Dr. Richard, who was back in town. Gehbauer was diagnosed with some form of acute indigestion or an ailment producing symptoms of nervousness. Dr. Richard prescribed some tonic and checked back on him at 11:00 A.M., finding his problem resolved.

At Orleans Parish Prison, Lewis Lyons spent a quiet morning, ate breakfast, and appeared not the least bit worried about his fate. Captain Rennyson gingerly rebuked him for falling asleep in court the previous day, but Lyons denied that he had done such a thing. In fact, he claimed that he had been wide awake the entire time, in spite of what others observed.

While jurors waited for the trial to resume, one of the men had his "talking machine" delivered to the jury room. The jurors jubilantly gathered around this early version of the record player and listened to an assortment of music, the sound filtering downstairs to the second floor, where it was heard by newspaper reporters.

When court convened, Judge Chretien announced that, after a thorough review of the law, he decided to overrule Generelly's objection.

"No sir, he did not," Dr. Danna answered, referring to whether Lyons had spoken to him irrationally.

"That's all," the district attorney said.

With Generelly's cross-examination yielding nothing, Dudley Sneed, a *States* reporter, testified that he visited the defendant numerous times while in the hospital and later at the prison. Like Dr. Danna, Sneed denied ever hearing Lyons speak irrationally. His answer came after the defense's objection was overruled.

Dr. Richard Salter, another oculist, took the stand. After stating his credentials, he testified that he had examined Lyons's eye the day before. Generelly immediately objected.

"This time I make it with force," he proclaimed. "No examination made at this time of this man's eyes, three months after the occurrence, is admissible in evidence."

But Judge Chretien overruled the objection, and the defense again reserved a bill of exception. Dr. Salter testified that he saw no evidence of a choked disc during his examination of Lyons's right eye. Further, he stated that there was no evidence that a choked disc causes mental illness.

Two additional oculists, Drs. Ernest Bobin and H. Manning Fish, testified that they had also examined Lyons the day before. Both concurred with Dr. Salter's findings, based on their experiences and after a careful review of the medical literature.

Dr. Richard Salter on the stand, with stenographer Sturges Adams (1903). (Courtesy NOLA.com/The *Times-Picayune*)

James Fitzsimmons, a bartender who worked at a saloon frequented by Lyons, testified that Lyons was a sensible fellow. But on cross-examination, he admitted that he hadn't spent a great deal of time conversing with him and may have missed when Lyons spoke "wild things."

At this juncture, Luzenberg produced the Civil District Court record of Lyons's bench trial and asked that it be entered into evidence. A copy of the transcript had been submitted to the defense the previous night. Luzenberg's point was to highlight certain sections of the record where corrections and erasures had been made, as Lyons had asserted in his letter to Denegre. This was an attempt by the State to prove that Lyons's letter about the transcription errors was not a rant by a madman but rather based on a legitimate, though minor, grievance he had with the stenographer, Leslie Bobb.

Seven additional non-expert rebuttal witnesses followed, including Lena Heffner, Lyons's former landlady. None of the witnesses saw Lyons acting irrationally in their presence.

Dr. Alexander G. Maylie, the State's expert witness on mental illness, was the last rebuttal witness called on Tuesday afternoon. As a practicing physician for over fifteen years, a visiting physician at Charity Hospital and affiliated with Touro Infirmary, Dr. Maylie had been associated with the coroner's office between 1892 and 1896 and for the past twenty years had made a special study of mental illness. In preparation for the trial, Luzenberg asked him to examine Lyons and render his unbiased opinion of the man. Dr. Maylie visited the defendant on six occasions.

Based on his careful review of Lyons's writings, interview of Lyons's family and friends, physical examination, and question-and-answer sessions with Lyons, Dr. Maylie concluded that the defendant was "absolutely sane."

Generelly and Doyle grilled the doctor for the remaining part of the afternoon, before the jury asked for a toilet break. But while the jurors were upstairs, one of the deputy sheriffs returned to the courtroom to report that Henry Gehbauer had taken ill again. Judge Chretien sent for Dr. Richard. Whatever the origin of Gehbauer's distress, it had little effect upon the rest of the jurors, as one of them cranked up the phonograph and the rest gathered around to listen and sing. With Gehbauer's medical status uncertain, court adjourned until the following morning. (Gehbauer's mysterious illness resolved within hours.)

Wednesday, November 18, was a cold day in New Orleans, with temperatures expected to remain in the forties. Coupled with the steam boilers not properly functioning that day, the entire courthouse was frigid when the trial resumed at 9:30. Few spectators braved the temperatures to attend the last morning of testimony.

Judge Chretien's teeth clattered from the cold as Dr. Maylie resumed his seat in the witness box. The defense tried in vain to get the doctor to admit that Lyons's writings pointed to insanity, but not even Lyons's suicide attempt convinced Dr. Maylie.

"Suicide may be an evidence of insanity, but sane people also sometimes commit suicide," he proclaimed.

Eight additional rebuttal witnesses were called before court recessed for lunch, including Zach Spearing, who was finally able to testify about the fraud perpetrated upon him by Lyons. But the testimonies of Margaret Wallace and Alvin Mabius were of particular interest.

Mrs. Wallace knew Lyons for thirty years and rented a house from him next door to his property on Hillary Street. Mabius owned a jewelry shop in Lyons's Carrollton neighborhood. Both individuals portrayed the defendant as a wife beater. On several occasions after Lyons's 1895 arrest, Wallace saw the defendant beat his wife and once witnessed him knocking her to the ground. Mabius, who knew Lyons for six years, saw Mrs. Lyons's face bruised and testified that she appeared "downhearted" when she came to his shop one day.

When court reconvened at 1:30, twelve additional rebuttal witnesses were called, but George Denegre, whose name came up several times during the trial, seemed to reap the most interest from the spectators. Serving as Lyons's arbitrator during his dispute with Gurley, Denegre stated that he found nothing improper in Gurley's handling of the lawsuit but admitted that he might have filed the paperwork "somewhat differently" than Gurley had done.

One of the last three remaining rebuttal witnesses to take the stand was Dr. Mioton, the assistant coroner, who had conducted over two thousand autopsies during his career. He testified that even if a microscopic examination of the brain was performed, it couldn't prove that a person suffered from insanity. Short of an organic cause to explain the development of insanity, such as a cranial tumor, it was difficult to diagnosis such a condition by an autopsy alone. Clearly, this was to counter Dr. LeMonnier's prediction that a diseased brain would be found upon Lyons's death.

To reinforce the testimony of Wallace and Mabius, Luzenberg produced a court record dated August 6, 1896. In it, Lyons was charged with assault and battery, which was pled down to simple assault. A conviction would carry a twenty-dollar fine or thirty days in jail. The July 3, 1896, incident was perpetrated upon Kate Barringer, a widow, a year after Lyons's arrest. If Lyons could commit violence upon women, it wasn't a stretch for jurors to assume he could do the same upon a man. After two additional rebuttal witnesses, the State rested its case.

Generelly jumped at the opportunity to repudiate the State's claim that Lyons abused women, Kate Barringer in particular. He produced a letter that she wrote to the sitting judge at the time. She explained that she stole Lyons's watch and chain at one of the saloons they patronized. She didn't indicate in her letter why she took the items, but one possible reason was that she was financially desperate. Her husband, Charles William Barringer, had died of alcoholism at age thirty-eight in February 1896, just months before the incident. In any event, she wrote that a quarrel ensued between her and Lyons, resulting in her tearing his shirt and Lyons shoving her back. It's possible that eyewitnesses, who didn't know that Barringer had initiated the squabble, lodged the original complaint against Lyons. It's also possible that Barringer had no direct knowledge of Lyons's subsequent arrest.

She explained in her letter that she spoke to the district attorney, who later advised Lyons to plead guilty to simple assault. Lyons complied and the judge fined him twenty dollars, in spite of his innocence. This was still a time of chivalry, and no gentleman dared threaten or attack a widowed lady without repercussions, regardless of the circumstances.

Feeling remorseful, Barringer wrote to the judge asking him to remit the fine, though it's not known if the judge complied. By 1903, the judge was dead, and Barringer was not called as a surrebuttal witness because she died of tuberculosis three years earlier.

Generelly, having dispensed with that matter, called his only surrebuttal witness to the stand, Dr. LeMonnier. The witness stated that he had met with Dr. Mioton about the various documents entered into evidence, and Dr. Mioton, speaking in French, told him the tenor of the letters was melancholic. Dr. LeMonnier equated that to a form of insanity, though personally he considered the letters to be examples of "delirium of persecution." In any case, in his opinion, the letters pointed to the writings of an insane man.

During cross-examination, Luzenberg asked Dr. LeMonnier to express his view of the State's various expert witnesses. He replied that they were all honest in their opinions but age and experience would eventually change their views about the defendant's state of mind.

By 5:00, both sides rested, and court recessed until 6:30. It was agreed that closing arguments would begin thereafter and continue until midnight, if necessary. By the time court reconvened, every seat was taken, with standing room only in the aisles. Among the horde of spectators was an unusually large number of civil-trial attorneys, who rarely saw the inside of a criminal courtroom.

Samuel Montgomery, the assistant district attorney, informed the jury they shouldered a burden of great responsibility not only because a life was at stake but because a man's life had been taken. In order to prove murder, the State had to show the crime was premeditated and carried out with malice. He asserted that the State had established this without question. And regarding the defense's claim that Lyons was insane when he murdered—

"Insanity, oh, insanity, what crimes are committed in thy name?" Montgomery proclaimed. "How many asylums do you think we would have to erect if all such men as this were pronounced insane?"

According to the State, the defense had to prove by a preponderance of the evidence that Lyons was insane at the time he murdered Gurley. Montgomery stated that the evidence proved otherwise. He then painstakingly chronicled the murder and reviewed Lyons's various correspondences and concluded that Lyons wasn't insane when he murdered Gurley or attempted suicide.

"If this is insanity, then any train robber who holds up an express messenger is insane. There can be no doubt as to his guilt." Montgomery ended with a simple plea to the jury. "Duty to man, duty to God, demands that you find him guilty."

The jury was allowed to retire for a few minutes before Warren Doyle spoke for the defense. He reminded the jury that they were not a body of avengers for the murder of the district attorney. Rather, their duty was to determine if Lyons was guilty or not of murder. He then explained the various classifications of homicide. The last category, and the one more relevant to his argument, was that the slayer's mind was in such a condition that he couldn't distinguish between right and wrong. Doyle declared that his client was insane at the time of the murder and therefore could not be held responsible for his crime.

Doyle spent considerable time discussing Dr. LeMonnier's opinion of Lyons, which had largely been based on his extensive knowledge and experience in dealing with the mentally ill, rather than the State's younger and less experienced expert witnesses, who "relied on their books" to prove their point.

Then Doyle contrasted Lyons's life before and after his 1895 arrest, to illustrate his slow downward spiral into insanity.

And not to alienate the jurors by disparaging the victim, Doyle ended his argument by paying tribute to Gurley, whom he admired and considered a friend. Thereafter, Joseph Generelly rose to his feet to complete the defense's summation.

Generelly gave a brief account of the murder, then stated that of all of the physicians who had testified, the opinions of only two mattered—those of Drs. LeMonnier and Maylie. Generelly added that the former physician was eminently more qualified to render an opinion than the latter. He then implored the jurors to look at his client and asked them to explain why Lyons had aged as he had.

"Now, what is the cause of this emaciated form?" Generelly asked. He reminded the jury that Dr. Maylie had examined his client and found nothing physically wrong to explain his weight loss. "Dr. LeMonnier told the truth when he said it is insanity, the worst malady that attacks the human race. I would rather my tongue would cleave to my mouth than stand here and plead in behalf of the murderer of J. Ward Gurley."

Like his law partner, Generelly then took an opportunity to praise the deceased district attorney before his closing remark.

"That poor man there is subject for the lunatic asylum," Generelly stated, as the clock chimed 12:30 A.M.

The State would have the final word later that morning. Court adjourned until 10:30.

A packed audience heard Luzenberg's closing argument when court reconvened on Thursday, November 19. He addressed the jury for three and a quarter hours, discussing the murder, praising the noble victim, and reviewing the testimony of some defense witnesses that seemed to paint a picture of a vindictive man rather than an insane one. Piece by piece and page by page, he meticulously presented the various documents written by Lyons to prove his point. He then addressed Lyons's Civil District Court record, transcribed by Leslie Bobb, to illustrate that Lyons wasn't laboring under any

Lewis W. Lyons (November 1903). (Courtesy Colin O'Key)

delusions when he accused the stenographer of altering the record. Some errors had occurred, though they were trivial in nature and never rose to acts of criminality.

He discussed Dr. Maylie's opinion that Lyons was not insane and, more importantly, that suicide wasn't always a sign of insanity. Luzenberg even took a jab at Dr. Jones's testimony, the defense witness who claimed that a choked disc pointed to insanity. Luzenberg maintained that such a conclusion was highly suspect among the State's oculists who testified. Of course, Generelly interrupted him for disparaging and misconstruing Dr. Jones's conclusions. He went so far as to instruct Sturges Adams, the court stenographer, to read aloud the doctor's exact testimony. But in the end, such a tactic made no difference to the jury during their deliberation.

When Luzenberg's closing argument ended at 1:45, Judge Chretien charged the jury by defining murder and manslaughter and instructing them in matters of law. They could only base their verdict upon evidence presented at trial, nothing else. The jury was given five possible outcomes: guilty as charged and punishable by death; guilty without capital punishment; guilty of manslaughter, which carried imprisonment not to exceed twenty years and a fine not to exceed two thousand dollars; not guilty, in which case the prisoner would be released; and finally, not guilty by reason of insanity, in which case the court would order Lyons to an insane asylum.

With the judge's instructions complete, a recess was called at 2:10, and the jurors were escorted upstairs for lunch. Their deliberations began during or after their meal. On the first ballot, every member of the jury believed that Lewis Lyons was sane at the time of the murder, though two jurors voted guilty without capital punishment. On the second ballot, only one man held out for life imprisonment. Some people speculated the holdout was Henry Gehbauer. On the third ballot, after a total of twenty-five minutes of deliberations, Lyons's fate was sealed.

Meanwhile, deputies led Lyons to the sheriff's office for lunch in the company of his wife, Clara, sister, Miss Chattie, and brother, Wilson. For whatever reason, his aged mother remained at home. After a short visit, Lyons asked his family not to return to the courtroom for the reading of the verdict. He realized that, in the best scenario, he would be condemned to a mental hospital for life, though he probably knew that was a slim possibility.

Judge Chretien had barely returned from lunch when a deputy sheriff whispered in his ear that the jury had reached a verdict. The judge's jocular mood quickly changed to absolute seriousness when he received the news.

"In the twinkling of an eye," the *Daily Picayune* reported, the courtroom quickly filled with an immense crowd, all eager to learn the fate of the accused murderer of J. Ward Gurley.

Lyons sat to the left of his attorneys and briefly stared at the jury box as the twelve men took their seats. He momentarily shuffled his feet and let out two or three low coughs before settling into his standard indifference to the court's proceedings. With Luzenberg and his assistants present, Judge Chretien ascended the bench and his court was called to order.

"Gentlemen of the jury, have you agreed upon a verdict?" Minute Clerk Arthur Desmond asked.

"We have," Foreman William Faust slowly replied, as he passed the verdict to Desmond.

The verdict was then forwarded to Judge Chretien to review before he returned the slip of paper to the minute clerk to read.

"Guilty as charged," Desmond stated.

The verdict took no one by surprise, except Generelly and Doyle, who were astonished by the judgment. One observer thought that Lyons might not have heard the pronouncement, due to its brevity. Lyons had risen to his feet to hear the verdict, but "there was not a tremor about him" when it was read, the *Daily Picayune* reported. "He [stood] just as he had been sitting, as motionless as the sphinx."

After the jury was polled as to their verdict, Luzenberg broke his silence, asking the court to extend thanks to Generelly and Doyle. Luzenberg realized that both men had sacrificed much as Lyons's court-appointed attorneys. Judge Chretien agreed and then thanked and discharged the jury. The twelve men departed, eager to rejoin their families after such a prolonged absence.

None of the jurors was more willing to leave the courthouse than Henry Gehbauer. Reporters soon found him at his residence, 524 Orange Street, in bed under the careful watch of his wife and children. He had taken ill again and complained of lack of sleep. Whatever the origin of his poor health, it wasn't fatal. The father of nine children, Henry Philip Gehbauer lived another twenty-eight years and died on November 9, 1931, from organic valvular heart disease at the age of sixty-eight.

Lyons's defense team might have been duly discharged of their responsibility upon the jury's verdict, but before the court adjourned Generelly announced that his team intended to file a motion for a new trial, based on the bills of exception the defense had filed. This case was far from over.

After Lyons was remanded to prison, he was transferred to death row, located on the second floor in the north wing of the prison. There he awaited his official sentencing by Judge Chretien.

After Lyons arrived at his new cell, he told reporters the trial had proven that Mellen and Gurley mishandled his lawsuit, based upon Denegre's testimony, though this was a gross distortion of what he said. Lyons further stated that Leslie Bobb had erred in the transcription of his bench trial. Lyons felt at last vindicated, and he took the opportunity to express his appreciation for his defense team.

"The boys were honest and conscientious," Lyons told reporters, "and I do not blame them in any way for having lost the case."

Chapter Thirteen

His Sentencing and Unforeseen Brothers

Mr. Lyons, you were charged with the murder of John Ward Gurley.

Judge Frank Chretien

On Friday, November 20, 1903, the day after Lewis Lyons was convicted of the murder of J. Ward Gurley, New Orleans experienced a third consecutive day of cold weather, with the temperature hovering around thirty-seven degrees by sunrise. It wasn't expected to get much warmer by the start of the business day. With the adjournment of Judge Chretien's court until Monday, December 7, and the cancellation of Judge Baker's court due to the cold weather, the courthouse resembled a virtual ghost town. Nonetheless, the building didn't stay quiet for long. On the top of the list of cases pending before Judge Chretien were the murder trials of Charles "Shotgun" Foley and Samuel Sparo.

Foley stood accused of the murder of Richard Flynn, alias "Rat Tooth," a well-known, small-time criminal associate of his. In spring 1902, Foley labored under the false belief that Flynn had turned police informant and implicated him in a recent warehouse robbery. Both men had a history of petty larceny, and Foley two counts of assault and battery, for which he served briefly in Orleans Parish Prison. By the time of the murder, Foley had added grand larceny to his criminal history. During the evening of April 7, 1902, a quarrel broke out between the two supposed friends and ended with Foley firing multiple shots at Flynn. His partner died several days later, swearing on his deathbed that he never implicated his partner in the warehouse robbery. Foley's original trial date was set for mid-August 1902, but numerous stays were granted on account of the unknown whereabouts of a key witness.

Samuel Sparo was accused of the August 9, 1903, murder of Antonio Luciano, a revenge killing. It was another in a long line of Mafia slayings in the city. District Attorney Chandler Luzenberg prosecuted both murder trials, though the Sparo trial was destined to be one of the most peculiar and ironic murder cases of his long and illustrious career.

Before Luzenberg assumed the reins of district attorney, he served as Luciano's defense attorney, who was himself accused of a Mafia murder. Luzenberg successfully defended his client, planting the seeds of doubt in the minds of the jury as to his client's sanity. Luciano was acquitted in mid-February 1903 and walked out of the courthouse a free man, only to be murdered by Sparo six months later. Sparo befriended Luciano several months after his acquittal and, when the opportunity presented itself, fired four bullets into Luciano, killing him almost instantly.

Foley, twenty-six years old at the time and married with a child, went on trial on December 15, 1903, a week after Judge Chretien reconvened his court following his abbreviated holiday. Samuel Montgomery served as the chief prosecutor. At 6:00 P.M., after fifteen minutes of deliberation, the jury found Foley guilty of capital murder. In early February 1904, Luzenberg successfully prosecuted Sparo.

Two weeks after the Sparo conviction, Luzenberg successfully prosecuted a fourth man, Moses G. Lewis, an African-American who was convicted of the November 11, 1903, rape of a thirteen-year-old white girl. Though the girl survived the attack, Lewis was sentenced to death, as rape was a capital offense. A month later, Luzenberg successfully prosecuted a fifth man, Louis Sejours, who was convicted on March 1, 1904, of the July 14, 1903, murder of Robert Edward Reid.

By all accounts, 1903 was a bloody year in New Orleans, with the homicide rate up from the previous year, from forty-nine to fifty-seven killings. The police also reported a total of 335 cases where someone had been wounded by gunfire or stabbed. All told that year, New Orleans police made over 16,000 arrests, out of a population of just over 287,000.

These statistics were not unusual for a city with a long history of violence. It would only get worse as the population grew. But what was unique about the crime statistics of 1903 was that the five aforementioned men ended up sharing death row by the first week of March 1904. At no time in the city's history had so many condemned prisoners been housed at Orleans Parish Prison. This unprecedented event began with the capital murder conviction of Lewis W. Lyons in November 1903.

⌖ ⌖ ⌖

The day following Lyons's guilty verdict, the prisoner, in the company of Captain Rennyson, returned to Charity Hospital, as his left eye had received little medical attention during the two-week trial. Lyons complained that his eye was causing him considerable pain, which Dr. Jones attended to.

Upon Lyons's return to death row, reporters found him "exceeding well," though he continued to complain about his eye. Also, regarding the trial's outcome, Lyons "did not appear to care what happened to him or to realize that the Jury had found him guilty and that the only sentence he could receive was the death penalty." The *Daily Picayune* added that Lyons "was communicative and pleasant, and nothing appears to worry him at all" and that he "really looked better than he had for some time past."

Nothing that Lyons told reporters that day amounted to headline news. Rather, he spoke of trivial matters, such as he was doing quite well and had rested quietly the previous night, in spite of the frigid temperatures. He had received two blankets during the night that kept him warm. He continued to praise the services of his attorneys, saying he "could not have had any better or more faithful or hard-working lawyers," though he did register one minor complaint about Dr. LeMonnier. He thought his ten-hour testimony stretched over three days was overkill, though he was grateful to the man. In truth, the totality of Dr. LeMonnier's testimony probably bored him to tears. He knew he wasn't insane.

After the reporters departed, Lyons spent an hour or more visiting with his wife under the watch of James McLaughlin, a prison trustee. McLaughlin was instructed not to leave his side and to observe him closely, should he attempt to harm himself. Lyons had been on suicide watch before, but now that he was a convicted murderer, tensions heightened among prison officials, though the thought of suicide was the farthest thing from his mind.

Generelly's first task in arguing for a new trial was to obtain a copy of the court transcript. Sturges Adams had taken down the fifteen-day trial in shorthand, so it was anybody's guess when the typed version would be available for review.

Meanwhile, Lyons spent a relatively quiet weekend. His brother, Wilson, visited on Sunday, along with Dr. LeMonnier. During his lengthy stay, the doctor enlightened Lyons as to why he had so painstakingly explained his opinion on the stand. The doctor had probably read in the newspaper about Lyons's comments related to his protracted testimony.

On Monday November 23, Lyons was escorted to Charity Hospital for his routine eye examination, performed by Dr. Jones. He continued to complain about his eye pain and headaches but nothing that was debilitating in nature. Later that day, his family visited him.

On Tuesday, reporters found Lyons sitting in his cell, looking rather bored. He told them that they had erred in printing his thoughts about Dr. LeMonnier. Apparently, he felt some remorse over his comments, especially after meeting with the doctor on Sunday. He stated that what the newspapers had printed was simply not true.

During the interview, Lyons took another swipe at Delos Mellen, though what he said about his former attorney wasn't published. Undeniably, it wasn't too flattering. For his part, Mellen was likely pleased that his former client was locked up on death row.

Regarding questions about his health, Lyons continued to express that he felt okay and indicated that his left eye was drying up, though his left ear was draining fluid again. Whether it appeared clear or infected is not known. In any event, some degree of infection had resurfaced. Without the benefit of antibiotics, it was going to be a difficult problem to treat.

Captain Rennyson had earlier promised that he would send Lyons a set of dominoes—one of his favorite games—a checkerboard, and a pack of playing cards, but by Tuesday the games hadn't arrived. Lyons told reporters that he believed the warden had probably forgotten about it. He was hoping that Rennyson would read about it in the newspaper and be reminded of his promise.

Ever mindful of a possible suicide attempt, two jail keepers constantly watched Lyons's every move, a standard protocol, though he didn't seem to mind. He had no intention of killing himself and liked the extra company. Resigned to his fate, he softened his attitude towards peace officers and became more sociable with them.

On Monday, December 7, Judge Chretien granted Generelly and Doyle a fifteen-day extension for filing their application for a new trial. This was likely requested because Adams had not completed transcribing his notes. In any case, the new deadline came and went, and it wasn't until January 15, 1904, that they filed their lengthy motion for a new trial with the court. It claimed that the verdict was contrary to the law and evidence and that the court had erred specifically in overruling the defense's objections to the testimonies of Parody; Frank Reitmeyer, the newspaper reporter; Mellen; and several other State witnesses. In fact, the defense cited all forty-eight of their overruled objections as causes to request a new trial. Oral arguments were set for January 22. As a result, Judge Chretien indefinitely postponed Lyons's formal sentencing, which had been scheduled for January 15.

But the date to hear arguments for a new trial came and went. Likely, Luzenberg asked for a postponement, as the State was preparing its case against Samuel Sparo. The Sparo trial started on Tuesday, January 26, with a guilty verdict reached on February 4 after three minutes of deliberation, one of the quickest verdicts on record. Five minutes after the verdict was read, Sparo joined Lyons and Charles Foley on death row.

⌖⌖⌖

Of the three condemned prisoners on death row, Sparo seemed to be the most nervous when he arrived. He had resided up to that time in relative luxury in one of the private rooms on the third floor, the same area where Lyons had convalesced after his release from Charity Hospital. Costing Sparo $2.50 per week, his room was spacious and included a cot, rather than the standard canvas hammock that was provided to the general prisoner population. Now that Sparo was on death row, he found himself having to sleep on the floor on a pallet or mattress. There were no hammocks available to the condemned prisoners, as the dangling ropes might have provided them a means to end their lives. Sparo's initial nervousness might have been rooted in his change of scenery (now bare walls and tight quarters) and lack of a comfortable bed.

Two days after Sparo's conviction, reporters visited the trio and observed the Sicilian native pacing the corridor in front of his cell. Claiming that he was innocent and hoping to be granted a new trial, he seemed to have a good appetite that day when lunch was served. Sparo and Foley consumed the meal, consisting of a chunk of fatty meat—mostly fat—and a large piece of bread, without complaints. Lyons, on the other hand, didn't miss the opportunity to register his displeasure about the prison chow.

"I gave my dog better food than this when I was at liberty," he told reporters.

None of the condemned men were given forks or knives with their meals. They were only allowed a tablespoon to eat with, a precautionary measure for all prisoners on death row. In addition, two deputy sheriffs were constantly on guard near the cells to prevent any disturbances or acts of self-destruction.

With the matter of *State v. Sparo* finally settled, though Sparo's attorneys still needed to file a motion for a new trial, Friday, February 12 was set aside to hear oral arguments in the Lyons case. But by then, Judge Chretien had already determined his course of action when Generelly and Doyle began to argue their case, followed by Luzenberg for the State. After reviewing the litany of bills of exception included in the defense's motion for a new trial, he saw no basis in law to set aside the conviction. Listening to the disappointing news in court were Lyons's wife, sister, and brother.

After Judge Chretien overruled the motion, Lyons was brought into the courtroom for sentencing, assuming virtually the same fixed position he held during the trial, with his face shielded from view and his back to everyone but the judge. A camera had been set up near one of the side windows to take a photograph of his front, though the only image the photographer managed to take was of his back. Lyons was aware of the camera's position and wanted no part of the photo shoot.

Judge Chretien was about to pronounce sentence upon Lyons when he was interrupted by the defense. Generelly and Doyle handed the judge a written plea of present insanity. The statement read that Lyons was currently "laboring under such defect of reason from disease of the mind as not to know the nature or quality of the act." They asked the court to stay all proceedings. Both attorneys sensed that Judge Chretien would overrule their motion and had plan B conveniently tucked inside a coat pocket: a request that Lyons's state of mind be reevaluated.

Judge Chretien was wise enough that he must have been known such a preemptive move might be made. He stated that it would require the appointment of a Commission de Lunatico Inquirendo to decide the issue. The defense agreed and planned to file a separate motion as soon as possible.

Because of the Carnival season and other personal matters, Generelly didn't file his motion until Friday, February 19, three days after Mardi Gras. The following Tuesday, Judge Chretien granted his motion and appointed a three-member commission—Drs. George Hays, superintendent of the State Insane Asylum; Jefferson Bloom, house surgeon at Charity Hospital; and Quitman Kohnke, president of the Board of Health for New Orleans. The physicians were given the task of establishing Lyons's current state of mind and presenting their findings in open court to Judge Chretien and a jury of twelve men. In other words, Lyons could escape his death sentence if the physicians rendered Lyons insane and the jury went along. By law, a finding of insanity would make Lyons ineligible to be sentenced to death.

District Attorney Luzenberg must have been livid when he heard Judge Chretien's decision in court. The following day, the *Daily Picayune* equated the ruling to a retrial of the Lyons murder case. The *Picayune* wasn't alone among the other New Orleans dailies in telegraphing their displeasure with Judge Chretien's order. Everyone held various degrees of distain for the murderer of J. Ward Gurley.

It's not known what motivated Judge Chretien to do so—second thoughts or the political and social winds blowing against him—but on March 16, he revoked his order that the commission report their findings to a jury. Instead, the physicians would report directly to him. Everyone was pleased with his reversal, except for Lyons's defense team. Generelly and Doyle took exception to the ruling. The *Daily Picayune* suggested that the gentlemen might take the matter up with the Louisiana Supreme Court.

Meanwhile, on February 18, thirty-one-year-old Moses G. Lewis was convicted in Judge Chretien's chambers of raping the daughter of Victor Kientz and Maria Turck Kientz, both natives of Germany. The victim, Caroline Mary Elizabeth Kientz, though she was always referred to as Elizabeth Kientz, was born in New Orleans on August 14, 1890. Fortunately, her mother never had to endure the family's outrage, as she died in February 1892, years before the sexual assaults began. The year following her mother's death, Elizabeth's father, a truck farmer, began to employ Lewis as a laborer, a position he held with the family until his arrest on November 11, 1903. Between those times, Victor remarried, and by June 1900, Lewis was listed as a "day laborer" with the Kientz family, according to census data.

During his one-day trial, Elizabeth testified that Lewis repeatedly molested her. The *Daily Picayune* chose not to print the sordid details of his many attacks on the young girl. It was enough to say that Elizabeth described on the stand "a state of depravity seldom heard of, and confessed that Lewis, had outraged her four years ago when she was but 9 years old." The last time Elizabeth was assaulted, the day of Lewis's arrest, he allegedly threatened to kill her and her family if she ever spoke about his actions.

Lewis was also suspected of being involved in the June 22, 1900, drowning death of Elizabeth's older brother, Nicholas Aloysius "Alois" Kientz, though such suspicions came to light only after Lewis was charged with rape. During the early morning hours, eleven-year-old Alois was found at the bottom of the family's "well," though it likely was a cistern, given the topography of the area. In 1900, the family lived at 1337 Kentucky Street. Nevertheless, though Lewis never denied sexually assaulting the girl, he went to his grave swearing he had nothing to do with the boy's death.

The general prisoner population was segregated, but that was not the case on death row. Soon after his conviction, Moses Lewis found himself housed in the same unit as his white counterparts.

The lunacy commission, chaired by Dr. Hays, began their task within two day of their appointments, though they would not deliver their finding to Judge Chretien until the second week of May. In the interim, on March 1, Louis Sejours, alias "Dago Louis," age twenty-eight, went on trial before Judge Joshua Baker for the murder of Robert Reid, a dry-goods clerk. Between one and two o'clock in the morning on July 14, 1903, Sejours got into a scuffle in front of Emile Baumann's saloon and oyster bar, 1041 Canal Street at the corner of Rampart, with Pvt. Garfield Bower, an artillerist stationed at Jackson Barracks. Sejours, a hot-tempered man, falsely believed that Bower had insulted his lady companion as the pair walked past Bower, who stood in front of the drinking establishment. During the ensuing confrontation, Sejours pulled out a revolver and shot at Bower, missing him.

Patrons in the saloon, including Reid and a number of other soldiers, rushed out to investigate the sound of gunfire. Reid got as far as the side door on Rampart Street when he was struck in the chest by a second shot fired by Sejours, causing him to stagger back into the saloon. He died shortly afterwards. Sejours fired a third shot before fleeing the scene.

Sejours, testifying on his own behalf, swore he was home at the time of the shooting and nowhere near the area. Countless eyewitnesses testified to the contrary. The jury began their deliberations at 11:15 P.M. and returned a guilty verdict at midnight. Sejours's utter disregard for human life weighed heavily on the jury's decision. His capital murder conviction now placed five men on death row.

On March 11, Judge Chretien formally sentenced Moses Lewis to death, with Charles Foley sentenced on April 4. Samuel Sparo followed suit on May 9. Judge Baker refused to grant Sejours a new trial and sentenced him to death on March 25. It would fall under the purview of the new governor, Newton Blanchard, to later fix the various dates of execution. By the second week of May, only Lewis Lyons waited for his formal sentencing.

On Friday morning, May 13, 1904, Judge Chretien handed Minute Clerk Arthur Desmond the report of the Commission de Lunatico Inquirendo for filing. Dated May 12, 1904, the report left nothing ambiguous about the commission's conclusions. Individually and collectively, the members had examined, interviewed, and observed Lyons and had carefully reviewed the "voluminous court records and documents" pertaining to his trial. The commissioners made clear that they had determined that the self-inflicted wound to the head didn't penetrate the brain to any degree that would cause a post-crime mental defect in Lyons.

"While he appears and acts as one deeply affected by a sense of great wrong suffered, and profoundly moved by a feeling of strong resentment," the report read, "Lewis W. Lyons is not insane, and is in a mental condition of full responsibility."

The implications of this report were clear. All that was left for Judge Chretien to do was to pass sentence on the prisoner, though he had yet to decide what day he would do so. Nonetheless, with Judge Chretien's summer recess scheduled to begin on June 1, it was clear that sentencing would have to occur within the next two weeks.

Shortly after two o'clock that Friday, a flurry of activity began in the courthouse. Luzenberg had received a note at his office indicating that Lyons had committed suicide. Not knowing if there was any truth to the story, the district attorney quickly dispatched his aide, Special Officer John Trainor, to the prison. As incredible as the news was, it was not out of the range of possibility that such an event had occurred. After all, the commission had essentially sealed Lyons's fate.

Trainor thought the report of Lyons's suicide was nonsense. He had just left death row a few minutes before and saw Lyons very much alive and well. Luzenberg told him to go anyway. In the company of Captain Rennyson, Trainor arrived at Lyons's cell to find him asleep on his pallet. Trainor had one of the guards shake him awake, just to be sure. Lyons rubbed his eyes in astonishment when he was told why he had been roused from his deep slumber. During this brief inspection, Lyons exchanged few words with his prisoner keepers, other than to ask Captain Rennyson what had become of the silver studs that were attached to a shirt he had worn. The jewelry had disappeared.

On Saturday, Judge Chretien announced that on Wednesday, May 18, Lewis Lyons would be sentenced, though his death sentence was never in doubt. The only question that remained was how soon Governor Blanchard would set the execution. Meanwhile, Generelly and Doyle turned their attention towards the Louisiana Supreme Court.

When Lyons entered Judge Chretien's chambers for sentencing, he walked towards the defense table with his shoulders drooped and his head turned slightly to the left so he could better use his good right eye. He looked feeble but in relative good health, and he assumed his typical nonchalant attitude towards the criminal proceedings.

The court's first order of business was to allow Lyons's defense team to file three bills of exception prior to sentencing. Generelly and Doyle still raised the issue of Lyons's present insanity and wished to introduce their own evidence to prove so. In addition, because the commission's report was not sworn to, the defense claimed that it could not be taken as evidence. Judge Chretien naturally overruled the exceptions, at which time Generelly notified the court that he would file a motion for a suspensive appeal with the Louisiana Supreme Court. Afterwards, Judge Chretien instructed Lyons to stand and asked if he had anything to say prior to sentencing. Lyons made no audible response and shook his head no.

"Mr. Lyons, you were charged with the murder of John Ward Gurley," Judge Chretien began. "You were tried by a jury selected by you and the State. You were given an absolutely fair and impartial trial, giving you the opportunity of proving the issue which you raised fairly and honestly."

The judge proceeded to state that the jury found no tenable evidence supporting the defense's claim of insanity and that an appointed commission had so confirmed that Lewis Lyons was sane. He further declared that the crime "was one that shocked the moral senses" of the citizenry of New Orleans and "was committed without any cause or provocation." Judge Chretien then sentenced Lyons to be hanged by the neck until dead. The governor would fix the date of his execution. "And may God have mercy on your soul," he prayed.

Unmoved by his sentence of death, Lyons left the courtroom with his shoulders still stooped. Escorted across the "bridge of sighs" that connected the second floors of the courthouse and prison, Lyons was returned to death row.

Two days after Lyons's sentence, Captain Rennyson moved the condemned inmates to the tower. He explained that this location was safer and obviously more isolated. With only four cells at his disposal, Rennyson paired Foley and Sejours in Cell No. 1. Lewis was placed in No. 2, followed by Lyons and Sparo in No. 3 and 4, respectively.

When told of the move, Lyons took it in stride and only shrugged his shoulders in response. But the remaining prisoners voiced their displeasure to the warden and, after the move, to their attorneys. With the governor not fixing any of their execution dates as yet, the inmates thought it was premature to transfer them to the tower. But their attorneys told them otherwise. According to state law, the minute the jury found them guilty of capital murder, the prison warden could transfer them as he pleased.

Foley turned white when he was told of the move, the finality of his fate at last sinking in. Sparo looked worried, his dark eyes resembling "the orbs of a despairing animal just before the rise and fall of the death horn," the *Daily Picayune* reported, a veiled reference to playing "Taps" at his funeral. Sejours grew pale, then flushed, as he expressed that he had been railroaded by the court.

When the prisoners reached the fourth floor, they were escorted up the narrow, winding stairs to the tower, guarded in front and rear by deputy sheriffs. One deputy sheriff also walked along the edge of the railing beside Lyons, to prevent him from possibly throwing himself over the side. Prison officials still believed that Lyons would attempt suicide by whatever means.

Past the iron gate that separated the stairway from the wide, paved gallery on the upper floor, Sparo was ushered to his cell. He could peer down into a portion of Yard No. 7, where the hangings were initially to take place. Nervous at the prospect of being placed alone in a cell, Sparo begged Captain Rennyson to pair him with someone.

"I don't sleep well at night, Captain; I lika company," he said in broken English. "Please let me go in with Lyons."

Rennyson told Sparo that no amount of begging would change his mind. "Lyons is a good prisoner to keep by himself," he explained. "We can watch him better when he is alone. You stay where you are."

Sparo fretted that the spirit of Antonio Luciano, his murdered victim, might pay him a visit now that he was in the tower. Rennyson attempted to relieve his fears or maybe poke fun at him.

"Tony won't bother you. The light's too bright out here in the gallery at night, and the watch never sleeps."

Captain Rennyson soon disappeared from the floor, and Sparo walked dejected into his prison cell. He sat on the edge of his iron cot and rested his head in his hands. Within seconds, he was lost in melancholy thought.

For Lewis Lyons, there was nothing to do but resign himself to the fact that the tower would be his home, shared with his unforeseen brothers until his final day. Meanwhile, his attorneys attempted every legal maneuver at their disposal, hoping to spare him from the hangman's noose. Their efforts to secure a new trial ultimately failed, but the energies they expended demonstrated to the city that though justice eventually prevailed, Lyons was never underserved.

Chapter Fourteen

Awaiting Death

Hanging is a queer calling for any man of any race to follow.

Capt. Archibald Rennyson

On May 26, 1904, eight days after Lyons was sentenced to death, Joseph Generelly filed an appeal with the Louisiana Supreme Court. The brief included more than fifty bills of exception filed during and after the murder trial. Generelly also had Sturges Adams forward the 188-page court transcription to the High Court for their review. With the jurists scheduled to start their summer recess on July 1, oral arguments were set for June 11, though Generelly knew it was going to be difficult for him to meet that deadline. Within days of the announced date, he filed a petition for a continuance.

During the January 1904 statewide elections, Generelly's law partner, Warren Doyle, was elected to the state legislature, representing the city's Second Ward. The legislative body began their regular session on May 9, so with Doyle in the thick of his elective duties in Baton Rouge, Generelly decided to seek relief with the High Court.

On May 31, after receiving Generelly's petition, Chief Justice Joseph Breaux instructed him to appear as scheduled on June 11 and at that time make his motion for a continuance before the entire bench. When the court granted him the extension until mid-November, District Attorney Luzenberg was disappointed, to say the least. He felt that the Supreme Court would never vacate the lower court's verdict and had hoped the matter would be decided as soon as possible. Nevertheless, with Doyle unavailable and the defense needing extra time to prepare for oral arguments, the court indulged them.

In the meantime, on June 6, the Louisiana Supreme Court affirmed the murder conviction of Charles Foley, though a petition for a rehearing was filed five days later. By then, Generelly had assumed the role of Foley's counselor, too. He was given until June 18 to file his brief, though he was able to complete the task one day earlier. The court wasted no time and on June 20 refused the rehearing. All that remained was for Governor Blanchard to fix the date of Foley's execution.

The prospects for Moses Lewis, the convicted rapist, were no better. That same month the High Court affirmed his conviction and death sentence. On June 13, John Q. Flynn, Lewis's attorney, announced that he would not apply for a rehearing. He knew it would be a pointless endeavor. In addition, the *Item* wrote, "The members of Lewis's family [had] given up all hope of saving his neck in the face of public opinion." The brutal crime of rape was bad enough, but given that an African-American man had raped an underage white girl at the turn of the twentieth century and he never denied the crime, there was little expectation that the Supreme Court would agree to rehear the case. Nevertheless, there was always the chance that the Board of Pardons might commute his sentence from death to life behind bars.

On August 25, 1904, Governor Blanchard signed the death warrants of Lewis and Foley, setting the date of their dual executions for Friday, September 23. They would be the first executions at the new prison since July 24, 1896, when James "Greasy Jim" Murray, another African-American, was hanged for the murder of private watchman Michael Cotter.

Now that there were two confirmed executions and perhaps as many as three more to follow, Captain Rennyson was besieged by would-be executioners hoping to be hired. It was a repeat of the previous year's scenario when another African-American prisoner was scheduled to be hanged. George Thompson was twice convicted and twice sentenced to death for the 1889 Christmas Day murder of Robert "Bill Draws" Johnson. The victim was allegedly "a black bully" of the neighborhood who had a long criminal history including murder and had spent several terms in the state penitentiary in Baton Rouge. Thompson was sentenced to death for Johnson's murder and had spent some time on death row since his first conviction in June 1901. Several weeks prior to his March 13, 1903, execution date, droves of hangmen showed up at the parish prison eager to be hired by the warden. Only the last-minute commutation of Thompson's sentence to life in prison spared Captain Rennyson the laborious task of having to select a hangman.

"Hanging is a queer calling for any man of any race to follow," Rennyson said. "Nearly all the applicants for the job of killing a fellow-creature appeared to be in the business more to gratify some morbid, blood-thirsty impulse, than for the money there was to be gained."

In the past, Rennyson had seen his share of would-be hangmen who came to his office seeking the job. It didn't matter if there was a pending execution or not. Some of the men professed their skill at quickly breaking the victim's neck to spare him needless pain. Other hangmen touted their years of experience, while others admitted they knew nothing of hangings but were eager and ready to learn.

One such experienced executioner who had called on Rennyson was a light-skinned African-American named Taylor, not to be confused with "Hangman" Taylor, who executed Etienne Deschamps in 1892. ("Hangman" Taylor's first name, Joe, finally surfaced in the *Daily Picayune* in April 1896.) This current hangman carried with him a model of the gallows he used at previous executions in Mississippi and elsewhere. He was particularly proud of his model trapdoor design, which was made of cigar-box wood. Among the accessories were tiny ropes, counterweights, and a noose so that Rennyson could visualize how the contraption worked. Taylor gave the miniature gallows as a gift to the warden, who kept the device in his office as a curiosity to share with his visitors. After the model had gathered sufficient dust and cobwebs, Rennyson asked a reporter to take it off his hands. The newspaperman collected various oddities that showed up at the city morgue and had quite a collection of relics at his home. But his wife vetoed his plans to bring home the miniature gallows. That was a line she wasn't willing to cross.

Among the prospective hangmen who came calling during the summer of 1904 were two boys, not more than eighteen years old, who asked for the privilege of hanging Lewis and Foley. Their youth and inexperience ruled them out. John Broadus, from Mobile, Alabama, read about the upcoming executions in one of the New Orleans dailies and offered his services to Captain Rennyson at fifty dollars per man.

Several African-American prisoners also longed for a chance to play executioner. According to the *Daily Picayune,* one of the men admitted that "he didn't 'zackly' know how to build a gallows, but he guessed if the Captain would have the thing erected he could knot the ropes and do the swinging part of the business, all right." In the end, with a surplus of hangmen to choose from, Rennyson knew he would have no problem hiring someone, though by the first week of July he had whittled down his list to two experienced candidates, Frank Johnston being one. Ultimately chosen, he wasn't informed until the day before the execution. The chosen hangman was usually sworn in as a special deputy, serving in that capacity until his job was complete.

On June 21, Dr. Mioton, the assistant coroner, visited the five condemned men to evaluate their health. He did this at least weekly. Dr. Mioton found

Lewis and Sparo the most troubled among the prisoners. Lewis was so nervous "and altogether impoverished" that Dr. Mioton prescribed a tonic for him. Sparo's emotional state was not as severe, but it was evident to the doctor that his death-row experience was eating at his psyche because he looked so emaciated. "The native brightness has gone from his eyes and they give forth nothing but a listless, droopy stare," the *Item* reported.

The other prisoners still appeared unshaken by the unfolding events, even though Foley's fate had been sealed. Lyons treated his doom with his customary indifference. Foley had a similar reaction, though he expressed anger at the unfairness of his prosecution and sentence of death. Sejours laughed at his impending death and voiced that he was tired of waiting to die. He thought the governor should move more quickly to fix his execution date.

The first week of July was spent constructing the gallows in Yard No. 7, even though the governor had yet to set the date of Lewis and Foley's hanging. With both men having failed in their appeals before the Louisiana Supreme Court, Rennyson knew it was only a matter of time before the governor signed the death warrants. Up in the tower, the prisoners "could distinctly hear the clang and clatter of the carpenters' hammers" as the construction progressed.

On July 2, carpenters spent most of the day working on the trapdoors that would simultaneously send Lewis and Foley to their deaths. Each trapdoor was fitted, weighed, and held in place by a single lever. A single cut of the rope would cause both trapdoors to swing down, and the weights tied to the ends underneath would prevent the boards from rebounding and striking the prisoners as they dangled. In addition, the structure's frame, with the exception of a little trim work, was completed by that date. It was hoped that everything would be finished by July 5, including the application of two coats of gray paint.

The location of the gallows didn't sit well with one prominent attorney. Though his name wasn't revealed, his office was located on the upper floor of the Hennen Building, the eleven-story office complex shared by scores of attorneys, including Generelly and Doyle. Built in 1893, the Hennen Building was officially New Orleans's first skyscraper. From his upper perch and four blocks from the prison walls, the attorney could see into the prison yard and witness the execution, if he was so inclined; he was not. He protested to Captain Rennyson, asking that the structure be dismantled and placed in another exercise yard away from his window view. He declared that the sight of the gallows caused him and his stenographer undue nervousness and psychological pain. Rennyson sympathized, but at this late stage, he wasn't about to tear down and relocate it. He did, however, promise to screen the structure with some kind of drape.

On Sunday, July 24, reporters arrived at the tower to interview the prisoners. None of the men seemed particularly worried now that the gallows structure was complete and that two executions would soon commence. Instead, they only expressed either boredom or concern about their close confinement.

Louis Sejours, who shared a cell with Foley, stated that their space was too small to comfortably accommodate both of them. He was a large-framed man who had performed hard, manual labor. Sejours wasn't used to being confined in such a small space and rendered inactive for long stretches of time. He had to spend most of his days lying on his bed. At least he and others didn't have to sleep on a pallet on the floor now that they had moved to the tower. Not a reading man and choosing to engage in only limited conversation with Foley, Sejours expressed that he often thought about happier days, when he was free. Given the hopelessness of his situation, he wished that his execution was closer at hand than it was.

Charles Foley appeared more hopeful than the other men, expressing confidence that the Board of Pardons would eventually commute his death sentence. Still, he complained that he had been given an "unfair deal" at his trial.

The *Daily Picayune* reported that Samuel Sparo, "the swarthy-faced, sunken-jawed Mafiaman," remained deeply depressed as he sat alone in his cell. "His features [stood] out with distinction, under the tight parchment-like skin," as he appeared to be melting away, looking thinner each time reporters visited him.

Lyons appeared to be the most talkative of the men that day—an unusual thing, according to one reporter. For some time before that, Lyons had been very selective about whom he spoke to and guarded in what he said.

Lyons appeared to have aged considerably since his July 1903 arrest. His snowy-white beard now reached his upper chest, making him look decades older than his forty-five years (his next birthday was in mid-August), and he covered his partially bald head with a blue cap. He also lost a good deal of subcutaneous fat in his cheeks, though that may have been difficult to ascertain given his beard, his jaws sunken "beneath the mass of white whiskers." His nostrils appeared very thin, his damaged left eye was completely closed, and his right tear duct had sealed. Thus, his right eye no longer watered.

Every evening, in the company of one of the deputy sheriffs, Lyons and Sparo were paired and given an hour's walk in one of the exercise yards. The men strolled along the yard's perimeter wall, engaging in small talk, while the rest of the prisoners in the tower awaited their turn. The men kept this route unless the weather interfered.

Besides these walks, a day spent on death row consisted of being served three meals. Breakfast and supper were usually light, consisting of bread and a beverage (tea or milk), with a more substantial meal (meat, soup, beans, and/or some other vegetable) provided at lunch. In addition, each morning the prisoners were permitted to freshen themselves using the communal sink or tub, along with using the toilet as needed.

Family visitations helped break up the monotony of death row for the inmates and lifted their spirits, though these were allowed only within the confines of a booth. This structure contained a wall and screened window that separated both sides, preventing the parties from passing things or physically touching. There was always the fear that someone might hand the prisoner a contraband object, including a means to end his life. Only the State reserved that right. In addition, prisoners were only allowed a fifteen-minute visit per guest.

On August 26, the day after Governor Blanchard affixed his signature to the death warrants of Foley and Lewis, a *Daily Picayune* reporter broke the news to the condemned men. (It would be several days before the official signed warrants were delivered to the prison.)

Lewis was walking back to his cell after the departure of a female visitor when the reporter, accompanied by Deputy Sheriff William "Billy" Fineran, called him back.

"Did you hear the news, Mose?" the reporter asked. He was often referred to by his nickname, "Mose," rather than his given name, Moses.

"From Baton Rouge, mister?" Lewis asked. He immediately moved closer to the gallery bars, his interest piqued. "No sir. What is it?"

"The governor has fixed the twenty-third of next month for your execution," he replied. "Signed the death warrant to-day." In truth, the governor had signed the warrants the day before. Lewis was startled but took the news in stride.

"Well," he said, catching his breath, "I can't help it. If I've got to go, all right!"

At the other end of the corridor was Foley's and Sejours's cell. Both men jumped out of their beds during the conversation and pressed their ears against their locked inner cell door to listen more attentively. Sparo, whose cell was closer to the discussion, did the same. Even Lyons rose from his bed to hear the conversation.

"What day did you say it was—the twenty-third?" Foley called out.

"Yes," the reported responded. Foley retreated to the rear of his cell and carried on a brief inaudible conversation with Sejours.

Meanwhile, Lewis informed the reporter that there was still a chance that the Board of Pardons might commute his sentence if an application was filed. But the reporter replied that when his attorney suggested such a move, his mother had made it known "that if it was God's will that her son should die on the gallows, he would meet that end, and, if God chose to save him, he would be saved."

"That's not so," cried Lewis. "That would be a fine thing for a mother to say about her son, wouldn't it?" He had previously heard the same story and confronted his mother about its truth. "She said it wasn't true," Lewis told the reporter, "and I'd take her word before I would Lawyer Flynn's."

Lewis was correct, because John Flynn applied to the Board of Pardons for a commutation of sentence. They would not render a decision until a week before the scheduled execution.

When the reporter asked Lewis if he feared the gallows, he became rather "boisterous in his merriment at the thought of such a thing," the *Daily Picayune* recounted.

"Afraid? What, me, afraid?" he bellowed in laughter. "Why, I'll go down in that yard and climb them steps, all right, and never show a tremble, that I will, you see if I don't."

It turned out he spoke the truth. Lewis returned to his cell, and Foley was brought to the reporter, who stood on the other side of barred wall. Showing no fear, Foley insisted that "he hadn't been given a square deal."

"Why, they wouldn't even let me show up the character of the man I killed," Foley declared, "and the State's best witness was so drunk that they had to delay the case a day for him to sober up."

He expressed his opinion that Judge Chretien had appointed someone who had very little experience as a criminal-defense attorney. But he said it was okay. He'd get his justice in Heaven before God, who he knew would judge him fairer.

"Maybe he'll show his justice too, as regards those people who have helped hound me to the gallows," Foley added. "My wife and child and my mother—it's when I think of them that I feel my position. For myself, I don't care much if I have to die on the gallows. I guess I can meet my fate as bravely as another."

But Foley insisted that he wasn't quite ready to die. He knew that his family and friends were working diligently on his behalf, as he maintained that he had killed in self-defense.

Returning to his cell, Foley sat on the side of his bed and rested his head in his hands. The evening meal was soon served, described as a "gloomy function" set in a melancholy atmosphere.

Now that the execution date had been fixed, Captain Rennyson instructed his guards to be ever vigilant for any signs of self-destruction. It had been eight years since the last execution, and none of his men had ever served as death watchmen in the tower before.

The news that the death warrants were signed took prison officers by surprise. Everyone had assumed the governor would wait until the Board of Pardons forwarded a recommendation to him, as both men had applied for a commutation of sentence. But to date, the board had taken no action.

The Board of Pardons was composed of two permanent members—the lieutenant governor (J. Y. Sanders) and attorney general (Walter Guion)—and an ad hoc member—the presiding judge who had sentenced the prisoner in question. In both of these cases, that was Judge Chretien. Their inaction stemmed from Sanders having taken sick some weeks before. Thus, it was unlikely they would reach any decision until sometime in September, after Sanders recuperated.

Meanwhile, on Monday, August 29, Sheriff Reilley received the death warrants. It would be the responsibility of the sheriff's department to read the warrants to Foley and Lewis at the appropriate time. But soon after their delivery, it was discovered that the documents contained factual errors that required them to be returned to Baton Rouge for modifications.

When the corrected warrants arrived Thursday morning, Sheriff Reilley ordered them read to the prisoners as soon as possible. He passed the responsibility on to his son-in-law, Captain Rennyson, with Chief Deputy Patrick agreeing to read the warrants at eleven o'clock. At the designated hour, Rennyson and King, along with five other members of the sheriff's department and prison and several members of the press, ascended the three flights of stairs to the fourth floor of the prison. They stood there for a minute to catch their breaths before continuing their journey up the steep and narrow stairway to the tower.

Entering the gallery, Rennyson ordered one of the guards to retrieve Charles Foley from his cell. Foley appeared with a handkerchief in one hand and wearing a pair of dark trousers and a light pink undershirt. He approached his side of the barred wall, as King stood on the other side with his arms folded and the warrants in hand. Taking a few steps forward, King read the document with a trembling voice as he announced the hanging would occur between noon and two o'clock on Friday, September 23. Foley stood unmoved, intently focused on every word spoken. King then asked if he had anything to say.

"No sir," Foley replied.

The deputy then expressed his regret at having to read the warrant and instructed Foley to prepare for death, as it appeared his case was hopeless.

"I am ready," Foley responded, as he stood with his arms folded. He then turned about and retreated to his cell.

Moses Lewis was then brought forth, wearing a pair of dark denim trousers and an undershirt that only covered his chest and shoulders. King read almost the identical death warrant, again expressing his regret and telling him to prepare for death.

"If it's got to be, it has to be," Lewis replied when asked if he had anything to say. He then turned and walked back to his cell.

If any of the witnesses expected a wailing display of cowardice by the prisoners during the reading of their death warrants, they were greatly disappointed. If anything, the inmates' unyielding nerve in light of their impending deaths caused some of the men to admire the condemned prisoners. The press from that point forward viewed both men as made of sterner stuff than what they previously imagined.

⊕⊕⊕

The Board of Pardons didn't meet to discuss the Foley and Lewis cases until Tuesday afternoon, September 13, and then no action was taken. Foley insisted that he had shot in self-defense. Scores of people, including the entire jury who had found Foley guilty, affixed their signatures to the application seeking a commutation of his sentence. Regarding Lewis, his attorney's argument, flimsy as it was, insisted that his client hadn't committed rape as strictly defined by law. Rather, he had engaged in a consensual affair with the young girl for several years before rape was alleged. Between then and his arrest, he has only guilty of "visiting the girl frequently." The matter was settled three days later when the Board of Pardons refused to recommend a commutation of both sentences.

"I expected such a result," Foley responded when Captain Rennyson told him of the board's decision. "Last Monday, I told the deputy sheriffs that I felt the board would do me up."

By then, the gallows had been disassembled in Yard No. 7 and reassembled in the center of the Colored Yard. It's possible that the attorney who had raised concerns about seeing the gallows from his office window had persuaded parish officials to relocate the contraption to a less conspicuous space. To ensure that no one could witness the executions by climbing a telephone pole or standing atop some other high-rise building in the general proximity, Rennyson planned to hang a tarpaulin across the yard to block the view.

The original two-person trapdoor was then replaced to accommodate only one man at a time. It had been discovered that the old design was too unreliable. Thus, Foley and Lewis would die separately.

In spite of the decision of the Board of Pardons, neither Foley nor his family gave up hope. Foley could get a rehearing before the board, or the governor might read the transcript of his trial. Before Blanchard was elected governor, he served as an associate justice on the Louisiana Supreme Court. Foley believed that if Blanchard was given an opportunity to review the court record, his expertise with the law might persuade him to see things differently. At the very least, Foley and his family planned to spend the next week doing everything in their power to convince the governor to grant a respite. Lewis was less optimistic about his chances.

"Well, the Lord's will be done," Lewis responded to the announcement of the board's decision. "I have made my peace with God, and I am ready to die."

During that era, his crime and race were clearly strikes against him, and he resigned himself to his fate. He later told reporters that he trusted that the Lord had forgiven him. He promised everyone that he would die bravely and expected to go to Heaven. He had lately taken up religion and saw a priest on a weekly basis, having confessed his sins and embraced Catholicism.

On Sunday afternoon, September 18, reporters revisited the condemned prisoners, describing Foley and Lewis as "virtually dying men, although they [were] sound in mind and body and in excellent health."

"It will be murder to hang me," Foley proclaimed. "I killed [Richard] Flynn, yes, but it was in self-defense."

When asked if he had given up hope, he responded no. He intended to forward a letter to Governor Blanchard, who was expected to arrive in New Orleans on Monday evening. The governor planned to attend the Judicial Convention on Tuesday and the City Convention on Wednesday. At the latter event, Democratic Party candidates would be chosen for the upcoming local elections, which corresponded with the November presidential election. With the governor staying at the St. Charles Hotel, five blocks from the prison, Foley hoped his letter would reach the chief executive in time for him to stay his execution.

"The governor is a just man, and in him I may find the relief I seek," Foley explained to the reporters. He was convinced that the governor would see how unjust his punishment was when, in self-defense, he took the life of "Rat Tooth" Flynn.

Charles Foley did not receive the news he so desperately sought until the day before his scheduled execution. Through the efforts of his stepfather, Frank Rhodes, his mother, his wife, and his attorneys, Warren Doyle and Joseph Generelly, the Board of Pardons finally recommended to the governor that a respite be granted to Foley until they could hear some newfound evidence from a previously unknown witness.

On Thursday afternoon, September 22, moments before Governor Blanchard was to board a train for his return trip to Baton Rouge, the board's recommendation reached the station. The governor quickly responded and granted Foley a two-week reprieve, pending the findings of the board.

"Board has recommended a respite for you," one reporter informed Foley after the decision was known.

"Yes?" Foley responded from his cell, as he sighed in great relief at the good news. "God is good, sure enough."

All the other condemned prisoners, except Lewis, offered congratulations to Foley, as he fully expected the Board of Pardons to commute his sentence in the coming days. For his part, Moses Lewis expected to swing on the gallows the following day. Nothing, it seemed, could stop his execution as he spent the last full day of his life high atop the prison.

Down below, a group of African-American prisoners busied themselves with last-minute preparations, which included covering with heavy, white canvas the sides of the yard facing Gravier and Saratoga streets. It was hoped that any curiosity seekers wanting to see the execution from outside the prison walls would be precluded from doing so; it didn't happen.

Standing on the gallows and supervising the workers was a "medium-size, smooth-shaven, heavy-jawed and compactly built white man," as the *Daily Picayune* described the hangman. Wearing dark clothes and a broad-brimmed black alpine hat, and calmly smoking a cigar, the man entertained questions from reporters after they knew what duties he would perform the following day. He winked and called himself Shepard, though his real name was Frank

Johnston. It would be Johnston's first execution at Orleans Parish Prison. He calmly explained how he became an executioner and how he planned to hang Moses Lewis, his eighteenth execution. His matter-of-fact language and nonchalant mannerisms regarding his history of executions took most observers by surprise. These were not traits that reporters were used to seeing in a hangman. The men marveled at his confidence, which had probably won him the job when Captain Rennyson chose him that day.

After his selection, Johnston was allowed to visit the tower that evening. He was eyeing Lewis's size and gaging his weight, along with Foley's. Though Foley had been given a temporary reprieve, Johnston suspected his stay would be short-lived. Prior to leaving the floor, the hangman told Foley, "Good-by, old man; guess I'll be back in two weeks to see how you take it."

Johnston's comment wasn't appreciated by the prisoners, who came to believe he took morbid pleasure in his duties, especially when he cited examples of gruesome executions he had participated in. One such hanging, presumably early in Johnston's career, involved placing a five-eighths–inch-diameter rope around the neck of a 208-pound man and then dropping him nine feet. The hanging produced instant death. But Johnston had miscalculated the height of the fall based upon the prisoner's weight and, compounding his error, had used an undersized rope. The net effect caused the prisoner to be decapitated. Unquestionably, the hangman gave assurances to Captain Rennyson that such a ghastly mistake would never be repeated.

On Friday, September 23, Moses Lewis met death as bravely as any person could, without a whimper in his voice or a tremor in his gait. His pulse was recorded at seventy-two beats per minute just prior to the release of the trapdoor, a remarkable clinical finding for a man moments from death. His newly found faith had finally fortified his resolve to meet his Maker, confident of his place in the afterlife.

"We'll meet in Heaven, Father," Lewis told the assistant rector of St. Joseph Catholic Church, smiling as the pair stood on the gallows' platform. "Yes, my son," Rev. James Devine responded, trying his best to suppress his tears as he gently stroked the condemned man's shoulders. Moments later, the rector took his leave and walked halfway down the steps before stopping to await the cutting of the rope. After binding Lewis's arms and legs and placing the noose around his neck, Johnston pulled a black death cap over his head. As his face disappeared from view, Lewis was seen calmly praying in silence.

At 12:32 P.M., Moses Lewis went to his death as the trapdoor swung down. His body plunged eight feet before the rope snapped his neck, terminating his descent. "His body spun once or twice on the rope's end, and contractions and relaxation of the muscles were noticeable, but these horrors soon ceased," the *Daily Picayune* reported.

Scores of onlookers within the prison walls witnessed Lewis's execution. In spite of the best efforts to shield the hanging from outsiders, it was observed from neighboring structures, including the Hennen Building. Using binoculars, spectators could easily see the execution from high atop its observation deck.

Prior to leaving the tower and seeing the crowds gathering inside the yard and outside the prison, Lewis commented, "There's enough of 'em to look at me die." He was sadly right. It was something that didn't go unnoticed by Lewis Lyons. That day he swore he would have no gawking at his execution.

Lewis's body dangled for ten minutes and fifteen seconds before it was cut down and laid on a table below the gallows. An autopsy performed by Dr. Mioton revealed what was obvious to all. Moses Lewis had died from a fractured neck. The body was transferred to the funeral home of (Widow Albert P.) Boyer and (James) Taylor Company, located at 1309 St. Philip Street, and later interred at St. Roch Cemetery. Survived by his parents, Joseph and Caroline Lewis, and siblings, Moses H. Lewis was thirty-two years old.

In spite of the many sexual assaults he perpetrated upon his victim, Elizabeth Kientz, the young girl went on with her life, eventually marrying William Lobrano on October 26, 1910, in New Orleans. The couple had three children. In early 1921, the Lobrano family relocated to Los Angeles, California, and was soon joined by Elizabeth's father, Victor, her stepmother, Amelia Stoll Kientz, and their six children. Her father died in February 1926 at age sixty-four. With a long history of rheumatic heart disease and having experienced repeated strokes over the years, Elizabeth passed away on August 20, 1973, the result of congestive heart failure. She was buried three days later at Inglewood Park Cemetery, in Inglewood, California, where she last resided. Survived by two of her children (her husband and middle child died in 1957 and 1965, respectively), Elizabeth Kientz Lobrano was eighty-three years old.

The fate of Charles Foley wasn't known until Wednesday, October 5, when the Board of Pardons refused to act on the evidence brought before them. Though Doyle was able to secure the testimony of an eyewitness who stated Foley had shot his victim in self-defense, the prosecution produced a witness who countered that account. In the end, the board refused to accept any of the new testimonies and voted to uphold the original murder conviction. Foley's family traveled to Baton Rouge seeking an audience with the governor, but the chief executive declined to counter the actions of his Board of Pardons. Foley's execution was set for Friday, October 7.

Like Lewis two weeks before, Foley bravely faced the situation before him. "At no time through the dragging hours leading up to the doom moment did the young prisoner show the faintest sign of breaking down," the *Daily Picayune* reported. He even joked with the prison guards that he would have to change his voter registration from the Second Ward, where his family currently lived, to the Fourth Ward, where he was to be buried.

At 12:36 P.M., Foley plunged into eternity, dropping six feet. "His body paused in its flight, with a jolt and suddenness sufficient to fracture the neck bone, and death must have been easy and nearly instantaneous," the *Daily Picayune* reported. Again, it seemed that Frank Johnston, the executioner, had done his job proficiently.

Charles Foley (1904). (Courtesy NOLA.com/The *Times-Picayune*)

The body dangled for twelve more minutes before the autopsy was performed. The body was then released and transferred to Patrick McMahon, an undertaker; his business was located at 1114 Dryades Street. Foley's funeral later took place at the home of his stepfather and mother, 919 Poeyfarre Street, with the burial at St. Patrick Cemetery No. 2 on City Park Avenue. Leaving behind his wife and a four-year-old daughter, Charles Foley was twenty-six years old.

The presidential and local elections that occurred the following month ousted some of the elected and appointed members of the criminal-justice system in Orleans Parish. Terrence Reilley, the current criminal sheriff who was not nominated for reelection by the Democratic Party, was replaced by Matthew Long. During the first week of December, Long appointed Richard Meredith the new warden of Orleans Parish Prison, replacing Captain Rennyson. In addition, Luzenberg failed to be nominated to the Democratic ticket. In his stead, J. Porter Parker won the election in a three-way race for Orleans Parish district attorney. And finally, Dr. Joseph O'Hara replaced Dr. Richard as the parish coroner.

November 1904 was also important in terms of the remaining three condemned prisoners at Orleans Parish Prison. Sometime during the month, Sejours's case was argued before the Louisiana Supreme Court. Meanwhile, representing Lyons, Generelly and Doyle finally presented their arguments for a new trial on November 12, followed by Sparo's attorney on November 26. Sejours learned his fate on December 5, when the Supreme Court affirmed the lower court's judgment. On December 19, Lyons and Sparo learned that the court had also sustained their original verdicts. Only a commutation of their sentences by the Board of Pardons or governor could save them now from the executioner. Lewis Lyons had no illusions about his fate, though his attorneys continued to work feverishly to spare him from the hangman.

Chapter Fifteen

THE DOOMED TOWER

I want to be buried in the old cemetery in Carrollton.

Lewis W. Lyons

On Saturday, December 17, 1904, two days before the Louisiana Supreme Court rendered its opinion regarding the Lyons and Sparo appeals, the heralds of the upcoming Christmas holiday season were heard everywhere in the city, as young boys blew their tin horns and the sounds of celebratory fireworks filled the air. Virtually everyone in New Orleans was getting into the Christmas spirit, except the three remaining condemned men housed in the prison's doomed tower. With nothing to look forward to, the prisoners could only reflect upon Christmases past, though for the men those memories just added to their despondency.

"Have I any Christmas memories?" Sejours repeated a reporter's question. "Yes, I have. No particular ones, but still, recollections that aren't pleasant to me now. I remember how, when a little boy, I always welcomed Santa Claus—he was so good to me then, and I was his firm believer. But how can I compare those days to these—the days of childhood and freedom, to the days of sorrow and a prison?"

Lyons was less inclined to speak to reporters, stating he was in no mood to reminiscence about past holidays. But he seemed to relish the years when he was a successful businessman "in a home of comfort and plenty," the *Daily Picayune* recounted.

Sparo was even more reluctant to talk. Nervous and easily agitated, he paced the corridor in front of his cell, with his head bowed to his chest and his hands clasped behind his back as reporters peppered him with questions. "The very mention of the word Christmas seemed to throw the convicted felon into a high state of nervousness," one reporter wrote.

"Me know nodin', Christimus," Sparo uttered with a thick Italian accent. "He bad time for me." He promptly walked back into his cell. The interview was over.

In spite of the expressed gloom, by Christmas Day parts of the prison were lavishly decorated for the holiday. Wreaths made with evergreens and embellished with cotton balls covered the front gate and strings of moss adorned the front corridor leading to the bullring, which itself was decorated with ropes of moss, cotton, palmetto leaves, and pine needles. Even some of the barred walls in the tower were wrapped with moss and sprinkled with balls of cotton. Adding to the festive mood, Christmas fell on Sunday and Sundays were a normal visiting day.

When Mass was celebrated that morning in the chapel, only Sejours chose to attend. Sparo, who was Catholic, declined, and Lyons's Protestant leaning excluded him, though he didn't attend any religious service that day. For lunch, everyone feasted on "turkey, cranberry sauce, rice, potatoes, and other delicious things," according to the *Daily Picayune,* "along with a big cup of wine and plate of fancy cakes [for dessert]."

On Tuesday, January 3, 1905, Joseph Generelly filed a petition with the Supreme Court seeking a rehearing for Lyons. Sparo's attorney did the same, though Thomas D. Flynn, Sejours's attorney, chose a different route. Knowing it was pointless to do so, Flynn instead prepared a lengthy petition to the Board of Pardons seeking clemency for his client. There was ample evidence to show that Sejours had not acted with malice or forethought when he murdered Robert Reid instead of his intended victim. Regardless of the circumstances, this was not a case of premeditated or capital murder. Thus, Flynn hoped the board would commute his sentence. The Board of Pardons planned to meet later that month to decide the matter.

In the meantime, on January 14, Governor Blanchard fixed the execution date for Louis Sejours for Friday, February 17. Sheriff Long had been expecting the arrival of Sejours's death warrant since the beginning of the year, so he was surprised to learn about it from a newspaper reporter at his office, rather than in an official communique from governor.

When told by reporters of his execution date, Sejours, standing at the door of his cell, responded, "I have nothing to say for publication." Calm and unconcerned, he whistled a bit and continued to chew on a toothpick.

Lyons was lying on his bed with his back to his cell door, smoking and reading the newspaper, when he heard the conversation a short distance away. Turning his head slightly to better hear, he nonchalantly returned to his paper after learning the date.

It wasn't until the afternoon of January 28 that the Board of Pardons met regarding the application filed on Louis Sejours's behalf. To the great joy of Sejours and his family, the board recommended to the governor that his death sentence be commuted to life imprisonment. Likely aiding in their decision were Luzenberg's expressed second thoughts about the initial charge. Months after the trial, he commented that he never expected the jury to convict Sejours of capital murder. After much reflection, he came to believe that the crime lacked malice or premeditation.

Governor Blanchard didn't receive the recommendation until three days later, and it didn't became official until February 13. Nevertheless, by then the commutation of sentence was only a formality. It was rare that a governor would counter the board's recommendation, though prior to that time the governor had expressed opposition to granting any form of leniency. Only after a careful review of the record did he change his mind.

"God bless you! Thank Heavens for this news," Sejours said, with tears in his eyes, when Sheriff Long told him of the board's recommendation.

After his death sentence was commuted, Sejours was transferred out of the tower. On April 1, 1905, he was relocated to the state penitentiary in Baton Rouge to serve out his life sentence. In March 1909 he began to apply for a pardon, without success. It wasn't until Sejours' third attempt, in October 1916, that the Board of Pardons finally recommended his release for time served for the 1903 murder of Robert Reid. Sejours returned to New Orleans, eventually remarried a widow, Eugenie Casteix Yrle, and lived an uneventful life in the city until his death on February 3, 1946, from respiratory failure, exacerbated by congestive heart failure. Leaving behind his wife and at least one son from his previous marriage, Louis Henry Sejours was seventy-one years old.

Lewis Lyons and Samuel Sparo would never live to see old age. Their date with the gallows was sealed on January 31, 1905, after the Louisiana Supreme Court refused both men's request for a rehearing. Within a few days of the news, Generelly and Doyle sought a writ of mandamus from Judge Chretien, which he refused. There would be no repeat impaneling of a lunatic commission for Lyons, though both attorneys refused to give up.

Their next move came on February 11 when they sought immediate relief with the Supreme Court, asking the jurists to order Judge Chretien to show cause as to why he had refused to issue the writ. But the following day, the court sustained Judge Chretien's refusal. Lyons's last option was to appeal to the Board of Pardons and hope they commuted his death sentence as they had done with Louis Sejours.

Knowing that options were running out for both condemned prisoners,

Governor Blanchard sought their court transcripts. As a former jurist, he wanted to review both cases before fixing a date for each man's execution. On Saturday, February 25, confident that Lyons had received a fair trial, Blanchard set the fourth Friday in March as his execution date. Only the Board of Pardons could interfere with carrying out the governor's warrant.

Captain Meredith received the telegraph from the governor's office that evening but chose to delay the news, wanting Lyons to get one more good night's rest. He had every intention of delivering the bad news in person the next morning but circumstances intervened.

As was Lyons's routine upon awakening, he asked the guards for a copy of the *Daily Picayune*. Each morning he scanned the pages for any news about his case. The guards knew about the execution date before giving him the paper. As Lyons flipped through the pages, the guards watched for his reaction. On the third page, he read what he undoubtedly had prepared for. Lewis Lyons was to hang on March 24, 1905, unless his mother's efforts prevailed. Behind the scenes, she had been tirelessly preparing a petition for a commutation of his sentence or pardon from the Board of Pardons.

As was characteristic of Lyons, when he learned the date he reacted without worry or bother and continued to scan the newspaper until Mrs. O'Connor brought him breakfast. He carried on a lively conversation with her, as if it was any other day.

Sparo's sour mood quickly lifted and he smiled for the first time in a long while after he realized the governor had yet to set his date with the hangman. He even went so far as to coax the prison cat into his cell, where he surrendered a portion of his breakfast to the animal. The feline was probably placed in the tower to take care on any rodent problems. Occasionally during mealtimes, the creature would enter a prisoner's cell, searching for leftovers.

After breakfast, Sparo was allowed to go in Lyons's cell to offer comfort, but Lyons needed no consolation and eventually begged him away. Besides, Sparo spoke terrible English, and Lyons didn't speak or understand a word of Italian. Unwanted, Sparo returned to his cell and amused himself by talking to the cat, which didn't seem to care what language he spoke, as long as she was fed.

Down below in the Colored Yard, the gruesome gallows that had ended the lives of Moses Lewis and Charles Foley remained as a stark reminder that the structure would not be torn down and stored away until two more prisoners met their deaths. Meanwhile, the African-American prisoners who used the exercise yard were often seen on warm days sunbathing on the gallows' platform or hanging their laundry on the wooden beams and railing to dry. It was a peculiar sight for anyone peering down from the tower.

On Wednesday morning, March 1, 1905, Charity R. Wilson Lyons, Lewis Lyons's mother, unexpectedly died at her home, 3718 Pitt Street, where she lived with one of her daughters, Miss Chattie. Ill for some time and undoubtedly strained by her son's situation, Mrs. Lyons passed away from heart disease at age seventy-three. Lyons was notified of his mother's death, but his reaction wasn't reported to the newspapers. Mrs. Lyons's funeral was held at her home but delayed until Friday afternoon, as one of her daughters, Mary Lyons Decan Jones, who resided with her husband and family in Philadelphia, needed time to travel to the city. Mrs. Lyons was later interred at Lafayette Cemetery No. 1 in the family tomb with her late husband.

The day after the funeral, which Lyons did not attend, Sheriff Long, Captain Meredith, Chief Deputy Sheriff Patrick King, and several reporters went to the tower, where King read Lyons's death warrant, which had finally been delivered to the sheriff. "Lyons listened attentively, but took the event just as stoically as he had all matters pertaining to his trial and proceedings in court," the *Daily Picayune* reported. Meanwhile, Sparo stood at his cell door and listened, knowing he would soon hear the same pronouncement.

"I have nothing at all to say," Lyons responded when asked if he had any comments.

Afterwards, Lyons returned to Cell No. 1, which had been assigned to him sometime following the previous year's executions. (Sparo was moved to Cell No. 3.) Back in his confined quarters, Lyons immersed himself in reading a book, which was a passion of his. Besides his daily walks in the exercise yard, Lyons loved playing cards with the guards and developed a reputation as a fine poker player who won more times than he lost.

On March 11, after completing his review of the Sparo transcript, the governor fixed Friday, April 21 as his execution date. It was later changed to April 28, when it was realized that the original date fell on Good Friday.

On Friday, March 17, one week before Lyons's scheduled execution, the Board of Pardons met at the office of Attorney General Walter Guion. Along with Lieutenant Governor Sanders and Judge Chretien, the board heard from Dr. LeMonnier and Miss Chattie, summoned by Generelly and Doyle on behalf of their client. Dr. LeMonnier reiterated what he had testified to during the trial, along with supplying the board with an update on Lyons's mental state. He continued to insist that Lyons was insane.

Miss Chattie then gave an impassioned defense for why her brother shouldn't be hanged. She never asked for leniency from the board, but only justice instead, insisting that he was insane and should not be executed. But she realized that if the board didn't commute his sentence, then "God's will be done."

The Board of Pardons decided two cases that day, refusing to intervene in Lyons's original sentence but commuting a death sentence to life in imprisonment for an African-American. Since the latter crime occurred in Red River Parish, Judge Chretien played no part in the unanimous decision; that was left to Judge Porter, the sitting trial judge.

Miss Chattie and her oldest sister, Mary Jones, wasted no time after receiving the disappointing news. Governor Blanchard happened to be in the city, staying again at the St. Charles Hotel. The day after the board's decision, the sisters sought an audience with the chief executive, but the meeting proved fruitless. The governor had already reviewed Lyons's case and refused to counter the decision of the Board of Pardons.

⌖ ⌖ ⌖

Lyons spent his last Monday visiting with his brother, Wilson, and various members of the clergy, including those of the Episcopal and Catholic faiths, though he aligned with the former as a Protestant. Rev. Ernest Rennie, the curate of St. Paul's Episcopal Church, had become an almost daily visitor to the tower, along with Rev. Jacob Helinski, another assistant rector serving at St. Joseph Catholic Church, and the Sisters of the Order of Mercy. Reverend Helinski had been the spiritual advisor for Charles Foley and continued his priestly rounds after his execution.

Lyons's attitude about organized religion had dramatically shifted away from skepticism now that his death approached. He warmly greeted those members of the clergy who visited him. During that week, Lyons was particularly anxious to see Rev. Alexander Gordon Bakewell, the curate of Trinity Episcopal Chapel on South Rampart Street, but the minister was suffering from influenza at the time. Rev. John Miller would eventually visit in his place.

For his part, Samuel Sparo spent most of his time praying and seemed to have found great consolation in religion, as Lyons had done. Because of his obvious language barrier, Sparo was visited by a priest who spoke fluent Italian.

During Monday's visit with his brother, Lyons inadvertently forgot to inform him about his burial wishes. Not wanting to wait until the next scheduled visit on Wednesday, Lyons penned a letter that evening. "The missive's brevity and pointedness showed the practical man," the *Daily Picayune* stated. "Its plain expression made clear the stoic, and its whole tenor was in accord with the known temperament of the writer." If ever there was proof that Lewis Lyons was sane, his concise, rationally written letter about his burial wishes was it.

"I want to be buried in the old cemetery in Carrollton," Lyons wrote to his brother. "The aged sexton of the cemetery knows the exact spot where I want my body to lie. Find him, and let my burial be as I wish it." He most likely wanted to be buried near his firstborn, a victim of the city's yellow-fever epidemic of 1897.

Lyons passed the letter to the watchman, who forwarded it to Captain Meredith for his approval. All written communications had to be reviewed by the warden before being sent out. Satisfied that the letter contained no infractions, Meredith placed it in a stamped envelope and had it delivered to the post office on Tuesday morning. Lyons appeared cheerful and relieved that his burial wishes were now public knowledge. The *Daily Picayune* published his letter on Wednesday morning.

As a precautionary measure, Sheriff Long shut down all general visitations to the tower as Lyons's execution date approached. Only the prisoner's immediate family, clergy, and members of the press were allowed to visit him. In addition, the standard twelve-hour shift was decreased to eight hours, with each prisoner assigned a watchman who sat inside the prisoner's cell, with a second officer stationed in the corridor.

When Sheriff Long arrived at the tower for his early-morning inspection on Wednesday, March 22, he found Lyons asleep and instructed the guards not to disturb him. The previous night had been a restless one for Lyons, keeping him from falling asleep until the predawn hours. He apparently had eaten something for supper that didn't agree with him.

Sometime after the sheriff's departure, Lyons awoke and appeared nervous, an odd behavior for Lyons as the guards had never seen him anxious before. In any event, by the time Mrs. O'Connor served him breakfast, he seemed to have snapped out of his uneasiness.

Captain Meredith entered the tower while Lyons was in the midst of eating his light breakfast. He was never a gluttonous eater. The captain greeted both prisoners, and they gestured back. As the captain was about to leave, Lyons called to him. Lyons requested that his few remaining hours be kept as quiet as possible, especially without newspaper reporters. He had no objections to being visited by family members and, by inference, members of the clergy, but being deluged by the press was a different matter. Captain Meredith agreed to honor his wishes, and Lyons thanked him in advance.

Late in the morning, after Lyons had read the newspaper and visited with his jail keepers, his brother, Wilson, and sister, Miss Chattie, arrived. Captain Meredith allowed them to stay as long as they wished, contrary to standard visitation rules. Lyons's wife, Clara, arrived after their departure but didn't stay long, greatly anguished by the visit.

On this day, Mrs. O'Connor had the unenviable duty of purchasing the clothes that Lyons would wear to his execution and be buried in. During his morning visit, Wilson Lyons had given her his brother's measurements and the money necessary to purchase the clothing and footwear.

On Thursday, March 23, last-minute preparation for the following day's execution was made in the Colored Yard. The gallows, which had originally been placed in the center of the brick-lined enclosure, was manually dragged to its new location at the corner of Saratoga and Gravier streets. It was hoped that this position would greatly hamper anyone's attempt to see the execution from outside the prison walls. Captain Meredith, experiencing his first execution as warden, didn't want a repeat of the spectacle observed when Lewis and Foley were executed. Scores of outsiders were still able to view the executions, in spite of the heavy canvas hung to block the scene.

Lyons also requested that his execution not turn into a carnival show, as the others had. The previous year, Captain Rennyson had issued numerous passes, allowing hundreds of people into the exercise yard to witness the hangings. For Lyons's sake, Captain Meredith put an end to that practice. The only visitor passes issued were for the fifteen state witnesses who were mandated by law to attend. These gentlemen would be ushered inside by way of the second-floor bridge that connected the prison with the courthouse. Additionally, the front gate on Gravier Street would be locked and the entire city block around the prison roped off after Friday's provisions were brought inside.

To prevent unnecessary eyeing from within the prison, all prisoners were locked inside their cells on the day of the execution. A canvas screen was placed around the two open ends of the gallows, to prevent everyone not directly connected to the hanging from seeing it unfold.

On the last full day of his life, Lyons woke after a restful night, having received a shot of whiskey from Sheriff Long the previous evening. The sheriff had learned of Lyons's uneasiness the night before. Upon rising, Lyons took a quick bath and then glanced over the morning newspaper while awaiting the arrival of his breakfast. Meanwhile, an African-American trustee appeared at his cell and handed him a morning "bracer." Sheriff Long wanted his prisoner to feel at ease throughout the day.

Though Thursday wasn't an official visitor's day at the prison, Captain Meredith allowed Lyons's family upstairs. Wilson and Miss Chattie, escorted by the warden and Reverend Miller, arrived at the tower at ten o'clock. During their time together, Lyons showed genuine interest towards the minister, who read passages from the Bible and recited various prayers. Lyons's siblings were often moved to tears, especially his sister, who did her best to hide her grief so as not to worsen the anguish that everyone felt.

At some point, Lyons bid a final farewell to his siblings, with Reverend Miller remaining to await the arrival of Mrs. Lyons and her five children. The warden escorted them in at two o'clock, and they visited for nearly four hours, during which time Clara convinced her husband to be baptized by Reverend Miller. During the family's tearful visit, two nuns from the Order of Mercy arrived to spiritually comfort the prisoner. By then, the nuns were well known to the prison population and beloved by all, including Lyons.

Likely, it was mutually agreed that none of Lyons's family would visit the following day. Normally, a Catholic-affiliated condemned prisoner would attend Mass with loved ones on his execution day. But since Lyons was not Catholic, no formal religious service (with family members present) was scheduled for Friday.

Near the end of the family visit, Clara implored the warden to allow her to kiss her husband goodbye. Moved by her appeal, and knowing this was her final visit, Captain Meredith discarded prison protocol and allowed Lyons to enter the gallery, where he was permitted to embrace and kiss his wife and children a final time. Lyons's oldest daughter, Chattie, nearly collapsed from her grief.

"Be good, Lewis," Clara gently admonished her husband, as the family departed the tower. Lyons stated that he would.

After their tearful departure, Lyons was warmly greeted by Mrs. O'Connor, who delivered his last evening meal. Surely suspecting that it had been an emotional and trying day for him, the prison matron asked Lyons how he was doing.

"I'm feeling all right," he responded in typical fashion.

By that hour, all preparations were nearly complete in the Colored Yard, including picking the executioner from among three applicants who sought the job. One of the candidates was the local African-American who had tried to convince Captain Rennyson of his skill with his gift of a miniature gallows. Skeptical of the man's ability, Captain Meredith awarded the job to Frank Johnston, who had proven himself a worthy executioner during the Lewis and Foley hangings.

Lyons retired to his bed later that evening, trying his best to fall asleep. It's not known if the sheriff supplied him with another nightcap. If he did, the alcoholic beverage failed to achieve its desired effect. Wracked with emotion and perhaps harboring some last-minute regrets, Lyons spent a near-sleepless night as the seconds ticked away until that fateful moment when he would be required to climb the steps of the gallows.

Epilogue

In Memoriam

I've only known two prisoners who didn't repent.

Mary O'Connor

After the execution of Lewis Lyons, Samuel Sparo was moved to his cell. Sparo's prior cage lay near the Saratoga Street end of the corridor and was, for unexplained reasons, poorly lighted. Sparo welcomed his new location, in spite of the smaller size. Now that he was the sole occupant of the tower, Sparo had free rein of the corridor when allowed out of his cell. He also became the supreme benefactor of the prison cat, affectionately named Miss Kitty, whom he fed on a daily basis with a bowl of milk and whatever leftovers he had. She became his constant companion.

Captain Meredith feared that some outside force might attempt to murder his prisoner before Sparo's execution, scheduled for Friday, April 28, 1905. Two days before the hanging, gossip reached Sheriff Long that the Mafia had hired a sharpshooter to assassinate Sparo. If the assassin was positioned atop a neighboring building, it was feared he could shoot Sparo while he exercised in the yard or, later, while he stood on the platform of the gallows. There was even concern that he might be shot while in his cell. Cell No. 1 was at an angle with one of the windows on the west side of the top floor, from "which a well-directed bullet [from Franklin Street] might speed," according to the *Daily Picayune.* Nothing came of the murder plot, except for some men placing bets that Sparo would die from a bullet instead of a rope. Nevertheless, just to be safe, the police ordered that building tops and galleries in the general vicinity be kept clear of people. In addition, Sparo was moved at midnight on Friday from Cell No. 1 to No. 2. The latter cage was out of reach of a would-be assassin's aim, with the courthouse blocking any other potential sightline from the north side.

Death by poison was another concern. If truth be told, it was the primary reason why Sparo was moved twelve hours before his scheduled execution.

Samuel Sparo (1905). (Courtesy NOLA.com/The *Times-Picayune*)

Sheriff Long suspected that Sparo was hiding something deleterious to his health in his old cell, smuggled in by some means. He feared that the prisoner would take the substance at the last moment, though nothing poisonous was ever found in Cell No. 1.

The poisoning of his food by outside forces was another possibility, so great care was taken during food preparation. Only Mrs. O'Connor was allowed to handle and prepare his food after the staples were brought inside the prison. No other outside food was allowed in for his consumption. In addition, when Sparo developed a severe cold the last week of March, only his doctor's prescribed medication could be administered; no home remedies were permitted.

As his execution date approached (the Board of Pardons refused to commute his sentence four days before the scheduled hanging), Sparo spent most of his time reading his prayer book, visiting with his priest and nuns, or conversing in broken English with Mrs. O'Connor during her rounds. On the morning of his death, he was allowed to attend Mass in the chapel with his wife, children, and a niece, where sorrowful farewells were exchanged. He hoped that his religious faith would finally strengthen his resolve to meet death not with a whimper but with steadfastness and dignity. It's possible he didn't want his loved ones to witness his march to the gallows; none attended his execution. But his resolve to bravely face death broke at the last moment while he stood on the gallows. Quivering in mortal fear, Sparo nearly lost his balance as he suddenly leaned against Captain Meredith for support. The stumble caused one of the nearby deputies to momentarily stand on the trapdoor with Sparo.

"Look out! Stand off the trap," Frank Johnston shouted to the deputy, who quickly moved away. Holding the cleaver in his hand, Johnston was moments away from severing the supporting rope that held the trapdoor in place.

Sparo's descent into eternity began precisely at 12:07 P.M. As with the previous three executions, Johnston's skill at terminating life was masterful. "An awful cry, muffled and dismal, came from under the blackcap as the body shot through seven feet of space, and the cry continued for the fraction of a moment and was smothered in a gurgling groan as the rope stayed the body's flight," one eyewitness reported.

Sparo's death was instantaneous, but the corpse dangled for twenty-one minutes before being cut down. Dr. O'Hara, the parish coroner, performed an autopsy. The neck was found to be fractured and the spinal cord completely severed. On Saratoga Street, Mrs. Sparo and her weeping children waited for the body to be brought out and placed in a waiting carriage for transport to Carrollton Cemetery. Sparo had asked his wife to bury him near his friend, Lewis Lyons.

The hanging produced some notoriety for the Sicilian native and for the hangman. The *Daily Picayune* described the event as the first Mafia execution in the United States. Leaving behind his wife and four children, the two youngest being twenty-month-old twin boys, Samuel Sparo was forty years old.

In spite of the tragedy that befell the relatives of Lewis Lyons, the family endured, though Lyons's sister, Miss Chattie, was the first to pass from this world after her brother's execution. Chattie Lyons was born in the city on June 30, 1865. For some odd reason, she was often listed in the newspapers as *Miss* Chattie Lyons. In reality, Chattie had married William R. Fagan on November 8, 1888. The couple never had children. By the time of the 1900 U.S. Census, Chattie was living with her sister Alice and brother-in-law Nadin Howard Moody and was listed as divorced. The shame of the divorce probably compelled Chattie to assume her maiden name. She eventually moved in with her mother and resided at the Pitt Street address until her death. Chattie E. Lyons died on November 30, 1908, at age forty-three from an unspecified form of cancer. She was interred in the Lyons family tomb in Lafayette Cemetery No. 1, where her parents were buried.

Clara Lyons, Lewis Lyons's wife, died on September 6, 1926, at her residence, 8322 Poplar Street, from chronic heart disease, kidney failure, and edema of the lungs. She was interred the following day in Carrollton Cemetery, likely at the gravesite of her husband and oldest child. Survived by three of her six children, Clara Wootan Lyons was seventy years old.

Wilson Lyons, the older brother, died on July 4, 1935, from a combination of heart disease and pneumonia at his residence, 1918 Tulane Avenue. Born in New Orleans on April 12, 1857, he married Mary Buckley on March 19, 1888. The couple was childless. On May 14, 1906, Mary died of heart disease at the age of forty-one and was buried in St. Patrick Cemetery. Within a year of her death, Wilson married Alice Bertin, though no children were born from that union either.

Wilson's funeral occurred the day following his death, and he also was interred in the Lyons family tomb. Leaving behind his wife, Wilson Joseph Wesley Lyons was seventy-eight years old. (Alice died as a patient in Charity Hospital on December 5, 1936, a victim of striatal syndrome and pseudo-pneumonia. Interred with her husband in the Lyons family tomb, Alice Bertin Lyons was fifty-five years old. Her maiden name was misspelled *Berlin* on the tomb.)

Lyons's executioner, Frank Johnston, quietly passed into obscurity. How many men he executed over his lifetime is not known, though by January 1911 he had placed a noose around the neck of forty-three condemned men. Johnston died on February 15, 1953, from cancer of the larynx, being a patient at Charity Hospital for the last three months of his life. He always loved a good cigar. A thirty-year inhabitant of the city, he resided at 1238 Dauphine Street at the time of his death and was employed as a night watchman. Single and buried at Cedar Rest Cemetery in Bay St. Louis, Mississippi, Francis "Frank" Elsworth Johnston was seventy-seven years old, though his death certificate incorrectly listed him as two years older.

Fernand DeRancé and Richard Kirwin, the officers who arrested Lewis Lyons that fateful day in July 1895, died within five months of one another. On January 15, 1908, DeRancé died unexpectedly from influenza at his residence, 1535 North Claiborne Avenue. Kirwin passed away on May 27 at his residence, 1809 Carrollton Avenue, from chronic kidney failure. At the time of their deaths, both men were still members of the police department, though they had long before severed their partnership.

Fernand DeRancé was born in the city in April 1852, the son of Dr. Henri DeRancé and Emma Lacoste. His father was a prominent physician in New Orleans and served for a time as coroner. Depending on the year, DeRancé's forename was listed in the U.S. Census, newspapers, or city directory as either *Ferdinand* or *Fernand,* with his surname spelled *DeRancé, De Rancé, de Rancé,* or *Rancé.* Some sources deleted the accent.

DeRancé joined the police force in 1884, after working for a number of years as a clerk at a cotton press. Five years later, he was appointed detective. In one of his many noteworthy criminal cases, he gathered evidence after the January 1889 murder of twelve-year-old Juliette Dietsh, the unfortunate victim of depraved mesmerist Dr. Etienne Deschamps. On October 25, 1905, when Victor Flotte, chief of detectives, unexpectedly died, DeRancé was promoted to his position, serving in that capacity until his death.

Troubled for a number of years with obesity and heart disease that left him barely able to walk, he contracted grippe (an archaic term for the flu) a few days before his death. DeRancé was granted a leave of absence in order to recover his health and strength. Never married, he planned a short vacation in Covington, across Lake Pontchartrain from New Orleans. At 9:45 A.M. on January 15, his sister found him dead, sitting in a comfortable position in his chair, as if sleeping. She had gone to his room to remind him of his intended trip. His funeral service was conducted the afternoon of January 16 at Sacred Heart of Jesus Catholic Church on Canal Street, with the burial in St. Louis Cemetery No. 2. Fernand DeRancé was fifty-five years old.

Richard "Dick" Kirwin was born in the city in August 1855 to John and Mary Kirwin, natives of Ireland who immigrated to the States in 1846. He worked as a house painter before joining the police force in January 1877, rising to the rank of corporal before resigning his position. Whatever the reason behind his resignation, he soon rejoined the force as a patrolman, married twenty-two-year-old Marie Cavanagh in 1878, and was appointed detective four years later. At the time of his death he was serving as the assistant chief of police, a position created after the death of Fernand DeRancé by his successor, James Reynolds.

In poor health for some time before his death, Kirwin left behind his wife and two grown children. Interred with Masonic rites in Metairie Cemetery, Richard Henry Kirwin was fifty-two years old.

Richard Kirwin (1908). (Courtesy NOLA.com/The *Times-Picayune*)

Of the sheriffs and prison wardens who served while Lewis Lyons was incarcerated, Sheriff Terrence Reilley was the first official to pass away, dying of a cerebral hemorrhage (stroke) at his residence, 1830 Canal Street. Shortly after midnight on July 29, 1918, Reilley rose from his bed to get a drink of water and minutes later was stricken and then died. As he was in good health otherwise, his death was unexpected.

Terrence Reilley was born in Ireland in May 1848, immigrating to the States as a young boy with his parents, who settled in New Orleans. After his formal education, he earned a living for a number of years as a tinsmith before switching to law enforcement. He served as a deputy under Sheriff John Fitzpatrick (1878-80) and during that time partnered with Remy Klock, a rising star in the department. In 1881, he was appointed docket clerk of the Louisiana Court of Appeals, serving until 1892, when he was appointed inspector of weights and measures. When Klock was non-sequentially reelected criminal sheriff in April 1900, he chose Reilley as his chief deputy. Klock's unexpected death the following November triggered Reilley's appointment to his unexpired term by Governor Heard. After leaving the sheriff's department, he worked a variety of jobs, including as a drayman, warehouseman, and clerk.

In February 1874, Reilley married Margaret King and from that union had seven children, including Catherine. She married Archibald Rennyson, who served as the prison warden during Reilley's term as sheriff. Reilley was also the brother-in-law of Matthew Long, who succeeded him as criminal sheriff of Orleans Parish. Long married his sister, Mary Reilley.

Reilley's funeral took place the afternoon of his death, with services conducted at St. Joseph Catholic Church. He was interred in Lafayette

Sheriff Terrence Reilley (1900). (Courtesy NOLA.com/The *Times-Picayune*)

Cemetery No. 1. Survived by three children (his wife had died in February 1914), Terrence M. Reilley, Sr., was seventy years old.

Capt. Richard Meredith, who served as Orleans Parish Prison warden during the final months of Lyons's incarceration, died of congestive heart disease at Hotel Dieu Hospital on September 2, 1928. He was born in New Orleans in January 1865 to John Meredith and Julia Kelleher. His first affiliation with law enforcement was as a court officer from 1888 to 1891, serving under Judge William B. Murphy of the First Recorder's Court. Under Sheriff Klock, he served as a deputy from 1892 to 1896 and again from 1900 until 1904 under Klock and Reilley. In December 1904, Reilley appointed him warden, a position he held until 1920. Meredith ran unsuccessfully for sheriff in 1920 and 1925, then served as the superintendent of the Orleans Parish levee board. At the time of his death he was a deputy state tax collector and resided at 4025 Cleveland Avenue. Meredith married Sidonia "Kate" Gomez on April 17, 1894, and from that union had seven children.

Capt. Richard Meredith (1912). (Courtesy NOLA.com/The *Times-Picayune*)

His funeral service, conducted at St. Patrick Catholic Church the day following his death, was attended by hundreds of city, parish, and state officials, as well as ex-inmates of the parish prison who remembered his kindness while serving as warden. Interred in St. Patrick Cemetery No. 3 and survived by his wife and five children, Richard Meredith was sixty-three years old.

Sheriff Matthew Long, who oversaw the executions of Lewis Lyons and Samuel Sparo, collapsed on Sunday morning, January 19, 1930, while attending Mass at St. Joseph Catholic Church. Taken to Charity Hospital several blocks away, he was pronounced dead a short time later. His death was attributed to chronic myocarditis with acute dilation of the heart.

Matthew Long was born in New Orleans on March 5, 1855, to Nicholas J. Long and Catherine Ryan, both natives of Ireland. Schooled at St. Joseph's School (for boys) and St. Mary's College (a high school) before finishing his formal education at Jesuits' College in New Orleans, he started his career at the Port of New Orleans, rising to manage a section of one of the municipal

Sheriff Matthew Long (1912). (Courtesy NOLA.com/The *Times-Picayune*)

district's wharves. He took a keen interest in politics and became a prominent member of the local Democratic Party. In November 1904, he was elected criminal sheriff of Orleans Parish and was reelected four times in succession. After leaving office, he served as a deputy in the state tax office until his retirement in 1925. Long married Mary Agnes Reilley on March 8, 1877, and from that union had nine children. At the time of his death he resided at 1912 Tulane Avenue.

Funeral services were conducted two days after his death at St. Joseph Catholic Church and he was interred in the Long-Lannan tomb in Metairie Cemetery. Survived by seven children (his wife died in April 1896), Matthew J. Long, Sr., was seventy-four years old.

Capt. Archibald Rennyson, the prison warden who accompanied Lewis Lyons on numerous visits to Charity Hospital, was pronounced dead at his home, 513 North St. Patrick Street, at 3:00 A.M. on April 23, 1947. He suffered a fatal coronary thrombosis (or occlusion) and acute myocarditis. He had a long history of arteriosclerotic heart disease.

Archibald "Archie" Rennyson was born in New Orleans in May 1870 to Henry Rennyson, a native of Ireland, and Elizabeth Myatt from England. His father came to the States as a young boy and was a prominent foundry man in the city up to the time of his death in August 1896. Archie took up his father's profession by 1890, working as a patternmaker and machinist. On July 19, 1894, he married Catherine Reilley and from that union had five children. Within three years, Rennyson entered into a partnership with his brother-in-law, Terrence Reilley, Jr., operating a furniture store at 236 South Rampart Street. When his father-in-law became criminal sheriff in November 1900, he was appointed warden of the parish prison, serving one four-year term.

From 1905 until 1920, when he was reappointed warden, Rennyson worked as a private contractor. His duties as captain of the parish prison ended in July 1925, when he resigned amid accusations that he had embezzled prison funds, a charge that was dismissed by the state attorney general the following October. He resumed his contractor business after his resignation and by 1930 was employed as an inspector for the State Board of Health, a position he held for at least a decade or more.

A private funeral service was conducted on April 24 at St. Anthony Catholic Church and he was interred in Metairie Cemetery. Survived by one child (his wife died in March 1926), Archibald Mitchell Rennyson was seventy-six years old.

Dr. Joseph Richard, the parish coroner, and his assistant, Capt. Aubrey

Parody, passed away decades apart. Dr. Richard died suddenly of gastritis at his home in Pearl River, Louisiana, during the predawn hours of May 31, 1917. Parody died on March 13, 1959, from a combination of diabetes and heart disease after being hospitalized for seven months at Veterans Administration Hospital in the city.

Joseph Richard was born on July 19, 1859, in Grand Coteau, Louisiana, one of many children of Theodule Victor Richard and Emily Amelie Peck. After completing his education at St. Charles College (a high school) in Grand Coteau, he enrolled at the University of Louisiana, graduating from medical school in 1882. He established his initial practice in Franklin, Louisiana, before relocating to New Orleans by 1892. Assuming his elected office as parish coroner in the spring of 1900, Dr. Richard served one four-year term.

On February 3, 1885, while living in Franklin, Dr. Richard married Catherine "Katie" Emma Birg and from that union had six children, though

Dr. Joseph Mentor V. Richard (1917). (Courtesy NOLA.com/The *Times-Picayune*)

two died as youngsters. Katie filed for divorce on June 2, 1904, claiming that her husband physically and emotionally abused her and, in mid-October 1901, abandoned her and failed to return. It is not known if the couple reconciled, but Katie was still married when she died of tuberculosis on March 1, 1905, at age forty-one. Dr. Richard remarried that year to Adrianna "Adrian" Pincus, eighteen years his junior, moving to Lake Charles by 1910. His wife's health immediately began to fail, and they relocated to Pearl River, presumably because she had family residing there. Buried the afternoon of his death and survived by his wife (Adrian died from heart disease on March 7, 1950, at age seventy-three) and four children from his previous marriage, Dr. Joseph Mentor Victor Richard was fifty-seven years old.

Abraham "Aubrey" Parody was born in the city on October 6, 1873, the eldest child of Lewis Parrody (the original surname spelling) from Russia and Charlotte Goldstein from Prussia (present-day Poland). His parents immigrated to the States separately and married in New Orleans on December 22, 1872.

During the summer of 1885, at the age of eleven, Aubrey graduated with honors from McDonogh No. 8, a public boys' school located at the corner of Constance and Ninth streets. Though he did not continue past the eighth grade, his lack of formal schooling didn't appear to hinder his ability to earn a living.

Parody found employment by the early 1890s as a clerk and by 1898 as a real-estate agent in partnership with Michael G. Lally, according to the city directory. For whatever reason, by June 1900 Parody returned to clerking for one of the local railroads. During the mid-1890s, Parody joined the Louisiana State National Guard, served during the Spanish-American War, and by 1900 was elected captain of Company C, First Louisiana Regiment. Sometime during the latter half of 1900 or in 1901 he married Edith Ruth Audry Guyol, a divorcee with three children, though her children were placed in a Catholic orphanage after the divorce. Years later those children joined their new family, which included six children from the Parody-Guyol union.

To fill a vacancy in the coroner's office in 1901, Dr. Richard appointed Parody his personal secretary or clerk. He faithfully served in that capacity until late February 1904, when he was indicted for petty larceny by the Orleans Parish grand jury. With little choice, Dr. Richard suspended him, pending the outcome of his legal troubles. On March 31, after a two-day trial and three minutes of deliberation, the jury found Parody not guilty. That evening, Parody tendered his resignation to the coroner.

Parody remained in New Orleans until 1908 working as a publisher, travel agent, and editor before relocating his family to the Empire State, where

Capt. Aubrey Parody (1904). (Courtesy NOLA.com/The *Times-Picayune*)

he continued to work as a publisher-editor. Edith died in September 1945 in New York City and Parody returned to New Orleans by 1950. His death certificate listed him as divorced and residing at 124 South Dupre Street.

His funeral service was conducted on March 15, 1959, at the funeral parlor of E. J. Ranson and Sons, Inc. on Elysian Fields Avenue, and he was interred in Lake Lawn Park Cemetery. Survived by four children, Abraham "Aubrey" Joseph Parody was eighty-five years old.

Mary O'Connor, the kindhearted prison matron who comforted and provided meals for the condemned prisoners, met her death on January 17, 1929, at the home of her daughter, Margaret Grace Hogan, 4125 Cleveland Avenue. A combination of heart and kidney disease, coupled with cellulitis of the neck, claimed her life.

When her husband, Jeremiah J. O'Connor, passed away in 1894, Mary was forced to find work, having four children to provide for. A friend of her late husband who knew Sheriff Klock was able to procure for her the position of matron of the parish prison. Taking her sewing machine with her on her first day at work, she made the female inmates hem the prison linen. Over the years, she encouraged the women to sew, knit, or crochet, "anything to take their minds off their troubles," she later commented.

She tirelessly worked at the prison for thirty years, doing all sorts of odd jobs. She dealt with hundreds of thieves, bootleggers, and murderers, including Lewis Lyons. Upon her leave, she had nothing but kind words to say regarding the criminal types she encountered, though there was always the exception.

"I've only known two prisoners who didn't repent," Mrs. O'Connor declared.

Lewis Lyons or the other death-row inmates housed in the tower between 1904 and 1905 weren't among the unrepentant, according to her. Remarkably, she was referring to two women who were convicted murderers, though both were spared the death sentence.

Her funeral service was held on January 18, at St. Anthony Catholic Church, with scores of individuals associated with the criminal-justice system attending. In addition, there was an outpouring of cards and letters delivered to her home from former inmates. Interred in Greenwood Cemetery and survived by three children, Mary O'Neil O'Connor, whom friends and associates affectionately called "Mother," was seventy-two years old.

Of the principal witnesses on the fateful day of Gurley's assassination, John Doran, the clerk who bolted from the reception room, was the first person to pass away. He died from cirrhosis of the liver on June 25, 1904. Born in the city on October 17, 1854, he was the oldest son of John D. Doran and Catherine Flood, natives of Ireland. He never married and at the time of his death resided at 216 South Roman Street, the home of his widowed sister, Ellen Doran Duffy. His funeral took place at the residence the following day, with his body placed in the Luke Duffy tomb in St. Patrick Cemetery No. 2. John D. Doran, Jr., was forty-nine years old.

William Shepard, the real-estate agent who heard the same gunfire as Doran, died of cardiac failure on August 23, 1910, at his home, 1462 Arabella Street. Though he had suffered from heart disease since June, his family didn't anticipate that he would die so quickly.

Born in the city on May 7, 1852, the son of William Crosby Shepard and Rebecca Knox, Shepard initially worked for his father in the crockery business until 1892, when he entered into a real-estate partnership with

William Shepard (1910). (Courtesy NOLA.com/ The *Times-Picayune*)

Eugene Hunter. He eventually went solo and became a highly respected and well-known agent in New Orleans. He married Anne Davis "Nannie" Atkinson on September 19, 1876, and the couple had three children, though one died at an early age. By the time of his death, Shepard was a member of several social and benevolent organizations and served as a major in the Washington Artillery, a unit in the Louisiana State National Guard. His funeral took place at his residence the day following his death, and he was laid to rest in Metairie Cemetery in the Atkinson family tomb. Survived by his wife and two daughters, William Lansing Shepard was fifty-eight years old.

Dr. Charles Buck, the dentist who briefly spoke with Lewis Lyons in front of the Macheca Building on the morning of the murder and saw the aftermath of the shooting, died at his residence, 2233 Brainard Street, on August 12, 1941. Having a history of heart and kidney disease, he suffered a cerebral hemorrhage and was laid to rest in St. Vincent De Paul Cemetery

No. 1 alongside his wife, Jane Augusta Morrison, who had passed away four years earlier. The couple was childless. A native of Baltimore, Maryland, Dr. Buck practiced dentistry in New Orleans between 1891 and 1918 and later became a pioneer in the state's gas and petroleum industry. Dr. Charles Collins Buck died at age eighty-two.

Dr. Valentine Irion, whose office was located directly across the corridor from Gurley, and who heard the fatal gunshots, passed away at his residence, 8013 Willow Street, during the evening of March 18, 1948, from heart disease brought on by hypertension. He also suffered from cancer of the tongue. Born on July 31, 1862, in Marksville, Louisiana, he earned an engineering degree from Louisiana State University in 1884 and then traveled to Switzerland, where for two years he studied dentistry under renowned dental surgeon Edward Doremus. Returning to the States, Dr. Irion entered the College of Dentistry, University of Maryland, and completed his studies in 1887. He initially practiced in Opelousas, married Helen Lastrapes on September 18, 1889, and had four children. In 1897, after serving in various civic positions in St. Landry Parish, Dr. Irion moved his family to New Orleans and eventually set up his dental practice in the Macheca Building. Active in local and state politics for many years, Dr. Irion was laid to rest in Masonic Cemetery No. 1 beside his wife, who had passed away the previous year. Survived by two daughters, Dr. Valentine King Irion was eighty-five years old.

George Terriberry, the attorney and a member of the coroner's jury who held Gurley in his arms as he drew his last breath, died of heart disease on October 19, 1948, at his residence, 1407 First Street. He had a long history of hypertension.

Born on February 10, 1875, in Galveston, Texas, Terriberry served as a private in the Louisiana Volunteers during the Spanish-American War and then attended Tulane University, where he earned a law degree in 1900. Serving as a state legislator, Terriberry married Miriam A. Patrick on July 26, 1905, though the couple remained childless. His funeral was held at his home on October 21, and he was interred in Metairie Cemetery alongside his wife, who had passed away eleven years earlier. George Hitchins Terriberry was seventy-three years old.

Alice Watling, Dr. Irion's stenographer who witnessed Lyons dragging Gurley through his office doorway, died of heart disease with acute cardiac dilation on Christmas morning 1948 at Touro Infirmary in New Orleans. Born in the city on July 15, 1876, and a lifelong resident, Alice was the oldest of eight children of William Watling of Ireland and Ellen Regan of New

Orleans. Never married, at the time of her death she resided at 1316 Calhoun Street. Her religious service was conducted on Sunday afternoon, December 26, at Holy Name of Jesus Catholic Church on St. Charles Avenue. Interred in St. Vincent De Paul Cemetery No. 1, and survived by two sisters, Alice M. Watling was seventy-two years old.

Robert Robinson, Gurley's office boy, died in Chicago, Illinois, on September 27, 1951, of an unknown cause. Born in New Orleans on June 23, 1888, and the oldest of six children of Robert James Robinson and Mary Boeckelmann, the lad likely obtained his position with Gurley through a family connection. In 1901, his father was employed as a railroad porter and two years later as a deputy sheriff in the First City Criminal Court.

Robinson found work beginning in 1907, if not earlier, as a clerk with the Illinois Central Railroad, located at 1100 South Front Street. He remained there for at least a dozen years. In 1908, he married eighteen-year-old Katherine Claverie and from that union had five children. The couple divorced during the early 1920s, with Robinson relocating to Chicago. His body was returned to New Orleans, with his funeral conducted on September 30 at St. Alphonsus Catholic Church on Constance Street. Interred in St. Joseph Cemetery No. 1 and survived by his five children, fourteen grandchildren, and two great-grandchildren, Robert Charles Robinson was sixty-three years old.

Of the attorneys and judges involved in Lyons's civil and later murder trial, Joseph Generelly, Lyons's lead defense attorney, was the first to pass away. On Monday evening, December 7, 1914, while at his residence, 1104 North Dupre Street, he suddenly complained of a headache and chest pain. Before his brother-in-law, a physician, could arrive at his home, Generelly lapsed into unconsciousness and died from a cerebral embolism and acute gastritis.

Generelly's law partnership with Warren Doyle dissolved sometime in late 1904 and he later partnered with another brother-in-law, Lionel Adams, before the latter's untimely death in September 1914 from a hemorrhagic stroke. Adams, a former district attorney of Orleans Parish, served as a special counsel for the State during the Deschamps murder case. Generelly was at Adams's side when he passed away, three months prior to his own death.

Generelly's funeral took place at his home, with a religious service performed at St. Rose de Lima Catholic Church. The service and burial were widely attended by city and state leaders, including the governor. Among the honorary pallbearers were Judge Frank Chretien, Chandler Luzenberg, and his old law partner Warren Doyle. Survived by his wife and six children and laid to rest in St. Louis Cemetery No. 2., Edward Joseph Generelly was thirty-nine years old.

Judge Thomas Ellis, who presided over Lyons's civil trial, died from chronic bronchitis at his home in Amite City, Louisiana, on August 2, 1918. He was still serving as the senior judge of the Civil District Court, Division A, when he passed away, a position he held for thirty years.

Thomas Ellis was born in Covington, Louisiana, on November 26, 1836. In October 1858, he married Martina Virginia Hamilton of Clarke County, Alabama, and from that union had eight children, though their first two died in infancy. Educated at Clinton Academy and later Centenary College of Louisiana, the forerunner of Louisiana State University, Ellis began practicing law during the late 1850s. He served during the Civil War as the captain of Company A, Eighteenth Louisiana Battalion Cavalry, and afterwards was elected to the Louisiana State Senate. During his tenure as judge, he taught law for a number of years at Tulane University. Survived by six children, he was laid to rest beside his late wife in Ellis Cemetery in Roseland, Louisiana. (Mrs. Ellis passed away in February 1891.) The Honorable Judge Thomas Cargill Warner Ellis was eighty-one years old.

Judge Frank Chretien, Lyons's criminal-trial judge, passed away on September 21, 1920, at his residence, 2323 Canal Street. Heart disease had forced him to take a respite from the bench beginning in January 1919. His funeral took place at his home the following day and he was laid to rest in St. Louis Cemetery No. 3. Survived by one daughter, the Honorable Judge Frank Dazincourt Chretien was seventy-one years old.

Delos Mellen, Gurley's old law partner, died suddenly from a paralytic stroke at his home in De Lisle, Mississippi, on the morning of February 23, 1933. Following Lyons's execution, Mellen uprooted his family and relocated to New York City in May 1906, where he continued to practice law for a number of years. Three years after the move, his wife, Corinne, died from cancer. Her body was brought back to New Orleans, where she was buried in her family's tomb in Lafayette Cemetery No. 1.

In his twilight years, Delos returned to his native state of Mississippi. Settling near the coast, he spent most of his time fishing, a fifty-year-old passion of his. His funeral took place in Gulfport before his body was transported to Natchez, his hometown, for burial in Natchez City Cemetery. Survived by two children, Delos Carpenter Mellen was seventy-three years old.

Warren Doyle outlived his former law partner by many years, passing away at his summer home in Lacombe, Louisiana, during the predawn hours of December 17, 1946. Pulmonary edema brought on by a coronary thrombosis ended his life.

Having served as a state representative between 1904 and 1908, Doyle was appointed assistant district attorney of Orleans Parish, serving in that capacity until 1912. Beginning in mid-November 1941, he served as the acting United States attorney for the Eastern District of Louisiana, until Pres. Franklin D. Roosevelt appointed a permanent replacement in late January 1942.

On the day of his death, Doyle's body was transported back to his residence in New Orleans, 1231 Nashville Avenue, where the funeral service was conducted that afternoon. He was laid to rest in Hope Mausoleum, 4841 Canal Street. Survived by his widow and three sons, John Warren Doyle was sixty-nine years old.

Chandler Luzenberg, who vigorously prosecuted Lewis Lyons, was the last of the major counselors connected to the murder trial to pass away, dying on September 4, 1950, at his son's residence, 5319 South Liberty Street. Cancer at the base of the tongue that had turned gangrenous was listed as his cause of death. He also suffered from senility and was in poor health the last nine months of his life.

After Lyons's execution, Luzenberg was elected outright district attorney of Orleans Parish in 1912 and served two terms. For a number of years, he also taught criminal law at Tulane University and for a time served on the Orleans Parish School Board. His wife, Jennie, died in February 1931.

Luzenberg's funeral took place on September 5 at Bultman Mortuary on St. Charles Avenue, with his internment at Lafayette Cemetery No. 1. Survived by two sons, Chandler Clement Luzenberg was eighty-three years old.

Within a year of the assassination of her husband, Marie Gurley moved to 5215 Pitt Street, along with her two stepdaughters, Aurora and Helen. Unfortunately for Marie, Gurley never revised his will, last executed on May 13, 1897, five years after the death of his first wife. At that time, he bequeathed all of his earthly possessions to her two daughters. As a result, Marie likely received none of her late husband's proceeds, which included the sale of their home on Henry Clay Avenue.

Aurora was the first to depart Marie's company, when she married Dr. Edward Larned McGehee, Jr., on September 7, 1904. By year's end, Marie and Helen had moved to 2033 Coliseum Street with Helen's grandmother, Rosamond Gurley; her uncles, Randolph and Hewes Gurley; and Hewes's family. By the time of Helen's marriage to Charles Congreve Carter on June 6, 1906, the Gurley household had relocated a short distance away to 1315 Jackson Avenue, where Marie's mother-in-law passed away on March 15, 1915, from influenza and senility at the age of eighty-seven. Marie had long parted company with the Gurley family, leaving New Orleans sometime in late 1908 or 1909. Her name was never again listed in the city directory after 1909.

Never remarrying, Marie eventually moved to Sacramento, where her niece worked as a bookkeeper. By April 1935, she had relocated to San Francisco, according to the U.S. Census. Eight years prior to her death, she was admitted to Napa State Hospital in Imola, an unincorporated community in Napa County, suffering from psychosis with cerebral arteriosclerosis. Marie died of bronchopneumonia at that facility on September 6, 1958, and was buried three days later in Holy Cross Catholic Cemetery in Colma, a small community south of San Francisco. Born on September 27, 1865, to natives of Alsace-Lorraine, a region now part of France, Marie Angela Homer Gurley died at age ninety-two.

The fourth floor of the Macheca Building no longer resembles the layout during the 1903 murder of J. Ward Gurley. The building's grounds have had a long and interesting history. The site at 828 Canal Street was previously occupied by the four-story Imperial Hotel, though other structures undoubtedly predated that building. Joseph R. Macheca, in partnership with John S. Sweet, in 1899 purchased the hotel, renamed the Imperial Stag Hotel, in hopes of making it a profitable enterprise, but other opportunities soon developed.

By the dawn of the twentieth century, businesses were beginning to concentrate on either side of lower Canal Street. Thus, a supply of office spaces along this corridor became a top priority. The demolition of the hotel began in April 1901, to make way for a new seven-story office building. Initially called the Imperial Office Building, the Macheca Building measured 65 feet along the street by 147 feet deep, with a steel-constructed frame and masonry exterior walls. It opened with great fanfare in late spring 1902. Containing approximately 150 rooms, it quickly filled to capacity with an assortment of tenants from the business and professional world. Such tenants included the Macheca Real Estate Company, a family-owned business, the New Orleans Cereal Company, the Prudential Insurance Company of America, a barbershop that also provided hot and cold baths, a business college, confectionery shop, hair salon, tobacco shop, and sewing-machine business. An assortment of physicians, attorneys, engineers, dentists, and other professionals also rented out office space.

There is an interesting sidebar related to the Macheca family, the building's namesake, and their indirect connection to the Etienne Deschamps murder case. Joseph's father, John Macheca (1851-1909), the patriarch of the family's fruit-import and later real-estate businesses, was the half-brother of Joseph R. Macheca (1874-1891), who was credited with establishing a Mafia organization in New Orleans. Joseph Macheca was subsequently arrested for his alleged involvement in the 1890 assassination of David Hennessy, the chief of police. He was among the victims who were murdered in March 1891 during the prison riot while Etienne Deschamps sat on death row for the murder of Juliette Dietsh.

In 1925, the Macheca Building was sold to the Leon Godchaux Clothing Company. Godchaux's had been an established clothing business since the 1840s and had operated at various locations in the city over the years. Prior to this latest move, Godchaux's was located at 531 Canal Street, three blocks down from the Macheca Building. By October 1925, all of the Macheca tenants were vacated as the building underwent a massive interior remodel. Godchaux's moved into its new location in June 1926, once the renovations costing $200,000 were complete.

In an unforeseen irony, the fourth floor where the murder occurred was designated for children's clothing. Part of the floor was also allocated as a safe zone where youngsters might entertain themselves while their parents shopped elsewhere in the building. Among the amusements placed on the floor was a merry-go-round.

The Macheca or Godchaux's Building was put on the National Register of Historical Places in January 1983 and sold that year to a private developer. Plans to convert the top two floors back into office spaces never materialized. Godchaux's continued to lease the bottom five floors until 1986, when the company was forced into bankruptcy. In 1987, Godchaux's liquidated its holdings, which at its peak in 1984 included eight stores. The current owner purchased the building in 1992, though by then the third through fifth floors were converted back into office spaces. To date, none of the offices has been leased. Stndrd Athletic Co., an apparel and footwear store, occupies the first floor, with the second floor used as a stockroom.

The criminal district courthouse and parish prison survived at its former location until 1931, when the entire complex was relocated to 2700 Tulane Avenue, between South Broad and South White streets. Afterwards, the old courthouse housed the First and Second Recorder's Court, the Traffic Court, and Night Court, until the building, along with the old First Precinct Station,

Stndrd Athletic Co. storefront, old Macheca Building, 828 Canal Street, in 2017. (Courtesy Christopher G. Peña)

were torn down in 1949. The Gravier Street prison was demolished in 1932. The old city block including Franklin Street, which no longer exists at that location, was swallowed up by the main branch of the New Orleans Public Library at the corner of Tulane and Loyola (a groundbreaking ceremony occurred on November 30, 1956); the Tulane University Medical Center complex, located farther up the block on Tulane; and a multistory building, formerly the Warwick Hotel, located on Gravier Street at the site of the old parish prison.

On July 20, 1903, Lewis Lyons entered the Macheca Building, took the elevator to the fourth floor, and fired his weapon five times in the rear office of J. Ward Gurley, killing the district attorney and nearly ending his life during the brief bedlam. The question of Lyons's guilt was never doubted by the newly appointed district attorney or a jury of his peers. But on March 24, 1905, as Lyons stood on the platform of the gallows with the noose carefully placed around his neck, this single question—was it really worth it?—*must* have momentarily entered his mind. Based upon the unapologetic stance he took from the time of the murder until his final days, Lyons must have thought it was, if he ever pondered such a question moments from his death. So in the end, the death over a diamond stud claimed two lives, while showering unimaginable pain and sorrow onto the families of both men and the city at large. It appeared that only the passage of time lessened the grief and shock that everyone felt on that ill-fated summer morning, an assassination committed in New Orleans so long ago.

Bibliography

Books

New Orleans City Guide: Written and Compiled by the Federal Writers' Project of the Works Progress Administration for the City of New Orleans. Boston: Houghton Mifflin, 1938.

Tallant, Robert. *Ready to Hang: Seven Famous New Orleans Murders.* 1952. Reprint, Gretna, LA: Pelican, 2012.

Louisiana State Archives, Baton Rouge

Certificates of Birth

Orleans Parish, Secretary of State, Vital Records, April 12, 1857-May 22, 1903.

Certificates of Death

Orleans Parish, Secretary of State, Vital Records, April 17, 1867-March 13, 1959.

Plaquemines Parish, Secretary of State, Vital Records, November 9, 1931.

St. Tammany Parish, Secretary of State, Vital Records, May 31, 1917-December 17, 1946.

Tangipahoa Parish, Secretary of State, Vital Records, August 2, 1918.

Certificates of Marriage

Orleans Parish, Secretary of State, Vital Records, December 22, 1872-October 26, 1910.

Louisiana Supreme Court Reports

Louisiana Annual Reports for 1897, Cases Argued and Determined in the Supreme Court of Louisiana, Vol. 49, Part I, Walter H. Rogers, Reporter, Case No. 12,240, *State v. John Scott,* January 18, 1897, pp. 253-70. New Orleans: F. F. Hansell & Bro., 1898.

Louisiana Annual Reports for 1899, Cases Argued and Determined in the Supreme Court of Louisiana, Vol. 51, From January 5, 1899, to June 30, 1899, Inclusive, Case No. 13,037, *Lyons v. Carroll et al.,* June 12, 1899, pp. 781-83. St. Paul: West, 1900.

Louisiana Reports, Vol. 107, Cases Argued and Determined in the Supreme Court of Louisiana, Juridical Year 1901-2, Case No. 12,757, *Lewis W. Lyons v. Daniel S. Carroll,* March 17, 1902, pp. 471-74. St. Paul: West, 1902.

Louisiana Reports, Vol. 113, Cases Argued and Determined in the Supreme Court of Louisiana at Terms Beginning First Monday of November 1903, First Monday of November 1904, Case No. 15,275, *State v. Lyons,* December 19, 1904, pp. 959-1001. St. Paul: West, 1905.

Louisiana Reports, Vol. 114, Cases Argued and Determined in the Supreme Court of Louisiana at Term Beginning First Monday of November 1904, Case No. 15,553, *State ex rel. Lyons v. Chretien, Judge,* February 11, 1905, pp. 81-84. St. Paul: West, 1905.

New Orleans Public Library Louisiana Division/City Archives

Orleans Parish Coroner's Office. *Records of Inquests and Views, 1887-1904.* Vol. 36. July 20, 1903. TH420, microfilm roll #28/903980. Autopsy record for J. Ward Gurley.

Newspapers

Cleveland Plain Dealer Magazine. October 17, 1909.
Daily Herald (Biloxi-Gulfport, MS). February 23, 1933.
Duluth News Tribune. November 7, 1909.
Macon Daily Telegraph. November 7, 1909.
New Orleans Daily Picayune. October 15, 1854-February 4, 1914.
New Orleans Daily States. June 1, 1917-September 4, 1928.
New Orleans Item. February 11, 1901-December 18, 1921.
New Orleans Times-Picayune. September 13, 1914-May 14, 1988.
Sunday Star (Washington, D.C.). January 8, 1911.

State of California, Department of Public Health Vital Records Sacramento, California

Certificates of Death

Los Angeles County, February 23, 1926-August 20, 1973.
Napa County, September 6, 1958.

Websites

http://babel.hathitrust.org
http://neworleanspubliclibrary.org
http://www.ancestry.com
http://www.findagrave.com
http://www.hancockcountyhistoricalsociety.com
https://archive.org
https://familysearch.org
https://prosecutingattorneys.org
https://www.genealogybank.com

INDEX